The Foundation of Hope

The Foundation of Hope

Turning Dreams into Reality

Edited by

R. JOHN ELFORD

LIVERPOOL HOPE UNIVERSITY COLLEGE

LIVERPOOL UNIVERSITY PRESS

First published 2003 by
Liverpool University Press
4 Cambridge Street
Liverpool L69 7ZU

British Library Cataloguing-in-Publication data
A British Library CIP record is available

ISBN 0-85323-519-8 cased
0-85323-529-5 limp

Typeset by Koinonia, Bury
Printed and bound in the European Union
by Biddles Ltd, Guildford and King's Lynn

Contents

—◦✠◦—

Acknowledgements

—◦✠◦—

A central part of the privilege of working in a university college or university is the opportunity to sustain discussions with colleagues, day-in, day-out, across a range of topics. The idea for this volume arose out of this. I am, therefore, personally indebted to and grateful for the willingness of some of those colleagues to engage in such debate, as they have so readily done in contributing to this book. No doubt we shall all change our views, on this or that, as discussions continue, but this volume is, at least, a reflection of some current thinking in Liverpool Hope University College.

So much of this has been inspired and encouraged by my senior colleague, Professor Simon Lee. For this reason it is a pleasure to thank him personally and wish him well in his future academic and administrative undertakings.

One other special appreciation goes to Mr Alfred Westwell who has graciously and so vigorously participated in the sub-editing and proofreading of the book.

R. JOHN ELFORD

Foreword

When we arrived in our respective diocese and archdiocese, the constitution of Liverpool Hope University College stated that the Governing Council was to be chaired in rotation by the Bishop and Archbishop of Liverpool. We duly served for a two-year term each, but were then happy to see the roles of chair and deputy opened to the wider Hope community, not least because, as the Dearing Report noted, chairs of governing councils need to be much more intimately involved in the governance of universities and colleges. We are pleased to continue to serve in other ways, as joint Presidents and trustees.

We would single out Hope at Everton as a major contribution to Liverpool's urban renewal. The diocese and archdiocese extend beyond the city, of course, as Hope does. We therefore also wish to commend the pioneering work of the Network of Hope in the North West. All these endeavours involve vision and the risks which so often go with its implementation. This is where creativity is so often to be found, as the history of Liverpool Hope has shown from the beginning and as its recent developments have shown in large measure.

We write on Maundy Thursday as the Pope has published a statement on the Eucharist and ecumenism. This reminds us that the ecumenical journey both for Hope and for the wider Christian family is complex, often sensitive and always challenging. It is not always easy to walk together with hope in our hearts, but this we must strive to do. Given both our history and the divided nature of the followers of Christ today, there remains often a sense of frustration, but debate must continue and must be vigorous, courteous and searching all at the same time.

It is good to welcome this book at the moment when Hope expresses its profound sense of gratitude, with which we concur, to Professor Simon Lee for his leadership over the past eight years. This is the moment, also, when we all welcome his successor Professor Gerald Pillay and wish him well in his new undertakings.

It is a privilege for us to be involved in the life and development of this university college and we commend this series of essays, all with different perspectives, to anyone concerned for the unity of the church, for theology and for higher education.

Liverpool, 17 April 2003   The Rt Revd James Stuart Jones,
                                                      Bishop of Liverpool

                                        The Most Reverend Patrick Altham Kelly,
                                                 Archbishop and Metropolitan

—◦✣◦—

Preface

R. JOHN ELFORD

—◦✣◦—

THIS book is both a celebration and an analysis of the creation of Liverpool Hope University College in 1996 and of some of its achievements to date, during an exciting period in British higher education. Its contents can only be a reflection of a wider whole. They are selected principally because, in their different ways, they capture something of that whole. In one sense, therefore, they are impressionistic, yet in another they deal with selected substantive issues. So much else that could have been essayed has had to be omitted. For example, no attempt has been made to discuss equally the 20 or so subjects taught in the modern and ever-developing Hope curriculum. Nor is there mention of the research activity that ranges across these subjects. In what follows, such issues come into focus only briefly, simply because they are illustrative of some point being made. All this is designed to make the book a livelier read than it otherwise would have been as a formal chronicle.

For such reasons, this collection of essays should not be read as a standard and traditional history of an institution. It is, rather, a snapshot of the contemporary development of a higher education institution which dates back to its principal origins in Warrington in 1844, in Mount Pleasant in 1856, and in Childwall in 1964. Above all, Liverpool Hope is now a single college community with roots in those earlier beginnings. It is, therefore, successor to a rich educational heritage in Liverpool, its environs and the wider region. For such a long time people have known and benefited from S. Katharine's, Notre Dame and Christ's; names that are part of the older educational and social history of the region. For a time they became the rather aridly styled Liverpool Institute of Higher Education. This could only ever have been the transitional device that it was. Its main and important achievement was that it patiently processed the many changes and rationalisations without which the new single college could not have come about. Liverpool Hope University College, familiarly known as Hope or Liverpool Hope, has now inherited the ring and resonance of the founding college trusts with a conviction that was, perhaps unavoidably, missing in the transitional years. That conviction is expressed in all areas of the modern college life, as will become representatively evident in what follows. For all these reasons and more, Hope is the modern expression of older living traditions which it does everything it can to take into itself and to render afresh. It also meets, as it must in an ever more competitive environment, the accountabilities and sheer market forces of present-day British higher education. Those of us who have been and are privileged to be part of this like to think, with due modesty, that it is a success story. We are fully mindful, however, that success is no more to be taken for granted today than it ever has been in the past. It always has to be worked at in the face of ever changing incremental pressures as well as sudden demands.

It will be clear throughout this volume that the Christian foundation of Hope is as strong as it ever was in formative periods of its history. This foundation is now ecumenical (though, as we shall see, it is not so entirely without difficulty). Hope's trustees are Roman Catholic and Anglican, and Methodism is now a part of the chaplaincy and college life. The mission statement, which is referred to throughout, ensures that Hope is now arguably one of the most mission-explicit Christian institutions in British higher education. It achieves this because it is positively open to students, staff and friends alike who are of other religious faiths or of secular persuasions. This is no platitude, it is both genuine and precious: the very key, that is, to the life of the present-day college community. Understanding something of all this at the outset will, it is intended, enable an enriched reading of what follows. This is part of the history and ongoing story of a living college community in the context of modern mass higher education. While that mass is politically and economically to be welcomed, it is only so welcomed here because it has not displaced those vital elements of the educational process which have to do with the personal, life-changing and ultimately socially transforming essences of what it means to become an educated individual.

More personally, the fifteen or so years I have been at Hope, in many guises and disguises, have been an important part of my life's work and ministry. They have at times been as impossible and as frustrating as any such work can and perhaps even needs to be. They have, at the same time, been a great privilege and constant joy, as well as sheer fun. The origin of this volume lies in the daily good conversations I have had with my senior colleague Professor Simon Lee about his vision for the college and what it is we have been trying to do to achieve it. Equally it lies in the wider engagement of that dialogue with colleagues throughout the college community and beyond.

After my own introductory chapter, we turn immediately to the Chair of the Governing Council, Sr Eileen Kelleher SND, writing in collaboration with others, about the student experience. This is unusual for two reasons. First, because this is the one thing usually missing from books on colleges and schools. So often one can learn everything about institutions without gaining the slightest inkling of how their most important members, their students, perceive them. In Hope, student response is held in constant regard because it is the barometer of whether or not, and particularly if not, we are achieving for our students what we aspire to achieve. Second, it is unusual in that the Chair of the Governing Council works so closely with the students' union and the many college staff and agencies which exist to serve the varied needs and aspects of student welfare.

The third chapter, contributed by Ms Sharon Bassett and Dr Helen O'Sullivan, explains in some detail how all this is actually maintained across a community now numbering some 7,000 or so students. Dr Bernard Longden then explores the background to Hope's commitment to widening the range of students who access undergraduate study. Dr Michael Ford, more widely known for his work as a BBC journalist and broadcaster, writes of his experience as a recent research student at Hope. This reminds us of the increasing importance in college life of the many postgraduate cohorts.

In Chapter 6, Bishop Ian Stuart writes about the life of the chaplaincy, which is at the heart of everything the college does. Dr Ian Sharp then gives an account of the activities of one of the four college deaneries. This is the Foundation Deanery, which is charged with oversight of all mission-related activities. Mention is made of the work of the Education Deanery in several places, most particularly within the section of Chapter 2 that has been contributed by Mrs Kathleen Hodgkinson. Space has precluded such explicit treatment of the work of the other two deaneries, Hope in the Community and the Arts and Sciences, though they are referred to throughout.

Professor Ian Markham explains in Chapter 8 how teaching and research in theology has recently been restructured. This is an activity in which he has played a central role. His successor as Liverpool Professor of Theology and Public Life, Professor Nicholas Sagovsky, then writes on his understanding of that subject. Next, Professor Kenneth Newport writes in detail about research in theology and religious studies. This is followed by a chapter by Professor John Hinnells on strategic research management. The relationship of the college's mission to vocation and profession in the education of teachers is discussed in the chapter contributed by Professor John Sullivan.

In the book's penultimate chapter, I write about the Hope at Everton development. The final chapter, by the departing Rector and Chief Executive, Professor Simon Lee, gives us his own account of some of the things he holds to have been important. It is a particular joy to us all that his successor Professor Gerald Pillay provides an afterword.

I am grateful to the authors here included for their willingness to respond as they have done to the invitation to write. I am sorry that the book does not afford space to include the similar contributions that could have been made by so many others. Just perhaps, however, this might be an encouragement to them to celebrate and analyse their doings in similar ways.

Finally, there is a proper appreciation running throughout to all who have contributed over the many years to the formation of Hope. More explicitly, the book is an appreciation of the contribution made to the life of the college by Professor Simon Lee during the eight years of his incumbency as Rector and Chief Executive. We all wish him well in his new post as Vice-Chancellor of Leeds Metropolitan University. At the same time, we welcome his successor Professor Gerald Pillay and wish him continued success, pleasure and blessing as he takes up his post.

CHAPTER I

From Urban Beginnings...

R. JOHN ELFORD

A S the preface has indicated, this book is a celebration and analysis of the achievements of Liverpool Hope University College and of the opportunities now presenting here. The 'college' designation is as important as its prefixes. The modern single institution is, as we shall see, derived from much older collegiate establishments that have meant so much to students and staff over the years. It focuses on the importance of personal interaction and development in the educational endeavour. Christians believe that all human beings are created in the image of God, but that for whatever reason that image in every individual is marred. Restoring that image is the central work of all Christian ministry. Christian education is a formalised part of that. While personal development of such a kind does, of course, occur in secular and larger institutions by dint of the commitment of individual staff members and in, for example, some halls of residence, it is that much easier to achieve and maintain in smaller ones. (The danger here, however, is that it can degenerate into an effete and ineffectual cosy intimacy. In these days of external account-ability and endless inspection this can be a serious weakness.) To work in a college like Hope is to experience the Christian mission at work in education. It is something to be celebrated and cherished. The challenge, of course, is to develop this at every opportunity. This is not always easy to achieve as the college grows numerically (which it has to do for its own good and viability) but it is always possible. As we shall see in later chapters, many of the modern facilities for student support, welfare and enjoyment of leisure at Hope are based on antecedent collegiate ones. They are also part of the fulfilment of Hope's shorter mission statement: 'Educating the whole person in mind, body and spirit'. This formulation is a constant and convenient reminder that higher education is a deeply personal and, at its best, life-changing experience. But even at times when we are most disposed to recognising this, we can scarce pinpoint its happening. All manner of influences, even serendipitous ones, interplay during the educational process, and it might be years later before we can even begin to identify, unravel and appreciate them for what they were.

The joy of working in a college like Hope, compared, say, with a larger university, is that it constantly provides opportunities to realise something of all this. Moreover, it does this never more effectively than at those times when staff and students alike can share the sheer exhilaration of the experience. Of course, life is not consciously like this all the time. Drains get blocked, things go wrong and cherished plans often come to nothing, but none of this thwarts a real vision for and experience of the educational process. This is more than enough to inspire successful college life. To participate in the continuum of such success is an educationalist's dream and a privilege.

Christian colleges and schools are all dedicated to some such understanding of the educational process. Of course, it is not achieved *only* in these places. Schools and colleges of other religions' institutions do the same thing, as do secular ones. The genuineness of this recognition is extremely important: it is not possible to participate in something as educationally protean as this if one even begins to think of it as an exclusive possession. Quite apart from the professional arrogance of that, it would also be a spiritual arrogance. Achieving excellence in Christian-inspired education need not be any better or different from achieving it in other ways. However, the daily life of a Christian college or school includes prayer and worship, which, put alongside the constant obligation to remember the intentions of trustees and the policies of governors, does help to maintain the vital focus. Here again, all this is perhaps most effective when we are least conscious of it. Our unselfconscious educational activities are probably our best. None of this, moreover, is the achievement of the few, not even the few who are regular in their prayers and devotion. In any Christian college or school there will be others, perhaps even the majority, who share the aims and objectives of such an educational vision without necessarily also sharing the Christian faith in which it is rooted. No church college or school could exist for long, let alone flourish, without co-operative goodwill of this kind. For this reason alone it deserves recognition and appreciation. Far more than that, however, it creates a wider forum for the challenge and stimulus which is vital to the well-being of the Christian vision. A church college or school that is aware of all this will be an open and dynamic place. It will welcome all manner of collaboration with others who might help to realise its central and cherished aims. Here it might well be remembered that the Christian faith is never better than when it loses its self-consciousness and gets on with the task in hand. Getting on with education in this way is what being a Christian educator in a wider secular environment is essentially all about. Much has been written and said about all this, and there is scarce space here to add more to it by way of introduction. However, what follows might well be the better understood if we keep such insights in mind, as we learn how this aspect of the foundation of Hope contributes to the wider whole. It will become self-evident that it all requires hard work and is ever incomplete. There is no room for the proverbial laurels, however successful we might think we have been with this achievement or that. Getting it right is always elusive and precarious. This alone is enough to make it exciting work. For some, as we have seen, it is the reason why it has to be rooted in the Christian vision, and in the faith and prayer which is central to that.

Hope is now entitled to use the 'university college' designation. This is because, in August 2002, it was awarded its own undergraduate degree-awarding powers by the Privy Council after a long process of detailed external inspection. It is, in fact, the first British higher education institution (HEI) to receive these powers under the present strict guidelines. Throughout the process leading to this success, the college was fully supported by the University of Liverpool. Pressure to make the application for undergraduate degree-awarding powers arose out of the Dearing Committee's review of higher education.[1] This proposed that the only colleges that should be permitted to use the prefix 'university' were either those wholly owned and governed by existing universities, or those that had been granted their own undergraduate degree-awarding powers. This was contested (to no avail) by Hope representatives during the Dearing consultation process, on the grounds that there was no desire in the college either to be owned and governed by the University of Liverpool, or to award any degrees other than those of that university. It later transpired that what was driving the direction of the review at this juncture was the government's desire to clamp down on instances of the alleged indiscriminate use by some institutions of the university prefix, in order to protect the international standing of Britain's universities. Some might suspect otherwise here, and detect a desire to rationalise British higher education, full stop. The non-university sector of higher education looks untidy, at the least, especially so since the polytechnics departed for the university sector in 1992. Pleas to the government that they should not interfere with the relationship between the university and its affiliated colleges here in Liverpool, which had worked for almost a century and was still working well, fell on deaf ears. Consequently, Hope took the government to Judicial Review, a process which was eventually abandoned only when it became clear that its success could only be assured in the distant and expensive European Courts. Now, happily, all this is in the past. For the immediate future, Hope now plans to award a combination of its own degrees and those of the University of Liverpool. The important thing to note here is that Hope degrees are externally examined and their quality assured in exactly the same way as those of the University of Liverpool. As a consequence, Hope now has an impressive array of high quality ratings to its credit. (Numerous other HEIs which are not in the university sector now seek to be in this position.)

The government White Paper of January 2003[2] might well necessitate yet further changes in the designation of the college. Some eighteen months ago the government announced that it was changing its then policy of imposing uniformity of content and achievement on all HEIs. This had come under criticism from the sector itself, which had seen the inconsistency of a policy that acknowledged the strengths of diversity in primary and secondary education but denied it in higher education. It clearly made no economic or educational sense to insist that all HEIs had to do all the same things. Nor did it make any regional sense, particularly in places like Liverpool where the college and the universities had always recognised differences between each other and had seen the economic and practical value of not competing unnecessarily. Ironically, other government policies had been encouraging this sort of co-operation at the same time as the uniformity demands were being imposed! All this inconsistency is now, at last, being sorted out. Different HEIs are to be supported in their differences. At the very least, this will enable higher education provision in an area like Liverpool to revert to the status quo ante. If only the government and its agencies had listened in the first place, one muses. However, listen it now thankfully has. At the time of writing, the 'university college' title is reserved for institutions which have the authority to award their own undergraduate degrees. Some HEIs also have postgraduate degree-awarding powers, and this prepares them for possible full university status. To achieve this, they must be able to demonstrate a critical mass of research excellence. 'This situation,' the White Paper acknowledges, 'is at odds with our belief that institutions should play to diverse strengths.'[3] Quite so, one might again add. The White Paper also takes the view that there is no necessary connection between academic research per se and teaching excellence. (No doubt, however, this will not be the last word on this hoary but important subject.) It is, therefore, proposed 'to change the system, so that the university title is awarded on the basis of taught degree-awarding powers, student numbers, and the range of subjects offered'.[4] This range, it is repeatedly made clear, must include the teaching of skills relevant to industry, business and commerce generally. It remains to be seen how these new proposals will translate into forthcoming legislation. However, they are essentially so very much in line with what the higher education sector generally has been strongly advising that it must be a reasonable expectation that they will emerge in some such form. If that happens, then yet another chapter will open in the remarkable story of Liverpool Hope: providing it can then meet the new criteria, there is no obvious reason why it should not become a university. That might well require an increase, already contemplated, in its established programme of skills teaching, which includes business studies, information technology, and initiatives such as *Unique Learning* (an initiative that is fully discussed in later chapters). It will also encourage the continuing improvement of the existing high rate of success in the assessment of teaching quality. With all this in place, and followed by other developments already in the strategic planning process, the attainment of full university status should be a realistic aspiration, providing, of course, that new legislation does indeed embody the proposals in the White Paper. Should that be the case, the college can still work, without deflection, to improve its well-established excellence in theological research and its programme for achieving the same in education. Both of these are essential to the mission, and are also subjects which are not taught at the University of Liverpool. All this is in line with the diversity and complementarity that the White Paper envisages. Managing higher education is never dull, to say the least. On the contrary, in recent years the college has been confronted by so many challenges and opportunities that one would scarce wish to have been anywhere else.

So much for the present; the antecedent history of Hope will only be rehearsed here in such outline as is necessary. This is not because its history is unimportant. To the contrary, if ever a modern institution has remained faithful to its origins then Liverpool Hope most certainly has. Rather, it is because that history is, for the most part, well known and well told elsewhere,[5] as well as because of the important claims on space made by all that follows.

The modern Liverpool Hope University College, founded as such in 1995, is a single entity, but it is made up of older parts and traditions which, in their various ways, still shape and complement its nature as a living community. They do this principally by their influence on its mission as an ecumenical (since 1979) Roman Catholic and Church of England foundation, with origins dating back to the middle decades of the nineteenth century. Horace Powys, the socially enlightened Rector of Warrington, was a man of great energy and vision. Family oral tradition still reports that he 'was never beaten by a horse'. Nor seemingly by much else either, one might observe. He became the first Secretary of the Chester Diocesan Board of Education, which had been set up in 1839 in response to a call from the Church of England National Society for the Promotion of the Education of the Poor, itself only established in 1811. The diocese was already active in the remarkable Sunday School movement of the period. (As is well known, this pioneered the education of the poor with remarkable results. It was soon to be followed by other such movements which in their different ways laid the foundations of the educational systems we now take for granted.) Church day-schools were a natural growth from all this and the widespread demand for them created an unprecedented need for teachers. The Chester Training College was founded in 1839, and still thrives in its highly developed modern form. The Warrington Training College followed in 1844. This was attached to a charity school for the education of the daughters of clergy, which dated back to 1697. It too still survives and thrives as St Elphin's, in Darley Dale in Derbyshire. Horace Powys steered both institutions in those early days. Their long-term success became inevitable, for the simple reason that they were responding to real needs that were not being attended to by others. The Warrington Training College moved to Childwall in 1930, after a sojourn in Battersea following a fire which destroyed the Warrington building in 1923. It became known as S. Katharine's College in 1938.

The Sisters of Notre Dame opened Our Lady's Training College in 1856. It was also referred to informally as 'Notre Dame' or as 'Mount Pleasant' (after its location). Our Lady's offered a broad-based education to women, who had access to a well-stocked library. Very soon, it became remarkably successful. This was largely due to the quality of the students and the ability of the sisters to combine the spiritual and academic disciplines in the curriculum. It has recently been importantly observed that all this was then more radical and innovative than what was happening in the Warrington Training College, where the more domestic expectations in the education of women were still evident.[6]

All this was characteristic of the way the churches had always responded to educational and social need. It was spontaneous and practical; it was also, to a point, impudent, for at least two reasons. It expressed a vision for mass education and it showed that women teachers were to be central to its delivery. Both of these things are now, thankfully, taken so much for granted that we can easily forget how radical they were in their time. More than that, they reflected a vision and commitment that laid the foundations for the widely successful modern church school and college presence in primary, secondary and higher education. For this historic reason, the church colleges and church university colleges still train more teachers for church and state schools than does any other sector of British higher education. In so doing, as is explored later in Chapter 12, they do much to bring a Christian cohesiveness to the content, as well as to the wider social setting, of the whole of primary and secondary education. Initial teacher education remains an important part of the work of Hope, accounting for some quarter of the total student body.

Church training colleges proliferated in the mid-nineteenth century, and several new ones appeared as late as the 1960s, among them Christ's College in Liverpool in 1964. Many, however, have either ceased to exist or now only remain as parts of larger and often secular institutions. However, some 16 remain, of which Liverpool Hope is one. They have all, like Hope, diversified their curriculum while remaining committed to their central obligations for teacher training and theology. As much as, if not more than, any of these others, Hope celebrates the origin of its mission in those early beginnings. It is also, importantly, an ecumenical venture. This remains of such central importance that it deserves comment.

The ecumenical vision in 1979 was born of a necessity which was prepared for, if not actually foreseen, in 1973 when the governing bodies of Notre Dame, Christ's and S. Katharine's colleges responded to the James Report of 1972 by setting up a joint committee to discuss federation. A year later, an Interim Federal Academic Council was established. By a remarkable coincidence, Christ's College had been built on Taggart Avenue in Childwall, directly opposite S. Katharine's. In 1973 the University of Liverpool agreed in principle to the colleges offering a general BA degree. At first, some students who had excelled in this were permitted to attend the university for a fourth year to attain a BA Honours degree. Few, in fact, did this. Such students were soon permitted to complete the fourth year at the colleges of 'the federation', as it was coming to be spoken of. In 1974, the Board of College Studies was set up by the University of Liverpool. This had quasi-faculty status and lasted until the Institute (as the federation was later known) was awarded accredited status in 1994. (It is perhaps salutary to reflect on the slower pace of development in times past by remembering that this was part of a relationship with the University of Liverpool which dated back to 1903.) High walls, only recently lowered in the Hope years, physically separated the two Childwall colleges, though good relations existed between them, and with Notre Dame. These good relationships were soon to serve them well. In the mid-1970s the government served Notre Dame and S. Katharine's colleges with notices of imminent closure, along with numerous others elsewhere in the country. Of the three colleges, only Christ's escaped this proposed fate. It had been founded by the Catholic Education Council and was proving remarkably successful. The closure notices brought these partners even closer together with a new urgency. The principals of the three colleges, Dr Geoffrey Barnard of S. Katharine's, Mgr Bernard Doyle of Christ's and Sr Catherine Hughes SND of Notre Dame, had the shared vision to create a new single ecumenical institution. Without this, nothing would have subsequently been possible. This development was timely in the sense that it was readily adopted by Archbishop Derek Worlock and Bishop David Sheppard as a major plank of their wider ecumenical vision for the city. On a historic visit to London, they secured from the Secretary of State for Education permission to create an ecumenical institute of higher education out of the three colleges. The story is often told that it was believed that he agreed to this only as an expedient, because he thought that it would not last long anyway. The Liverpool Institute of Higher Education was founded in 1979 when Dr James Burke, a leading Roman Catholic layman and Professor of Metallurgy at Swansea University, was appointed its first Rector. The inauguration service was held in the Metropolitan Cathedral. Notre Dame College disposed of its buildings in Mount Pleasant in 1980. Ironically, they were acquired by the then Liverpool

Polytechnic and are now the administrative headquarters of Liverpool John Moores University.

After 1979 there followed years of internal rationalisation. Notre Dame and Christ's colleges formally merged as a single Roman Catholic college at the time of the consolidation onto the Childwall site. Duplicate academic administrative and service provisions in the now two colleges were to be replaced by single ones. All this entailed progressive and at times rapid change. As a consequence, successive revisions of the Articles and Instruments of Government were required, and at times these could scarcely keep pace with developments. Such revisions were lengthy and invariably expensive, for the simple reason that they necessitated consultation with and approval from three sets of trustees: the Warrington Training College, the Catholic Education Council and the Sisters of Notre Dame. This, however, was to prove an immense benefit as the changes proceeded. It meant, quite simply, that the support of the trustees, the providers no less, was always kept on board. This has not always been the case elsewhere, and the years have unravelled some of the other federations of the 1970s. That between Ripon College and St John's York, for example, did not maintain separate trustees. As a consequence, nothing could be done by the Ripon interests when the campus was recently sold and its assets transferred to what is now named York St John. The answer, then, to the oft-asked question of how Hope came about in the way it has, is simply that it was through a succession of pragmatic and commonsense initiatives that were supported at all stages by the providing bodies.

This created at least the impression that a lot was always being achieved. However, as all this is ever more carefully studied, it might yet become apparent that the post-1979 rationalisations were too consuming of energies that were, perhaps largely unknowingly, inward-looking and still controlled by the status quo. Working practices of the staff, for example, did not noticeably change. Few engaged in research and there was some reluctance to accept the sort of accountability for the deployment of working time that might have opened up opportunity for it. As a result, there was little enthusiasm for innovation. However, important foundations were laid in diversifying the curriculum into combined-subject teaching for the new BA programmes. Gradually, the BA numbers grew until at the end of the 1980s they roughly equalled those on the BEd programmes. One strength in all this was the way the sophisticated timetable was constructed to deliver combined-subject teaching in blocks. This was in marked contrast to traditional universities, which are programmed to deliver single subjects within faculties, with those who wish to combine them having, for the most part, to do the best they can to fit things in. Without all this development in the Institute years, the modern college could not have emerged as it did.

By the late 1980s the general mood reflected an all-pervasive confidence in what was then thought to be a secure future. Little was realistically done to promote the life of the Institute externally, beyond maintaining the older college-based student recruitment networks that had long served it well. By 1988 the Liverpool Institute of Higher Education had some 1600 students. There was no general will to go beyond this number. However, the Teaching and Higher Education Act of 1988 created new circumstances which, it is now easy to see in retrospect, were to threaten what had become tantamount to complacency. The Act triggered an unprecedented growth in the number of students going to universities and colleges, and this in turn led to the transformation of the polytechnics into the new universities of 1992. For institutions with ambition, this expansion offered a free-for-all opportunity not to be missed. And missed it was not. Seemingly overnight, comparatively unknown polytechnics became credible, fully fledged universities. Liverpool Polytechnic, soon to become Liverpool John Moores University, joined enthusiastically in all of this. It rapidly grew from about 4,000 students to over 20,000. All this was going largely unnoticed by the Institute, even on its own doorstep. This rapid growth was to come to an end, of course, when the government introduced measures to cap the numbers of students it would fully fund. The only winners, by then, were those that had seized the opportunity while it lasted. Numbers of funded students were to be set in stone and still are, though institutions were at liberty to take as many as they liked on a fees-only basis (if they could afford to).

The ecumenical vision of 1979 centred on Roman Catholicism and Anglicanism. Since then, like ecumenism in Liverpool more generally, it has included the Methodists and other Free Churches. By dint largely of the helpful influence of individual governors along with that of successive Local District Chairmen and individual ministers, the Methodist church gradually became more prominent in the life of the Institute and, importantly, it has remained so. Hope also now embraces people of other faiths. For example, a prayer room is provided for the use of Muslims, and Muslim faith experiences are celebrated and valued. The present work of the ecumenical chaplaincy will be described fully in Chapter 6. However, by way of introduction, it merits some prefatory remarks here. While there was undoubtedly a time in the process of federation when there was a noticeably conscious awareness of whether this or that person holding this or that post was Roman Catholic or Anglican, and of whether one denomination was in any way more privileged than the other, all this has long since genuinely and thankfully passed. Representation on the Governing Council is now no longer predominantly Roman Catholic, and 'Anglican' places carefully include representatives of other denominations. Denominational sensitivities are still recognised, but they are less self-conscious and far more generous in their reciprocal trust. This is a credit to the churches involved and, as far as it goes, is a good example to others. It would, however, be disingenuous to pretend that the ecumenical spirit is expressed without difficulty here, any more or less than it is elsewhere. That difficulty is, moreover, graphically evident on the campus. Hope possesses three chapels. (The third, St Francis Xavier's Church at Hope at Everton, will be described later, in Chapter 13.) On the main campus, Hope Park in Childwall, there are two, the Roman Catholic Chapel of Christ's and Notre Dame, an impressive modern design used to model that of the later Metropolitan Cathedral, and the S. Katharine's Chapel, in the Allen Building (as the S. Katharine's main building is now known). Curious is it not, even to the casual observer, that all other duplicate provisions from older days have been rationalised – except this one! Curiouser still, given that yet older Catholic–Anglican divisions no longer prevail in college life. There is a genuine will in the college community that this duplication should cease and that there could be but one chapel on Hope Park where all could worship fully together. That does, for the most part, actually happen in the one chapel or the other. It does not do so, however, in the most important Christian act of worship, the Eucharist. The sacrament, that is, of nothing less than unity! The reason for this is that neither the Roman Catholic nor the Anglican churches want it; the former because officially it will not administer the sacrament to those it considers to be non-Catholics, and the latter because it mostly wants to worship only where the sacrament is administered freely to all. Another reason why some Anglicans want to keep a separate chapel is because to do otherwise would be to create the impression of a unity that does not, formally, exist. This situation is not, of course, unique. The same difficulty is experienced else-where. It is well known that many others in the Roman Catholic church simply redeem this situation by sharing the Eucharist with other Christians inform-ally, but that is not an option in the ecclesiastically comparatively high-profile life of the college. Would that it were.

By the early 1990s the long relationship of the Institute with the University of Liverpool had come to be governed by a validation agreement which operated through the Board of College Studies. This required that university staff be present at Institute subject management boards and that they be con-sulted over even the slightest innovation. Much goodwill prevailed, but it was, in effect, a tutelage relationship which could not last. The main reason for this was that the 1988 Act had created a level playing field of accountability for quality which was applied to universities and colleges alike. The validation agreement became anachronistic and only survived by being modified. This too was not to last. It was replaced by an accreditation agreement in 1994. This gave the college the autonomy to validate university undergraduate degrees on its own, in its range of subjects, without the obligatory presence and say-so of members of staff from the university. They were, however, frequently involved as invited external members of validation panels alongside those from elsewhere. None of this now left any continuing role for the Board of College Studies, which was duly disbanded. However, close working relationships that had served the university and the college well for so long were maintained, and still exist to mutual benefit. In all this, the administrative infrastructure of the Institute grew as needed, to meet the demands of implementing the new autonomy.

The way was now open for a series of rapid developments. Numbers of students at last increased, though, let it be known, on one significant occasion more by accident than design. Curriculum innovation took place in subjects such as business studies and fine art and design. Single-subject degrees proliferated. Postgraduate degrees were introduced, against the echo of older times which claimed that 'our students are not like that'. Institute students were, in fact, no different from any others and it did them no service to think otherwise. New quality-control systems were put in place along with a restructured committee management system. New systems of financial budgeting, control and auditing were also established. By the mid-1990s, all undergraduate degrees were modularised, and a new realism characterised the now single academic institution. Extensive building repair and maintenance programmes were completed. The 1960s Christ's and Notre Dame buildings were re-roofed and their windows replaced, and part of the S. Katharine's building was also re-roofed. The Alexander Jones Building was refurbished throughout. The use of every square inch of space in the colleges was reviewed, and subjects relocated as necessary. All this culminated in the construction of the Sheppard–Worlock Library, partly out of space vacated by the closure of the S. Katharine's dining-hall and the demolition of a ghastly 1960s kitchen block. The two existing libraries had long been coping only under great difficulty and this more than justified the £5.34m investment in the new building. It was opened to acclaim in 1997. In retrospect, this development was crucial for the imminent, but not at the time fully foreseen, numerical expansion of the institution. The Sheppard–Worlock Library is now open literally round the clock during term times and is proving itself more than capable of meeting ever-increasing demands on its services. It has since acquired a number of special collections. This project consumed financial resources which were denied to numerous other improvements required at the time. As a result, the rest of the campus was beginning to look and feel tired, apart, that is, from the enlargement of the (by now combined) students' union building and the provision of new science laboratories.

Much student social life and support up to this time was still largely based on the two individual college communities. They remained active in this way largely because the Institute had effectively failed to establish an identity of its own which could nurture them. At times, this created seemingly irresolvable internal dissonances. While the wisdom of establishing nothing less than a single institution was becoming ever more self-evident, the definition of one that was commensurate with the task of replacing all that the two colleges still did remained doggedly elusive. The introduction of degree-day celebrations in S. Katharine's in 1989 clearly demonstrated this. Prior to this, the only cele- bration of graduation was held in the University of Liverpool students' union. While this was enjoyable enough, it was perfunctory and clearly disconnected from anything else in the life of the colleges. They did each year maintain their Going Down Days but these had become anachronisms appealing only to a few, such as those who had been in residence in college throughout their studies. The whole-day format of the new degree-day celebrations was soon replicated in Christ's and Notre Dame with equal success. The numbers attending steadily increased year on year. Other such celebrations during the academic year kept alive the older graces of the life of the colleges which had meant so much to so many for so long. The colleges also worked closely with the students' union in all this, and together they succeeded in establishing new events such as the marquee Going Down Ball. That this all happened as it did is a testimony to how closely the two colleges were working together by this time. Such activities that were self-evidently desirable continued to be main- tained by the successor communities to the colleges, which became known as 'halls'. This carried on until an embracing effectiveness in all these things was established by what was soon to become Hope. Needless to say, new person- alities came (and mostly went) throughout all this, and perhaps my authorship of this chapter is living witness to the truism that it is the survivors, not just the victors, who write the histories! Members of staff who had served the colleges long and well were ever ready to assist in any way they could to maintain old traditions, develop them and create new ones. In turn, they set examples for newer staff to follow. As a result, members of the academic and ancillary staffs alike would go far out of their way to provide the energy and support that all this collegiate activity required. Many were heartened by the fact that there was such a visible will not to neglect, or fail to appreciate, the richness of spirit that such college life had always made possible.

The Liverpool Institute of Higher Education, which had come about out of dire necessity, had failed to find a new name for itself which could command the necessary acceptability and overall confidence. As a result, external per- ceptions were still largely of the two colleges which had, after all, been around for so long. Further to this, the suburban campus lent itself to a certain anonymity in both the city and wider region. Clearly, the pressing need was to find a new vision which could bring all these achievements together under a new name expressing the Institute's single identity. Nothing less would be able to channel a clearly nascent, but at times frustrated, self-confidence. And that, so to speak, is where *The Foundation of Hope* and this modern history book begins.

In 1995 Professor Simon Lee was appointed Rector and Chief Executive of what was then still the Institute. He had previously been Professor of Juris-prudence at Queen's University Belfast. At that time, the Rectorship was one of three posts reserved for practising Roman Catholics or Anglicans. (The other two were the Pro-Rectorships.) Simon Lee met this admirably. He was already nationally known as a Roman Catholic writer on contentious legal issues such as birth control and abortion. More than this, he clearly possessed in large measure the vision, energy and determination which the life of the Institute had come to need. One result was immediate. The new name was to be Hope. That was it: simple as that. (This name had previously been considered in passing but rejected.) Very soon, apprehensions about the new name were overcome, and in a remarkably short period its use became universally accepted, natural and widespread. Things soon started to come together as never before. The senior management facility was the Rectorate, consisting of the Rector and the two Pro-Rectors. (These latter were no longer designated as Heads of College, as they had been since the early 1980s. Residual parts of their former roles were now the responsibility of two Deans of Hall.) This Rectorate troika was supported by a Rectorate Advisory Group, made up of senior academics and administrators. An internal deanery structure focusing on the Foundation, Education, the Arts and Sciences, and the Community was established, and one of the Pro-Rectors (myself) became also the inaugural Foundation Dean. Later, the resignation of the other Pro-Rector Dr Susan O'Brien (on her appointment in 1999 to Staffordshire University) and my own semi-retirement led to the abolition of Pro-Rectorships, and to the four Deans taking on a stronger role in the Rectorate team. The 'halls' were soon discontinued as their functions were taken over by Hope and strengthened by new arrangements for student life and welfare. Along with all this, pre-existing developments such as those for the graduation ceremonies were developed and supported yet more fully. By this time, in fact, Hope was becoming solely responsible for all aspects of graduation, having taken over this responsibility from the University of Liverpool. The Hope brand was vigorously developed and marketed through a team set up explicitly for the purpose. New corporate colours and logos soon became known locally, nationally and increasingly internationally. Student numbers grew dramatically. This was undoubtedly facilitated by the extensive Hope advertising campaigns and the attention paid to campus visits and open days. Both of these were central to wider, vigorous and ongoing recruitment programmes. Even in the difficult current circumstances, recruiting is now well on track to meet the next planned expansion to 9,000 students. In all this, attention was paid to overseas recruitment, with the result that Hope now has students from 68 different countries. New leadership clearly commanded the support and respect that it needed to deliver rapid change and innovation. Part of the story of this is taken up in later chapters.

NOTES

1 *Higher Education in the Learning Society*, Report of the National Committee of Inquiry into Higher Education, chaired by Sir Ron (now Lord) Dearing, HMSO, July 1997.
2 *The Future of Higher Education*, January 2003, HMSO, 2003.
3 Ibid., p. 54.
4 Ibid., p. 55.
5 See, e.g., J. E. Hollinshead, ed., *In Thy Light: S. Katharine's College 1844–1994*, Liverpool Institute of Higher Education, 1994.
6 K. Lowden, 'Spirited Sisters: Anglican and Catholic contributions to women's teacher training in the nineteenth century', PhD thesis, University of Liverpool, 2002, p. 151.

CHAPTER 2

Celebrating
the Student Experience

EILEEN KELLEHER SND WITH OTHERS

'EDUCATING the whole person in mind, body and spirit' is the shorter
version of the mission statement of Liverpool Hope University College.
Expressed more fully, it includes the following statement:

> Liverpool Hope University College is an ecumenical Christian foundation
> which strives to provide opportunities for the well-rounded personal develop-
> ment of Christians and students from other faiths and beliefs, educating the
> whole person in mind, body and spirit, irrespective of age, social or ethnic
> origins or physical capacity, including in particular those who might
> otherwise not have had an opportunity to enter higher education.

The College Governing Council and staff constantly reflect on this. Governors
who interview candidates for posts emphasise the importance of the mission, so
that all who join the staff are aware of its relevance to life in the Hope community. The Rector and Chief Executive, Professor Simon Lee, keeps it very
much at the forefront of all that happens in Hope. In order to illustrate the
seriousness with which our students and staff accept and live out the mission, I
have, as Chair of Governors, chosen several areas of college life and invited a
number of staff and students to record some of their experiences. These illustrate the many reasons why students can be praised for, and congratulated on,
the use of their gifts for their own benefit and for that of the whole college
community. The areas are relationships between governors and the students'
union, recruitment and retention of students, Hope Across the Irish Sea, international students, student support, aspects of learning and teaching, and the
Network of Hope.

RELATIONSHIPS BETWEEN GOVERNORS AND THE STUDENTS' UNION

During my eight years as a governor of Liverpool Hope, I have observed that
the students' union has been represented on the Governing Council by a

succession of excellent presidents. The current president, Ms Kelly Parker, has participated in all Governing Council and academic board meetings over the past two years and has conducted herself with dignity. She is widely known. She presents informative reports on the activities of the union and its finances, and is unafraid to speak out for students' needs. As with former presidents, Kelly, ably assisted by Chris Shelley, the vice-president, is committed to the mission of the college, as is evidenced by the union's generous input into college activities such as Hope One World, Foundation Day celebrations, Graduation Days, open days, and welcoming students during Freshers' week. The students' union also welcomes prospective students visiting Hope, whether individually or in groups. Kelly leads the Students' Union Council in its care for students' concerns. It has representatives with responsibility for education and welfare, community service, athletics, academic affairs, entertainment, and clubs and societies. These latter are numerous and include the Christian Union, the folk group, the Hope One World group, the Jewish society, the history society, musical theatre, international students, the Irish society, the Colours of Hope gospel choir, Nyeusi and Moindi (black and Asian societies) and the Sri Lankan society.

The students' union and its president work very closely with the Rector and Chief Executive, the Chair of Governing Council, senior staff and the student services support team. The Hope gospel choir generates a vibrancy at ecumenical services. Along with members of the Governing Council, the Students' Union Council attends and supports many of the college activities at both Hope Park and Hope at Everton: art exhibitions, musical events and religious services. One memorable event when the students' union excelled in the generosity and warmth of its welcome is worth noting here. In June 2002, during the Football World Cup, Fr Mark Noonan, Principal of All Hallows College, Dublin, had been invited, along with four of his staff, to visit Liverpool Hope. This was their first visit, aimed at forging links between the two institutions. The day chosen happened to be the day when Ireland were playing Saudi Arabia. At the invitation of the president, and to give the usual Hope welcome to our visitors, we arranged their itinerary so as to include watching the match on the large-screen TV in the students' union bar. Our visitors were given the best seats in the house with a variety of refreshments to make them feel at home, and the Irish flag flying. I am sure that the All Hallows staff will remember Liverpool Hope for a number of reasons, but particularly for this warm and generous welcome from the students. It helped of course that Ireland won 3–1!

Members of the Governing Council always acknowledge the need to listen to the students. They appreciate their wisdom and insights as well as their wonderful tolerance of people and situations across the life of the college. The Students' Union Council is committed to raising concerns about student funding and student debt at both local and national level, and, at the time of writing, is involved in discussions on the government's recent White Paper on higher education.[1] Never have I seen students looking so crestfallen as on the day that the White Paper hit the headlines. The awareness that so many of their number would be carrying heavy debts into their first jobs, into new relationships and the setting up of new families, depressed them in a way they had never experienced before.

I have invited Kelly Parker, the union president, to contribute the closing lines of this section. She writes:

> To say that the students' union should be at the heart of an institution could be seen as a biased comment. One look at Hope gives the lie to this. The students' union at Liverpool Hope is a valued and respected part of the college. Union and college work hand in hand to ensure that the student experience is one that is well rounded, well supported and inclusive of all. Concern for the quality of that experience is shared by all.
>
> The union's main function is to facilitate, support and represent the needs of the student body. This is what each of our union officers endeavours to do. They enthusiastically and unreservedly ensure that each student's needs are met. This work also contributes to the officers' own individual development. As president, I am always ready to assist students who are in need of educational or welfare support. I am happy to meet with individuals or groups of students wishing to set up sporting or non-sporting clubs and societies. I also value being on hand when, for example, students come to collect their mail. Union sabbatical officers across the country well know that all of this means hard work on what often seem to be thankless tasks. Much of the time, one has to intervene to prevent simple misunderstandings getting out of hand. We work ridiculous hours and are under-paid. People might well ask why we do the job at all. The reply is that we do it because we are passionate about student welfare. It is also because our individual student experiences, in our various institutions, have been so positive that we welcome the opportunity to give something back. With all of this in mind, it is important to understand how we know that we are on the right track. One of my own measuring-sticks is our relationship with the staff and Governing Council of Hope. I submit regular reports to the Governing Council in order to be fully open and transparent about our activities, projects and business undertakings. I have found this an invaluable forum during my term of office. Liverpool Hope's governors are given the opportunity not only to question me about current actions, but also to offer their support, and perhaps make suggestions about how we might do better. This sort of relationship between the students' union and the Governing Council enriches the quality of our students' experience. I always welcome every opportunity to convey the student viewpoint to the Governing Council. This puts students' thinking at the very centre of Hope's thinking.

RECRUITMENT AND RETENTION OF STUDENTS

The recruitment of students and their retention are issues of concern for all higher education institutions. This is because of the need to maintain numbers and thereby to secure stable financing. However, for those of us who are immediately involved with the students, numbers and financing are very much in the background. We meet and listen to all kinds of students and their families. We become involved with their needs and with the wonder of their giftedness. Those who are engaged in recruitment activities attend careers fairs and seminars, and welcome prospective students at organised open days or on days requested by students at their own convenience.

Of all the recruitment activities that go on at Liverpool Hope, I shall concentrate on two aspects: Hope Across the Irish Sea, and the college's work with international students. The next two sections of the chapter will focus on these two topics in turn.

HOPE ACROSS THE IRISH SEA

For the last three years, my own most direct collaboration with students has been through a particular involvement with Hope Across the Irish Sea (HAIS). The HAIS project was an initiative of Professor Simon Lee, whose previous post had been at Queen's University Belfast. At first, HAIS was under the leadership of Paul Rafferty, who was succeeded by the present Co-ordinator of HAIS, Ms Gillian Atkinson. Gillian, who is herself from Northern Ireland and a former student of Liverpool Hope, writes,

> In 1999, the project Hope Across the Irish Sea was set up to raise the profile of Liverpool Hope in Ireland by developing links with schools, colleges and universities there. As a result of this development, the numbers from across the Irish Sea now studying at Hope have increased dramatically. These students bring to Hope so much of their culture, their warmth and their strong sense of community. There are currently around 500 students from Ireland studying at Hope, and with the increasing number of applications we are receiving from across the Irish Sea, this figure will rise further. Many Irish students are attracted to the 'village in a city' ethos that exists at Hope: it reminds them of the town or village where they come from. The college has links with schools and with colleges of further education across Northern Ireland. Links have also been made with schools in the Republic of Ireland, especially in the border areas. Members of staff visit schools regularly to make presentations, and school groups are invited to visit Liverpool Hope. This has proved extremely successful as it enables prospective students to get a taste of higher education and to meet current students, many of whom are themselves from Ireland.

The retention of these potential students has been a priority for Hope Across the Irish Sea, which provides support and advice to students at application stage, pre-arrival, and also when they are here at Hope. Many current students help with the pastoral support of incoming students by becoming mentors. Irish students also contribute to the social and cultural life at Hope. For students who enjoy Gaelic sports, there are men's and women's Gaelic football teams, a hurling team and plans for a camogie team. We also have talented musicians, and a couple of our students, such as Neil Morrison, have competed in the world championship for Irish dancing. These students all contribute to Hope's diversity.

In addition to the programme of visits to schools and FE colleges that Gillian Atkinson has referred to, students who have accepted a place at Hope are invited, along with their parents, to an orientation session a week or so before they depart for Liverpool to begin their first semester. Such sessions have been held in Derry, Belfast and Enniskillen. Parents are invited to events of this sort, because it is recognised that they are important in the students' decision-making processes.

Two places I am particularly interested in are Omagh and Donegal. School visits have been made across the whole of County Donegal from Carndonagh and Buncrana southwards to Letterkenny and Donegal Town, and staff and students from these places have also visited Liverpool Hope. It is a great privilege to be involved with these Irish students, their parents and teachers. The warmth of their welcome and hospitality, their openness, friendliness and generosity are blessings to behold by those of us who spend time with them. Prior to all this, I had visited all the counties of the Republic but had never been to Northern Ireland. I was amazed at what I found on my first visit. The goodness of the people shines so brightly that their politics remain hidden. The majority of people across Ireland get on happily with their lives and relate well with one another. It was around the time of my first visit that I read *Love in Chaos*, by Mary McAleese, President of Ireland. The foreword to the book was written by Archbishop Desmond Tutu, and I feel very much in tune with what he says about the people of Ireland:

> I came away from a late 1998 visit of both South and North of Ireland deeply impressed, deeply moved, by the hope that filled many people. I felt myself filled with hope that these marvellous people with a wonderful capacity to poke fun at themselves (like no other people I have encountered) would emerge on the other side of this chasm, ultimately reconciled and at peace with themselves, having come to revel in the glorious and rich diversity which was theirs. I met with political, religious and community leaders and was impressed that all did, indeed, want to establish a lasting peace. I spent some time with a remarkable group of peace activists in Belfast who were

working to build bridges in local communities. I attended a vibrant ecumenical celebration in a deeply polarized community.[2]

On my last visit to Omagh I was accompanied by two current students, Geoff Laird and Oonagh Mullin, who had themselves attended schools there. Listening to their well-prepared presentations to school groups, I was reminded yet again that Hope's students are our best ambassadors. Oonagh, a final-year BSc student, writes,

> Hope Across the Irish Sea has opened many doors for me. I mentor Irish students within college, and this has led to my being given the opportunity of mentoring secondary pupils in schools around Liverpool. This has proved a valuable exercise which has improved my presentation and my social and community skills. A particularly rewarding experience was a visit to Omagh with Sr Eileen and Geoff Laird, a second-year student. This was important to me as I visited my old grammar school. Our visit gave students there the chance to see exactly what Liverpool Hope has to offer them, both academically and socially. I hope that my personal reflections on the experience of Hope helped answer any queries they might have had about university student life.

Several Irish students from across a range of courses and levels have been asked to share some thoughts about their experience of coming from Ireland to Liverpool Hope. Their words tell something of their commitment to Hope and its mission and of Hope's commitment to them. They also show something of their 'Irishness' and their own particular interests. Mary Croarkin writes as follows:

> I am currently studying a secondary PGCE course in physical education. I came across to Liverpool in September 1999 to study for my degree in sport, recreation and physical education, and mathematics. This was my first time living away from home. I settled into Liverpool very quickly, because I met lots of people who ensured that I felt at home in my hall of residence and who genuinely wanted my first experience at Hope to be a positive one. I made lots of friends during my first few weeks in Liverpool at Irish Nights organised by the students' union or by HAIS. I also set up a ladies' Gaelic football team at Hope. This venture has kept me in touch with the sport I love and also enabled me to make new friends. As a team, we have travelled all over England for Gaelic competitions. This always left us feeling proud to represent the Irish game as Liverpool Hope students.
>
> I am now in my final year at college and, indeed, in my final year in Liverpool. Since starting at Hope, I have travelled back and forth on many occasions, and I regret that the time to leave has come so quickly. My college life has seen many positive experiences that I will never forget. I shall be sad to leave Liverpool Hope, as it has been the centre of my life for the last four

years. My dream is to become a PE teacher, and when I qualify in June 2003, I will have Liverpool Hope to thank for making that dream come true. If I had not taken the huge step of coming across to Liverpool, that dream would have remained a dream. I am also returning home a more independent and stronger person, with fantastic career opportunities available to me, and with many lifelong friends.

Brenda O'Neill writes,

Being a bit of a home-bird, I had always intended pursuing my third-level studies at home in Ireland, close to my family and friends. I had fixed ideas of where I wanted to go to college. Leaving my homeland in County Antrim was certainly not on my agenda. However, when things didn't work out for my chosen course, I reluctantly considered leaving home as an alternative. Liverpool Hope appealed to me; so late August 2001 found me at an interview in Belfast, with the Hope Across the Irish Sea team. They greatly reassured me and put me at my ease: I came away impressed but still a little reluctant. I followed this up with a visit to Liverpool where I was warmly welcomed by Mr Sean Gallagher, and shown round the college and the accommodation. Such was the hospitality, advice and assistance given, that September saw me arriving at Gerard Manley Hopkins Halls. There I spent a very happy year. I quickly settled in to both the university college and the halls, where I have made many good friends. Now as I progress through my second year, I am living in a house with friends made in first year. I am doing a primary teaching course with theology, which I enjoy. I am involved in a mentoring scheme through which further friendships with both staff and students are being cemented. Social life is good. Liverpool is a wonderful city, growing and modern with a friendly atmosphere. I love it here. Liverpool is now for me a home from home.

Seamus Deery comments,

I am currently in my second year studying for a BA Honours degree in history and sport studies. I come from a small town called Castleblaney, in County Monaghan. When considering my future in third-level education, Liverpool Hope became an obvious attraction. After some research and talking to previous students, Hope became my choice of university college. My first impression of coming to England was one of pure isolation. However, that soon changed as the enthusiasm and friendliness of the staff and students provided a warm, much appreciated atmosphere. The Gaelic football club has given me new friends and offered me the opportunity to further enhance my skills. Despite the disadvantage of the euro exchange rate, Hope has been a tremendous experience both academically and socially. It has given me the incentive to pursue a teaching career, which has always been my goal.

Carol Anne Seaye says,

> Moving away from home to university was a very daunting experience for
> me, and for my parents too. But on open day at Liverpool Hope I was
> introduced to HAIS, and the whole experience became a pleasant one.
> There was such a warm welcome, and none other than Professor Lee
> showed us around – the Rector himself! The whole concept of Hope Across
> the Irish Sea really came to life for me in Belfast, my home city, when new
> students and their parents met prior to the first semester in 2001. Here new
> friendships were forged and they have grown stronger over the past two
> years. This meeting gave me the confidence and the determination for the
> times ahead, as my parents and I knew there would always be someone to
> turn to for help. A year later I found myself back in Belfast helping the staff
> to welcome and reassure new first-year students at a similar orientation
> meeting. My time at Hope has been great! For the first time I feel fulfilled as
> a person, thanks to the encouragement I have received in Liverpool Hope.

INTERNATIONAL STUDENTS

I have invited Dr Keith Paterson, Director of International Students, and Ms
Jean Clarkson, who works with international students in the Education Deanery,
to help me compile this section of the chapter.

In the academic year 1996–97 just under 150 international students came to
study for one semester or more at Hope (writes Keith Paterson). Ninety-four
per cent were exchange students, mainly from European Union countries and
also from North America. Fewer than ten students were registered on programmes in the newly established Centre for English Language Studies (CELS).
By 2002–03, over 500 international students are registered on full-time courses
– almost a fourfold increase. Over this six-year period, the balance of different
categories of student has shifted. Exchange student numbers have dropped
markedly (from 134 to 55) while the numbers of fee-paying pre-degree English
language, undergraduate and postgraduate students have risen dramatically. In
1996 no overseas postgraduate student was enrolled, whereas in 2002–03 almost
150 such students are registered. Undergraduate numbers have seen a similar
growth and now reach over 100, and CELS recruit over 75 annually to full-
time courses. Income from overseas students was below £50,000 in 1996–97; it
is now close to one million pounds. Significantly, the number of countries from
which Hope draws students has tripled from fewer than 20 to 58 today. 'Hope
in the round' now emphatically means drawing on students round the world.

At the heart of this success story lies a commitment to internationalism
embedded in the Corporate Plan 2000–05 and supported by teamwork across
the college. The international project team has as its prime operational goal the
implementation of the corporate objectives, and meets regularly to monitor

and review progress. The work has many facets: arrangements for study abroad and student exchanges; marketing and overseas recruitment; student welfare and support; new collaborative partnerships; supporting research overseas; internationalisation of the curriculum; and development aid work with Hope One World. Our international strategy emphatically has a vision which goes beyond merely increasing fee-paying student numbers; it aims to ensure a high-quality personal and educational experience from the students' first moment of contact to the point where they complete their studies and begin their careers. Hope's mission emphasises widening access and reaching out beyond the confines of the city and region to embrace new initiatives around the globe. Students from overseas are an increasingly important and valued part of the Hope vision, bringing home the realities of globalisation and the fact that we are all members of a world community. Sharing experiences and creating and reinforcing positive images of tolerance and mutual respect are integral to the work we undertake. The benefits for all in terms of cultural and intellectual enrichment are considerable. Hope welcomes the diversity of traditions, cultures and challenges which this expanding international domain brings. Celebrating and building on this work will continue to be a high priority in the decade ahead.

In these days of conflict and hostility (writes Jean Clarkson) one aspect of Liverpool Hope's mission – to enhance diversity among the student community, to foster cross-cultural exchange and to encourage internationalism – becomes more pertinent than ever. The Education Deanery's aim of increasing the numbers of British students who have overseas experience has become a reality for hundreds of student teachers over the last ten years. Some have completed periods of teaching with Hope One World in the schools of Kinderdorf International SOS Children's Villages in Africa or Asia for periods of three weeks. Some students have taught in the international schools of Helsinki, Oslo, Denmark and Lithuania for longer periods of time to complete their block teaching experience. Yet other students have experience of schools in the USA, in Hope, Michigan, in Indiana or Pennsylvania, or in Alverno, Milwaukee. Few universities anywhere offer students the opportunity to teach in so many parts of the world as does Liverpool Hope. From Ladakh, at a height of 10,000 feet in the Indian Himalayas, with Tibetan teachers, to the sophisticated high-tech international school in Helsinki, Liverpool Hope student teachers have practised their chosen profession. In the schools of Hope One World's projects, students have not only taught all ages and raised funds, but have bought and donated vast quantities of resources, from books and mathematics equipment to clockwork radios. All this encourages children of the world to love learning. Many of our former students are now teachers in schools overseas. Some are in international schools such as Helsinki or Majorca, some are in far-flung schools in Australia, and others are continuing the work of Hope One

World, providing support and services for those in less privileged circumstances. The Education Deanery is proud of all the students who are brave
enough to tackle teaching experience in new and sometimes difficult circumstances and who provide an unforgettable experience for those children with
whom they come into contact.

As a testament to the value the Education Deanery places on international
experience, the new BA QTS degree programme has a designated slot in the
third year of the four-year course for students to spend abroad. This represents
a mini gap-year and students are offered European Union Socrates grants to
cover the cost of living in Europe. Additionally, a recent bid for funding, won
by Liverpool Hope and five other higher education institutions, provides an
opportunity for student teachers to receive a stipend of 2500 euros from the
Federation of International Post-Secondary Education EU/US to spend three
months in an American university. Here they will undertake a Certificate of
International Education, which will supplement their teaching qualifications.
There is no better thing than realising that people throughout the world have
fundamental needs and values, and no better way is this learned than by teaching
the children of the world, with their laughter, energy and joy of living.
Liverpool Hope student teachers have woven an educational web around the
world and are making a difference to children's learning all over the globe.

The following account, written by Suwani Gunawardena, a student from
Sri Lanka is illuminating.

> I completed a BA in sociology and history at Liverpool Hope and am now
> following an MSc in information technology. This has been made possible
> thanks to the flexibility of the academic programmes. My study has helped
> me to appreciate varied insights into life from the perspectives of different
> academic subjects. In all this, Hope staff and students alike have been warm,
> reassuring and helpful. Hope's growing international student population has
> enabled me to make many friends from around the world. The vibrant and
> friendly community at Hope has made it an interesting and comfortable
> place to be, especially as a student from Sri Lanka, coming from a very
> different educational and cultural background. Hope has become a second
> home to me. Clearly Liverpool Hope is not just involved in recruiting
> students; it has a long tradition of supporting and caring for them as well.
> The staff who have responsibility for international students organise
> numerous activities to help them feel at home both in Hope and in
> Liverpool. Recently I was invited to an evening meal in Keith Paterson's
> home with 30 students from India. His French wife is a wonderful cook. The
> company was superb and the students entertained us with Indian dance and
> song. It is not at all unusual for college staff to entertain students in their
> homes in this way.

A TRADITION OF STUDENT SUPPORT

None of what we have been hearing about happens by accident. Behind all the goodwill of the staff and the students there has to be a super-efficient administrative organisation. More than that, it also has to be one which is sympathetic to creating the sort of personal experiences and learning opportunities that we have now heard something of. Mrs Joy Mills who has just retired from the post of Registrar has been most recently responsible for much of this. I have asked her to contribute this section of the chapter.

A valued component of the experience of studying within a smaller institution has always been the sense that, as a student, you are not just a number or an anonymous face, but someone known (writes Joy Mills). Within Hope's constituent colleges, in the past, that situation was easy to take for granted. Yes, everyone had a personal tutor and, as elsewhere then and now, there was a system that provided an opportunity for tutor and tutee to meet and review progress and, where necessary, talk through anxieties or problems. However, the programmes of study were offered as year-long courses and, at least in the first year, most students worked with just one tutor in each of their three subjects. It was easy to know and be known, and relationships established in that first stage of study tended to endure and provide opportunity for support throughout. Sometimes, indeed, the best experiences by-passed the system as students chose to take their concerns to a tutor with whom they had weekly or perhaps even daily contact because she or he taught them. It was this tutor who would then establish the link by ensuring that the personal tutor was kept in the picture and that each college's Senior Tutor was able to maintain an overview and provide more formal support where necessary. Such relative informality was possible and safe when students were numbered in hundreds and tutors in tens.

Some worried in 1979 that what had been so easy and so successful in each of the former constituent colleges would become impossible, or at least more difficult, in the larger federated Liverpool Institute. The worry was unfounded. Shared values and the maintenance, through the 1980s, of a relatively stable staff–student ratio supported the continuance and expansion of the existing pattern to cope with the greater diversity of programmes on offer through that period. The real challenge to its continued effectiveness came with the increase in student numbers from the start of the 1990s and, more particularly, from the move towards a modular degree programme. This was formally approved for delivery from 1996, but had actually been developed and informally operated since 1994. Increased numbers overall, larger group sizes and the segmentation of each year's programme of study into what began as units of study and emerged as distinct modules, meant that even first-year students worked with, on average, three times as many different tutors as they had under the old structures. For most students the establishment of a firmly based link with a tutor in that first year became more difficult. Even the operation of the personal tutor system came under pressure because numbers were larger, and the likelihood of the assigned personal tutor also being one of the people teaching the student was massively reduced. Senior Tutors retained responsibility for dealing with major cases of difficulty and, as Hope developed further, the role evolved into denominational Deans of Hall. Their work was vital, especially for students whose difficulties were personal or health-related. These Deans, however, were not necessarily people that readily came to the mind if a student had academic difficulties.

The move from being a 'validated' to an 'accredited' institution in 1994 had already given rise to the setting up of award management committees. These committees were to take responsibility for ensuring that all students registered for an award were guaranteed comparability and consistency of experience and quality whatever their choice of subjects within, for example, either of the two major combined studies programmes, the BEd and the BA/BSc. The concerns of these committees and their chair, the Award Director, were of two kinds: for the nature, standard and operation of the programmes; and for the experience of students, including their support. In this context, the Award Directors took over from the Deans of Hall the responsibility for advice to and the support of students on these programmes. This ensured that such advice, even if it was of a personal nature, was based on a full knowledge of the student's academic position. It also enabled links to be established with other support facilities in the college, such as the counselling and welfare services.

The success of the new system depended on students continuing to feel that they were known and treated as individuals – a growing challenge as the numbers coming for such support and advice, within the BA/BSc programme alone, expanded year on year. Accurate records of meetings, shared with and agreed by the students, were essential. This ensured that both the advisor and those advised were clear about what should come next: that, where further meetings were needed, old ground did not have to be gone over, and that, where other groups within Hope – such as the registry or the counselling service – needed to be informed or involved, all parties were clear about what information was being passed on and what action was required or desirable.

By 1996, however, the number of students seeking support had expanded to such an extent that it was beyond the sole capacity of an Award Director, and so a team of associate directors was established. Records then acquired an additional importance. Students returning for further advice would not need to suffer delay by waiting for the advisor they had seen the first time to be available. They could take the first possible appointment and be sure that the person they were seeing would know what had gone before and could pick up the story at its latest stage, all within a context that provided appropriate confidentiality. Students soon had confidence in this system. By 2000, well over 1200 students a year were coming to the award office for support and the team of associate directors first doubled and then trebled in size. The time had come for formalising the college's commitment to an integrated student support service and COMPASS, which will be discussed fully in Chapter 3, was established. There might be over 7,000 students and the structures might appear more formal, but the tradition of concern for and support of the individual, who wants to be known and treated as such, remains intact.

WIDER ASPECTS OF LEARNING AND TEACHING

The 2003 White Paper on higher education stresses that 'Effective teaching and learning is essential if we are to promote excellence and opportunity in higher education. High quality teaching must be recognized and rewarded and best practice shared.'[3] In his statement to the House of Commons on the day of its publication, the minister called on universities 'to identify more clearly than they do now the way in which they address the great *missions* on the basis of which they were created'. He also stressed the need to emphasise the importance of good teaching: 'I am pleased to announce that the government is giving a far stronger focus on *teaching*', and added that 'all universities will, in future, be judged by their teaching achievement as much as by their research attainment'. Liverpool Hope University College comes from a tradition of over 150 years of excellence in teaching. Every effort is made to sustain and enhance this. It is fitting, therefore, that attention is given to some of the staff involved in this. These, again, can only be representative of many others. Mrs Kathleen Hodgkinson, Dean of Education, will write particularly about our mission and long tradition of teacher training. She will also mention recent developments in special needs education. Dr John Brinkman, Director of Management and Business Studies, will comment on that subject area's success in their recent external review by the Quality Assurance Agency, in which the panel found 'a culture of listening to what students have to say' and a 'positive, friendly atmosphere with clear evidence of a team spirit'. Dr Sue Thomas, Director of Psychology, will then write about teaching and learning in psychology. Finally, Dr Elizabeth Gayton, Head of School of Sciences and Social Sciences, will provide an overview, 1995–2003, of the *Unique Learning* course that is now an integral element of all undergraduate studies (other than teacher training).

Staff at Liverpool Hope are not immune to the temptation to think that 'things, especially students, aren't what they used to be' (writes Kathleen Hodgkinson). Within teacher education there have certainly been enormous changes. One thing, however, has not changed, and that is the motivation of those coming to Liverpool Hope to train as teachers. We now have around 1500 students on programmes leading to Qualified Teacher Status. These are, variously, undergraduate and postgraduate, full- and part-time, flexible or employment-based. Students prepare for early years, primary or secondary teaching. Most of the programmes are provided at Hope Park, but many are now located throughout the Network of Hope [see *The Network of Hope* section below]. There have been significant and welcome changes among the students presenting themselves for these courses. There is now a greater spread of applicants' ages. More are making a career change and more have family responsibilities. There is greater diversity of background, with more students who are the first in their families to undertake higher education. Some of these might well have left school without qualifications and returned to learning later, perhaps motivated by their own children's experiences of learning. There is more ethnic diversity than there was, although still not sufficient to reflect the population in the schools where the students will serve. There are, alas, fewer men training to be primary teachers and very few training to work with children in the early years.

Amid all these changes one thing remains constant. It is the fact that, overwhelmingly, students choose teaching in order to make a difference in children's lives. On application forms and in interviews, over the years the same message comes through: they all want to be part of the educational process for children. Sometimes this is clearly articulated, obviously the product of considerable thought and discussion; sometimes it is uttered hesitantly, as if the applicant is afraid of being considered foolishly idealistic. Often it is the result of substantial experience in schools or in voluntary work with children and young people. Interestingly, although there is a perception that the motivation to teach is likely to spring from the experience of having been taught by a particularly charismatic teacher (as in the advertising campaign *No-one forgets a good teacher*) this is not a motivating factor much mentioned by applicants. Enthusiasm for teaching is more likely to be based on the experience of having themselves already, in a small way, made a difference to a child or a young person. Sometimes this can be a tiny event – a 16-year-old on work experience in a school is placed with one child with learning difficulties and helps him 'grasp' an idea, or enables him to complete a task which other pupils are racing through unaided. Or, as another instance, a mature applicant – a solicitor in this case – who gained little satisfaction from his day job but enormous satisfaction from his voluntary contribution to a summer camp for disadvantaged youngsters, where he observed them gaining in confidence and self-esteem. Often this experience is related to working with a child with special needs, either in a school or voluntary setting or within the family, and many applicants express a wish to work in the area of special needs eventually.

The Education Deanery has constantly to react to all this. One way in which it has recently done so is to respond to the desire of students to make a contribution to the education of pupils with special needs. Staff of the Education Deanery were delighted when the Teacher Training Agency announced that, with the introduction in September 2002 of new standards for Qualified Teacher Status, universities would be permitted to offer primary teacher training courses which did not have a national curriculum subject as the specialist subject. Staff set to work immediately, assisted by the appointment from September 2002 of Professor Gavin Fairbairn who has had a lifetime of experience of working in special schools and in child and adult psychiatry. Together they set up a working group to write a new degree pathway in special needs. It included professionals from health, education and social work, and the public, private and voluntary sectors. It also included Hope staff from the psychology, sociology and health areas, as well as from education. Dr Alex Carson of the North East Wales Institute was a valuable member of the group, contributing both as an academic and as a parent of a child with special needs. The group worked well together and the course, or rather two courses, began to take shape. The reason for there being two courses was that it had been decided at an early stage to develop a foundation degree in special needs alongside the pathway within the honours degree programme. An essential feature would be some common teaching across the two; this would enable those studying for a foundation degree while still in employment and the full-time students taking special needs within the combined honours programme to be able to learn together and from each other. In the same way, members of the planning group were committed to offering the course to other students in the college who were studying for a combined honours degree. This was to enable the approach to special needs to entail a wider focus than the educational one alone. All this is absolutely in the spirit of Hope. It taps into the strong vein of altruism that is found among applicants to teacher training courses. It offers them, and many other students who will work in different fields, the opportunity to make a difference in the lives of others.

The Quality Assurance Agency review in 2001 of the management and business centre (writes John Brinkman) was to be the last such review prior to the external decision being made about whether Hope might be granted under-graduate degree-awarding powers in its own right. In these circumstances, none of us needed to be told that its outcome would be of critical importance. The review team comprised members from the University of Sussex, Queen's University Belfast and Bristol Business School. During their four-day scrutiny, the team investigated closely the provision on the following programmes: Business and Community Enterprise, the BA in Nursery Management, the BA in Professional Development, the MSc in Management, and the Institute of

Management programmes. The reviewers were particularly keen to speak to students from all the programmes, to observe teaching sessions (12 different sessions in all were seen) and to inspect samples of students' work from the previous three years. In particular, students' views are crucial to any inspection team's report, and the reviewers canvassed student opinion at every opportunity. Throughout the visit and in their final feedback, the reviewers commended the subject team for a wide range of aspects and examples of good practice. Exceptionally, the final feedback session consisted entirely of commendations, and mentioned no recommendations at all about how the quality of education might be improved! The fact that the management and business centre achieved a score of 24, the maximum possible score – an achievement matched by only 5 per cent of the country's business schools – is a mark of well-deserved recognition for the hard work, high quality and professional dedication of the staff of the management and business centre team, who benefited greatly from the positive support of their academic and support colleagues, and, very significantly, of the Hope students.

Psychology first became a subject area at the then Liverpool Institute of Higher Education in the early 1980s (writes Sue Thomas). In 1982 there was a Head of Department, Alex Potter, one other lecturer, Roger Clark, and two female students. Twenty years later there is a Subject Director, 17 lecturers and approximately 900 students located either at Hope Park or elsewhere across the Network of Hope. The courses are accredited by the British Psychological Society (BPS), which is the professional body for the discipline. The criteria for BPS recognition are strict: they ensure, among many other things, that students have access to adequate laboratory facilities and technical support. Such facilities at Hope have improved out of all recognition over the past seven years, since Professor Simon Lee arrived at Hope. Being encouraged to reflect on the curriculum and constantly develop it has enabled the psychology team to offer a level of provision that gives the student a wide range of choices. This feature was recently highlighted positively by the BPS, which also commended Hope for the support, both academic and pastoral, given to the students. I have myself had personal experience of this support: I first came to Hope as a mature undergraduate, and, having progressed from that point, I now know that I can continue to develop my career here.

Unique Learning (writes Elizabeth Gayton) is a course taken by all first-year undergraduate students at Hope. It grew out of comments made by Professor Lee during his first few weeks here in September 1995, when he challenged the academic community to look for ways of allowing Hope students to share some common experience regardless of their subject choice. The two modules, initially known as *Effective Studentship*, were informed by the concept of 'Hope Graduateness' and were shaped in response to the Dearing Report.[4] Later, the

term *Unique Learning* was adopted to highlight that this programme emphasised the individuality of the learning needs of each student. Every Hope tutor,
at all locations, works through a programme of study with a small group of
students for whom they provide personal and academic support. Recent years
have seen an increase in the diversity of the student intake to higher education.
Unique Learning has been one tool in Liverpool Hope's strategy to work with
staff and students to enrich teaching and enhance learning for today's students.
Evaluations show that the majority of students appreciate, at least in retrospect,
the benefits of working closely with their own tutor, and that they eventually
understand the significance of the modules' content and purpose. In addition,
tutors have been required to address the challenges of coping with diversity;
this in turn has enhanced their teaching of their own subject.

Time moves on, agendas change and modules evolve. Today the national
emphasis is on personal development planning. This is a structured and supported process whereby individuals reflect on their own learning, performance
and achievement to plan for their personal educational and career development. The government requires all institutions of higher education to have
policies and practices in place to implement this. Liverpool Hope's experience
with *Unique Learning* means that we are well placed for it. Elements of the
programme are being integrated into the content of academic subjects, while
the personal tutoring element will remain as a free-standing, credit-bearing
unit, encouraging students to enhance their subject knowledge and understanding by focusing on their own learning, and empowering them to plan
more effectively for their futures at Hope and beyond. The *Unique Learning*
project and these subsequent developments from it are further explored in
Chapter 3. As Professor Simon Lee departs, he leaves an academic community
whose members are more aware of their own learning and teaching issues, and
confident in their ability to apply this understanding to support the diverse
student intake of the present and future.

THE NETWORK OF HOPE

One of the most exciting developments in recent years has been the creation of
the Network of Hope. In 1997, Pat Mullin, one of the governors of Liverpool
Hope and also a governor at St John Rigby Sixth Form College, Wigan,
brought together John Crowley, Principal of St John Rigby, and Simon Lee,
Rector of Hope, to look into complementarities of mission and the possibility
of linking courses between the two institutions. On Shrove Tuesday, 24
February 1998, pancakes and champagne were enjoyed by a group of staff and
governors to celebrate the partnership of the two establishments. Since that
time, other further education sixth form colleges in the North West have also

begun working with Liverpool Hope in similar ways. As a result, there are now some one thousand Hope students on degree programmes located in various venues across the North West. Hope's mission and values are shared in this way with St John Rigby College, Wigan; Holy Cross College, Bury; and St Mary's College, Blackburn. Liverpool Hope and these colleges work together in partnership to develop routes of progression into higher education that aim to encourage and engage those who might feel that higher education is not for them. The aim is also to bring courses of higher education nearer to where people live. In 1999 the Network of Hope was formally established and the first of a series of applications was made to the Higher Education Funding Council for England (HEFCE) for additional student numbers based on the widening participation agenda. Further successful bids have been made in subsequent years.

The mission of Holy Cross College, Bury is 'to provide a high quality education within a community based upon gospel principles. The college aims to develop each person spiritually, morally and intellectually, and it welcomes students and staff of all faiths.' Holy Cross emphasises that the higher education opportunities available in Bury are delivered in partnership with Liverpool Hope University College. The partnership continues to go from strength to strength. Recruitment for September 2002 surpassed all expectations, and now over 350 adults are enrolled. Mr Mike O'Hara, Principal of Holy Cross, speaks of Liverpool Hope in his welcome to all new students. Those students who take Hope's courses are encouraged to reflect and report on their experiences. One of them writes, 'Circumstances stopped me continuing my education when I was 18 and now I have the opportunity to put this right. Studying at Holy Cross means that I can still be a full-time mum, keep my job, study for a degree and, in the long-term, qualify as a teacher.' Another explains, 'My course is a BA in IT and business. It is the right course, at a time that suits me, and it is just round the corner from home.' A third comments, 'My children have all grown up. I have wanted to study English for some time, because I want to be able to read literature with greater understanding and appreciation.' Yet another says, 'Studying for a degree in health and IT was instrumental in my recent promotion and will, I believe, be of great value in my future career development.'

Mr Mike Finley, Principal of St Mary's College, Blackburn, acknowledges that their partnership with Hope has enabled them to deliver their mission to a wider community, by providing degree and other courses to adult returners to education, so that their dreams can become a reality. Students regularly express their appreciation for being able to study part-time in a friendly and supportive environment. Many of them stress that they never thought that such an opportunity would ever be available to them. Gausiya Bade, who studies English and advanced early years education, says,

When I spoke to colleagues at work and told them that I was undertaking a degree in English literature, one lady said, 'You? … but your first language is not even English!' When I received my exam results, which were very good, I went to her and said, 'You know the degree you thought I couldn't do; well I have just got my results.' … It was a wonderful moment.

Taslim Umarji, who is studying psychology and health, comments,

Studying in the Network of Hope through St Mary's College has been a truly great experience so far. My results have been excellent, but I have been able to combine studying for a degree – my dream – with other personal commitments. The environment at SMC is very friendly and this has meant I have relaxed and remained at ease throughout the course.

Sadia Imran, who studies IT and geography, writes,

I am working in education but I need a degree to progress. At the moment I am supporting other teachers but because of my degree studies I have just been accepted onto a full-time primary PGCE course, which I am thrilled about. This is my dream come true; now I feel I am going to be recognised as someone able to help children make the future.

More widely still, Hope has established formal and informal partnerships with many other schools and colleges which are in sympathy with its mission. Among them are The Deanery High School, Wigan and the following Anglican secondary schools in Liverpool: Archbishop Blanch, St Margaret's and St Hilda's. Liverpool College is also included. Yet others are listed in note 25 on p. 63 of this volume. All this is part of a constantly developing programme of such collaboration.

This chapter began with the Liverpool Hope mission very much in mind. The intention throughout has been to show how that mission is reflected in the personal and learning experiences of a small selection of its students. Many others could have been included. The aim has been to encapsulate the experiences of many through the eyes of a few. It is, however, in the educational experiences of the many that the mission of Liverpool Hope is lived out. Working in partnership with other schools and colleges increasingly enables this to happen.

NOTES

1 *The Future of Higher Education*, January 2003, HMSO, 2003.
2 M. McAleese, *Love in Chaos*, New York, Continuum, 1999, pp. 9–10.
3 *The Future of Higher Education*.
4 *Higher Education in the Learning Society*, Report of the National Committee of Inquiry into Higher Education, chaired by Sir Ron (now Lord) Dearing, HMSO, July 1997.

Maintaining the Integrity of Student Support Services in Mass Higher Education

SHARON BASSETT AND HELEN O'SULLIVAN

THE last eight years have seen a significant change in the size and composition of the UK higher education student population. Framed by inconsistent government policy, tight funding arrangements (for both students and institutions) and a widening participation agenda encouraging more diversity than ever before, the complexity, pace and magnitude of this change has challenged the integrity of every higher education institution (HEI).

As the sector strives to meet the government's current inclusion target of 50 per cent of all 18–30-year-olds entering higher education by 2010, and influenced by the recent publication of a White Paper,[1] HEIs are today having to embrace marketing and create a more student-focused culture. In welcoming this as an opportunity, Liverpool Hope has built on its mission to educate the individual in mind, body and spirit and has developed a new mechanism for delivering support services that underpin the student experience and complement the courses on offer. The flexibility and responsiveness of this innovation in service provision has become an integral part of Hope's strategy to strengthen the foundation from which all students can flourish as individuals within mass higher education.

THE RECENT HISTORY OF STUDENT SUPPORT

The recent history of pastoral support at Hope is characterised by a change from one particular model of support to another. The imperative for this change was a mixture of internal and external factors but was driven by Hope's distinctive mission and ethos. Central to this is the aim to value each student as an individual. The student body is more diverse academically, socially and culturally. Students now have a wider variety of expectations of higher education and there is a broader range of aspirations after graduation. The challenge is therefore to adopt a model of student support that is responsive to students'

needs, flexible in its use of space, time and location, and that meets the increasingly high expectations of fee-paying students.

One of the traditional characteristics of British higher education has been
the provision of student support services, and this is especially strong in the
church colleges. The tradition may have developed because HEIs stood in loco
parentis until the age of majority was reduced from 21 to 18 in the 1960s, and
were therefore responsible for the students' moral and physical well-being as
well as their academic development. The front line of this support was often
the personal tutor, who was usually a lecturer in the student's main study area,
and a resident tutor who was a postgraduate student or a lecturer living in the
same hall of residence. The tutors worked in isolation, but would have been in
contact in the case of a very serious health or personal problem. At Hope, a
similar system had evolved. In addition there were Senior Tutors, one associated with each of the constituent colleges, and their role was to provide help
and guidance for the personal and residential tutors as well as dealing with
serious health or personal problems and disciplinary matters. As the constituent colleges made way for what were designated as 'halls', the role of Senior
Tutor evolved into that of Dean of Hall.

Russell Rowley has described four models of student service delivery.[2] The
models represent an increasing degree of integration with the rest of the
institution and move from a reactive to a proactive approach. With the Deans
of Hall, Hope was operating in a way that was very close to Rowley's first
model. The Deans worked relatively independently and would be involved
from the beginning to the solution of any particular problem, from the simple
to the complex. There was little networking of information, so that a student
could be having severe personal or health problems and yet their academic
tutors might never know. Students could suspend their studies or even withdraw from the college without that information being formally shared. Though
this approach was extremely effective and relevant to the culture and climate
that had existed at Hope's constituent colleges up to the early 1990s, with the
expansion of student numbers and a rapidly changing student cohort it became
time to develop a new model.

Given that it is impossible to separate out the factors that enable a student to
succeed, such as intellectual capacity, previous academic experience, financial
circumstances, family situation, or state of physical and mental well-being, it is
reasonable to argue that the services that support students should also be
managed holistically. A new system was introduced whereby all student
services would be co-ordinated under a Director of Student Services. The
name COMPASS was chosen as an acronym derived from the names of the
services that made it up, but more importantly to indicate that the system was a
one-start-shop that would help students to navigate their way through the

various support services. The most obvious manifestation of this was a COMPASS reception desk in a centrally located common room, staffed by personnel from the range of services that provide initial guidance for students. They all make a commitment to a half-day a week on the desk, answering general student enquiries. As the systems has developed, the staff members involved have become more aware of how their own particular service relates to other services, and of the sorts of issue that students are most concerned about. In addition, a COMPASS website provides a mechanism for students to make enquiries through an e-mail facility.

In its current operation, COMPASS is similar to Rowley's third model, in which student support systems are embedded in the organisational structure, there is liaison and support with senior managers and input into the students' learning activities. An example of this is the development of *Unique Learning* [see the *Personal Tutoring and Unique Learning* section below] which involves the integration of the personal tutoring system into a student learning opportunity.

So, how might Hope move its provision forward to the fully integrated model that Rowley argues is the most suitable for the changing culture of higher education? One key feature of the integrated model is an active and direct involvement in the learning and teaching process. The deanery structure at Hope provides a possible mechanism for such involvement. All academic activity is located within one of four deaneries that represent the four 'pillars' of the mission. One of these is the Foundation Deanery, which is home to those aspects of college life that most closely reflect the foundation and mission of the institution. Student services are located in the Foundation Deanery, and this makes a clear statement about their importance to the mission and to the life of Hope, as well as placing them in proximity to a range of academic staff in the area of theology and religious studies. One way for student services to develop its role in learning and teaching would be to take responsibility for the *Personal Development Planning* module that is currently being developed to replace *Unique Learning*. A step has been taken in this direction with the location of the Writing Centre, a key feature of Hope's learning and teaching strategy, within COMPASS. In this way, Rowley argues, student services can become more student-centred by being more issue-focused. By involving a service in the learning and teaching process (for example, careers service in the *Personal Development Planning* module) the service becomes more proactive than reactive and can then positively address those issues that stakeholders (students, employers and the wider community) want to see incorporated into the learning experience.

COMPASS: A NEW DIRECTION

The notion of a one-start-shop 'involving a real and physical presence dealing with client enquiries, ... diagnosing the clients' needs and referring them to the most appropriate provider'[3] not only indicated to students that COMPASS was a new start for support services at Hope but also that it recognised their changing needs. Higher education has become a complex business for students, involving not just the issue of choosing the right route and paying for it (fees, resources and living expenses) but also that of coping with concomitant emotional, mental and physical pressures. Thus, when students present themselves at the COMPASS desk, or are contacted by a concerned member of staff, they benefit from a collective force ready to deal with increasingly complex cases.

Operationally, this does not preclude students from using the system as a service network[4] and accessing one or more of the specialist teams directly. Of course, prior to COMPASS, this is how the system worked. Johnson and Scholes claim, however, that a well-functioning network of this nature is not easy to achieve, and initial gap analysis of Hope's support services proved them right, particularly over the difficulty of 'cross-selling' other services. From a strategic perspective, the one-start-shop arrangement allows for this cross-selling to take place in two ways: communication flows in a number of directions – top-down, bottom-up and horizontally across the teams; and, trends are identified centrally via information monitoring so that appropriate teams provide a support network for their colleagues as well as for their student clients. It is at this nerve centre that students learn about Hope's personal concern for them, through the many complementary student support services that are available to them both individually and collectively.[5]

The internal structure of COMPASS lends itself to the 'matrix' form of management. Although not widespread at Hope, this combination of structures (reporting simultaneously to senior management team members and, in this case, to the Director of COMPASS) has increased the quality and speed of decision-making through higher involvement and motivation.[6] Furthermore, through the Director of COMPASS, the system-paralysis often associated with conflicts of interest in such a structure has mostly been avoided. On a less positive note, the flexibility demanded by matrix management has led to a lack of clarity about the roles and responsibilities of some staff. This has required individuals to learn to work together in a more fluid and even ambiguous environment, but they are given ready access to more sources of help than ever before. One example of this can be found in the rapidly changing requirements regarding support for international students with disabilities. Addressing this issue and developing coherent policy has beneficially engaged colleagues from several service teams: for students with disabilities, for international students, and for finance. COMPASS does not have a specific service aimed at mature students, mainly because at Hope the mature students themselves represent such a diverse group. There are very significant differences in the needs and expectations of a 20-year-old who has worked for a couple of years, of a man in his early forties who is embarking on a career change while still supporting a family, or of a retired person who has a successful career behind her and is studying purely for personal interest. In addition, the matrix structure allowed for the development of a student-tracking system that could continually monitor the changing student experience. The main aim of this was to build student–student, student–Hope, student–staff, staff–staff and staff–Hope loyalty, by teaming up service providers and clients in an active effort to bridge both strategic and operational gaps. All this has enabled COMPASS to establish a clear and consistent approach to the management of complex variables.[7]

CHALLENGES TO EFFECTIVENESS

Strategy setting at Hope has traditionally been a mixture of Johnson and Scholes's 'planning view', that is, formal strategic planning using prescribed tools and techniques (usually based on HEFCE and other appropriate agency research) and their 'command view', that is, strategy developed 'through the direction of an individual or group, but not necessarily through formal planning'.[8] The introduction of COMPASS, however, created a deliberate emphasis on learning by doing – being more responsive to students and their needs and 'testing changes in strategy in small-scale steps', aptly called 'logical incrementalism'.[9] Not only did this open up the opportunity for frontline staff and students to have a broader influence on strategy making but it also allowed for a greater penetration of Hope's mission and values at each transaction point.

While noting the positive impact of this addition to Hope's strategic views, it is important to stress that such emergent approaches (command view and logical incrementalism) tend to unsettle those more comfortable with defining an exact strategy, outlining precise objectives at an early stage and detailing systematic follow-up. Although the relationship between planning of this nature and performance is an equivocal one,[10] the planning view does provide a structure that readily enables certain analytical processes, specific communication and system controls to operate effectively. However, it does little to promote sensitivity to those day-to-day variables[11] that are often identified 'by experimentation, trial and error, opportunism, and – quite literally – accident', which according to Collins and Porras[12] contribute to the best management strategies. The main point here is that no single approach is right. A balance of them is required.

Linking these strategic views with broader aspects of strategy making and implementation gives rise to a further challenge: the need to be aware of finite resources and to maximise Hope's use of them through ongoing review.[13] In this way, the challenge is to service effectively a continual cycle of learning that will inform the management of integrated support systems and communication. More specifically, in Hope's case this involves all of the following.

- Conducting ongoing effectiveness reviews of the matrix system. These help the Director of Student Services continually to re-focus attention on student service and satisfaction.
- Widening access to support services, mirroring module flexibility, students' choice and pace of study.
- Striking a balance between individual and customised solutions that are responsive to peak-time demand (in all locations) in order to improve efficiency without compromising integrity.
- Identifying staff training needs as student demand changes.
- Creating campaigns to raise students' awareness of the *real* and *virtual* aspects of COMPASS, encouraging them actively to manage their own higher education experience.
- Undertaking market research and interpreting direct feedback from (potential, current and graduating) students during recruitment initiatives and college-wide events, in order to shape the service and improve its effectiveness.

Now that students pay a proportion of their fees they have a heightened awareness of consumer rights in education. However, the time when 'the customer is always right' has long passed. Fifield and Gilligan[14] advise that there are customers in all markets that have begun to demand the impossible. Taking immediate action to fulfil such requests would not only spread resources too thinly but could endanger aspects of Hope's distinctiveness, such as ecumenism, inclusiveness and parity of esteem, that the college rightly values. On the other hand, such seemingly impossible demands can occasionally provide an insight into future trends and drive positive change at a greater pace than would otherwise occur, even if too slowly in the minds of the individuals or minority in question. In such cases, managing communication consistently and making learning the key (for both student and service provider) can increase satisfaction and minimise problems.

STUDENT LIFELINES

Supporting students now requires an understanding of their way of life in the college and outside it. In fact, it could be argued that the latter is the more difficult of the two for students to come to terms with, particularly when considering the transition from home life to student life for school leavers, from home country to the UK for those with international roots and, for the mature student, from full-time worker and/or parent to the challenge of combining employment, parenthood and a return to study.

In September 2001, COMPASS stressed the need to reach every student with a message of support, to combat the increasing number of cases of home-sickness, financial difficulty, personal and academic concerns. As a result, an annual programme of direct mail, targeted induction talks, intranet- and web-based communication now exists to educate all incoming and returning students, resident and non-resident alike, about the support available to them, and how to access it.

Students can only seek help if they know that a particular door is open to them and, of course, where and when it is open. They often literally experience 24-hour worry. This creates the need for COMPASS to provide round-the-clock support. Though this was not originally envisaged, it has taken on a new dimension through a growing network of service-oriented teams and on-line collaborations. Not only do careers, chaplaincy, counselling, disabilities specialists, the international office, personal tutors and student funds advisors offer confidential on-line support, but a relay of out-of-hours pastoral care is also available through the accommodation, chaplaincy, domestic, international welfare, resident tutors and security services. The students' union is also closely involved. The student counselling and health services have also pro-duced a comprehensive model for providing students with mental health support at any time of the day or night. By turning to this, the unexpected and the untimely can always be coped with successfully.

Such improvements to service quality have relied on opening consistent channels of communication, bringing together teams who, in the past, worked at a distance (not only geographical) from one another. An undertaking to familiarise each team with the work of other COMPASS members is another step towards participative system development.[15] This has resulted in the increased ability of frontline staff to give timely, consistent advice and deal with issues as they arise. Equally, the re-definition of some prime service roles, for example that of the resident tutor, has brought energy, innovation and a more hands-on approach to identifying and resolving such disparate issues as lifestyle differences, behavioural problems and even travel difficulties.

However, the key to managing increasing student numbers lies in the ability of the COMPASS teams to educate students to help themselves to deal with those issues that are more easily overcome.[16] Given the fact that a cultural change of such magnitude requires high-visibility actions and considerable initial support (for both the client and the service provider), only a small number of teams have so far initiated a move in this direction. For example,

'COMPASS On-Line' advises students whom to contact about specific areas of concern (this includes the provision of a list of direct-dial telephone numbers); a joint initiative between the award directors and the marketing team has developed a slate of web-based FAQs to deal with basic awards enquiries from both students and parents; and the students' union and resident tutors are increasingly involving students in the day-to-day running of particular facilities. In the constant challenge to meet students' needs and expectations, there can be no surer guarantee of success than understanding their experience, appreciating their views and sharing their vision for the future. This furthers Hope's mission to educate the whole student, in mind, body and spirit, in a mass system of higher education.

PRESSURE POINTS

As with most HEIs, the pressure points for students at Hope are reasonably predictable. They follow a cycle from arrivals, induction and registration (September), to first semester examinations (January) and through to second semester examinations (April/May), the subsequent issuing of results, graduation (July), possible further assessment (August) and recruitment support. All this is interspersed with surprise occurrences such as those associated with health-related issues. For emergencies that can be reasonably predicted (such as a case of meningitis within the student population) procedures have been laid down to help make the management of an incident run as smoothly and efficiently as possible. For unpredictable emergencies, a major incident plan has been developed and is reviewed regularly.

The start of each academic year sees first-year students facing the challenge of finding new support networks. For returning students, it is a time to reattach themselves to old ones. As a result, the pressure is on all COMPASS teams visibly to engage with students and their families and to raise their awareness of the support available. Some of the more common issues at this time include homesickness, lifestyle differences, getting to grips with registration and induction, understanding progression from one level to the next, being able to engage with the curriculum quickly for the eager student, self-discipline for others, and the management of money. In the initial weeks of the semester, these problems are addressed by daily action plans for all service providers, which give an indication of any new trends that might be foreseen. A recent development has been the introduction of induction mentors. These are members of academic staff who are allocated approximately 15 students directly after the students' first activity at Hope – a talk of welcome from the Rector. The induction mentors then lead their students on a tour of the campus and answer any immediate concerns or enquiries. These mentors then remain responsible for guiding their students through the induction and registration process, for example by accompanying them on an introductory visit to the library.

During this induction period, inter-team collaboration, led by the student records staff, facilitates the swifter electronic registration of student groups, and the programme introduces groups of new students to every aspect of college life. In this context, the term 'groups' refers to specific segments of the student body sharing common needs and expectations,[17] for example under-graduates, postgraduates, students in the Network of Hope and international students. These strategic groups are mapped through the process of examina-tions, the issuing of results and follow-up advice. This sequence, which even of itself can be quite stressful, propels each student through a cycle of attention to study skills, academic performance monitoring, health concerns, self-assessment, awards management and careers guidance. These identifiable student groups have common problems that can be pre-empted, allowing for a better co-ordination of resources, effort and experience in dealing with new issues. None of this, of course, obviates the continual need to identify cases that require individual attention. Recent developments here have included a faster response at examination results time, with specific targeting of advice, special guidance sessions and the provision of telephone support. While the number of students staying on their course has improved in the last two years as a result of such targeting, an even higher COMPASS profile could encourage more students to help themselves,[18] that is, to seek support at an earlier stage rather than when time and options are running out.

Even after the successful completion of a student's course the COMPASS teams have a contribution to make on Graduation Days, when they are avail-able to offer congratulation and encouragement to graduands and their families, and to foster the establishment of ongoing links with the college through alumni activities.

FLEXIBILITY AND THE MODULAR SCHEME

Hope's rates for non-completion of courses compare favourably with the national benchmark figures. Some institutions may have taken the decision to accept high drop-out rates as a consequence of their learning and teaching strategies and as an inevitable result of the decrease in the unit of resource made available to them. However, every student who does not complete her or his course represents a waste of physical and human resources for the student, and usually for the family and for the institution. In addition, there is often disappointment, damage to ambition and waste of intellectual potential. Hope's mission specifically precludes any notion of 'natural wastage' and, therefore, efforts are made to retain every student whose interests are best served in the pursuit of study.

The general adoption of modular schemes across UK higher education has been blamed for creating a climate in which students can easily lose confidence by accumulating, in a short space of time, a number of failed modules. Such cumulative early failure can then deny students any chance of progressing normally to their second year of study. When Hope set up its modular scheme it was determined to maintain its reputation for high academic standards. It also saw this as the opportunity to design a system that would promote a flexible approach to course design which would allow students who might experience difficulties the maximum chance of completing their studies. Academic standards are maintained by insisting that all modules are passed before a degree can be awarded (though not all necessarily count towards the degree classification). However, students may retake modules, suspend their studies and restart, study part-time for some of their courses, take additional modules and take elective modules in areas of general interest. Some recent data[19] shows that while 12 per cent of Hope students do not graduate at the end of their third year of study, 76.5 per cent of these have graduated within four years of starting. The degree classifications of those who take a further year of study are similar to those who complete within three years, which indicates that the reason for their needing to take extra time is not a lack of academic ability. These students often have health, financial or other personal problems, and the flexibility of the system enables them to change pace for a short period of time before successfully completing their studies.

Students are faced with a range of module choices and Hope provides academic and regulatory advice at the appropriate times in the form of 'module choice events'. Students are able to access full guidance on the regulations governing their programmes of study, and at the same time talk to an individual member of academic staff from their subject areas. By combining these two sorts of advice, students are able to design a modular programme that reflects their interests, capabilities and future aspirations.

Within a flexible modular structure, it can sometimes be difficult for students to understand the full implications of their choices for the longer-term progression in their studies. Students who are experiencing personal or academic problems that are likely to impede this progression will need high-quality advice on how to navigate the regulations to their best advantage. In order to provide this advice, Hope has set up an awards office for the undergraduate modular scheme (UMS). Students who are experiencing difficulties that might affect their progression are referred to the UMS awards office, staffed by a team of advisors (usually senior academics) who spend up to half a day a week offering guidance. Day-to-day advice about regulatory matters is provided by members of staff in the student records office. Furthermore, any student who presents to the registry or accommodation office saying that she or he wants to leave is directed towards the UMS awards office. Indeed, students may not de-register until they have spoken to an advisor from that office.

HOPE GRADUATENESS

In the early 1990s a debate gathered momentum across the higher education sector about what it means to be a graduate, and about the best way to ensure the maintenance of the standards for this across the range of institutions and courses. It was argued that it should be possible to define those skills and attributes that characterise all graduates and therefore benchmark minimum standards across all programmes of study in all institutions. In 1995 the Higher Education Quality Council (later replaced by the Quality Assurance Agency) published a paper entitled *What are Graduates? Clarifying the attributes of 'Graduateness'*.[20] This paper examined such questions as the notion of graduate-ness, the relationships between graduateness, core skills and personal trans-ferable skills, and how the attainment of graduateness might be verified. In contributing to this debate, Hope developed the concept by proposing the notion of a 'Hope Graduate'. It was argued that, as well as possessing those attributes common to all students engaged in the UK higher education system, the unique mission of Hope would enable the development of additional skills and personal qualities that would help to set the Hope Graduate apart. After considerable discussion, a series of skills, attributes and personal qualities were laid down as a statement of what the college community believed to be the unique set of benchmarks for all students graduating from Hope. Among the skills identified were the ability to reason across the arts and sciences; the ability to understand the ethical context in which the subjects studied are grounded; and the ability to contribute to current debate in those subjects.

Once the statement had been approved it was necessary to devise a mechanism to give students the opportunity to develop each of the skills, attributes and personal qualities. There were two main features of this. From September 1998, each module document across the entire provision was required to demonstrate how that module contributed to students' attainment of 'Hope Graduateness'. In addition, from September 1999, all students were required to take two first-year modules, named *Unique Learning* [see the *Personal Tutoring and Unique Learning* section below], whereby several qualities of Hope Graduateness (such as communication, teamwork, reasoning across the arts and sciences, critical thinking and ethical dimensions) were specifically introduced and developed. In the original Hope Graduateness project, the summation was meant to occur in the final year, where students would present a portfolio detailing evidence that they had achieved Hope Graduateness and could articulate to a range of external audiences (notably future employers) what this meant.

Much resource, time and creative effort went into *Unique Learning* and into making sure that other modules too enabled students to develop qualities of Hope Graduateness. However, similar progress was not made with managing the end of the process, and no mechanism was developed to enable students to demonstrate that they had achieved these qualities. Consequently, students did not get the opportunity fully to embrace the idea or understand its potential. In order to address this, Hope Graduateness was made the subject of a year-long review in 2000–01. The review panel was chaired by the Rector. It looked at various issues and took evidence from many sources. Several suggestions were put forward and evaluated, including the idea that students would be able to opt for a final-year module where they reflected on their development and compiled a portfolio of evidence to support their achievement of Hope Graduateness. The panel finally concluded that the notion of graduateness had been overtaken by many other developments across the sector such as benchmarking and programme specifications. The concept that a Hope Graduate has something unique to offer still resonates with colleagues, but the challenges of actually demonstrating categorically that each student had achieved a benchmark standard in each quality proved difficult to meet. The focus has now moved to enabling students to demonstrate for themselves their own personal development. Indeed, the latest version of *Unique Learning* (with the working title of *Personal Development Planning*) will have this as a central theme. With electronic profiling becoming more widespread and reliable, it may still be possible for Hope to develop a system whereby all students are able to demonstrate individually the unique way in which they have been touched by the Hope mission.

PERSONAL TUTORING AND UNIQUE LEARNING

Hope and its constituent colleges historically placed great value on the interaction between a student and her or his personal tutor. Until 1998 the personal tutoring arrangements followed a traditional model. Students were allocated to a personal tutor who then met all of her or his students at the beginning of the year and, after that, at the ad hoc request of the student. There was an excellent profiling system whereby students met with their personal tutor annually to discuss progress, career aspirations and any problems that they might be having academically or personally. This was well resourced, with whole days for it being made available from teaching time. Guidance was also contained in profiling booklets.

In the last few years of its operation, problems with the profiling system were becoming obvious. There were two main factors causing these problems: first, the worsening staff–student ratio and second, the increasing diversity of the student intake. By the last year of its operation, only a minority of students were participating in the process. At the same time, a team of academic staff was developing a level one course that would be taken by all students (apart from those undertaking initial teacher training). The aim of this course was to provide an effective transition to studying in higher education and to give an opportunity for developing key study skills and higher learning skills such as critical thinking.[21] An additional and equal aim, however, was to provide a mechanism for the delivery of a personal tutoring system. Weekly group meetings with the tutor facilitated this and gave regular opportunities to review progress. Within the course, there was also a modular unit on career and personal action planning. Naturally, not all students are particularly interested in career action planning, given the increased numbers of students who are retired and studying for personal interest. However, such students can prove a valuable resource when discussing the importance of work-related skills. This course became two 20-credit compulsory modules at level one. They were named *Effective Studentship* in the pilot and *Unique Learning* when extended to all students.

Unique Learning has run for three years and there have been some difficulties with its modules. For example, right from the pilot project, some teaching staff expressed concern that key study skills and critical thinking skills were better developed through the medium of the students' academic subjects. The application of the skills to subject contexts was increased in *Unique Learning* but was still not completely successful.[22] The academic board therefore took the decision in December 2002 to move the skills elements of *Unique Learning* into the subject modules. However, the main success of the modules has been to re-establish the link between students and their personal tutors. All students now see their personal tutor every week and engage at some level with personal and career action planning. The personal tutor (now referred to as personal and academic tutor) plays a role in monitoring the attendance of the student and intervenes when attendance is causing difficulties with progress. As *Unique Learning* is being redeveloped, personal development planning is assuming a dominant priority in the module and this will enable Hope to fulfil its requirements for progress filing and to reflect developments across the sector in this area.

NEW COMMUNICATIONS TECHNOLOGY

In a sweep of internal change, 1998 saw the introduction of *Hope Virtually Daily*, an intranet-based electronic newspaper. This gave Hope's mission, values and identity a far higher profile. With broad staff support and ownership, this e-newspaper soon became a popular medium through which to communicate wide-ranging issues, from operational practicalities and team support to the strategic management of change and brand building. It subsequently provided the perfect medium for the launch of COMPASS in 2001. However, COMPASS soon saw the potential for such technology to reach beyond the immediate audience for *Hope Virtually Daily*, mostly staff and a small group of students, to the altogether more remote, and even isolated, off-campus students. Working with the marketing department, the students' union, Award Directors, the chaplaincy, domestic services, the accommodation office and resident tutor teams, and in accordance with the newly implemented matrix form of management, such remote students were located and could be contacted. The effectiveness of COMPASS was thereby greatly extended – a development much appreciated by Hope students everywhere, whether in the Network of Hope or further afield in international communities.

Building an electronic and face-to-face network that allows students and service providers to become strategy setters[23] has led to the creation of new ideas and the implementation of new systems. It could be argued that the success of COMPASS relies on the fact that the college has approximately 7,000 students, notably less than local competitors. While size is an issue, however, it does not prevent an institution from developing a putting-the-student-first culture and enhancing capability through in-house learning opportunities, and the sharing of knowledge and resources.

Another aspect of new technology is, of course, the increasing availability of internet-based courses, or e-learning. The Higher Education Funding Council for England (HEFCE) has recently invested significant resources in setting up the e-University – a system for delivering on-line courses from UK universities. There is no doubt that improved electronic technologies have provided opportunities for geographically isolated students to engage effectively with higher education. In addition, internet-based learning and teaching have become a routine part of traditionally delivered courses. With the rapid growth of e-learning, more attention is being paid to the nature and quality of on-line provision. The traditional image of e-learning is that of a student working alone, perhaps communicating with her or his tutor through e-mail. However, research has consistently shown that students need to have human interaction even if they are taking an entirely e-learning course. For example, the Institute for Higher Education Policy, based in the USA, has recently published a set of benchmarks for good practice in e-learning that are based on research and case studies.[24] One of these benchmarks suggests that student interaction with both tutors and peers is essential and should be facilitated through a variety of means.

Hope has maintained its mission of valuing the individual in both supported distance learning (the part-time PGCE) and in e-learning (the BA in Nursery Management). Indeed, the first thing that students enrolled on the on-line Nursery Management course do is attend a weekend residential programme designed to introduce students to their tutors, the Hope ethos and their peers. In this way subsequent electronic contact will be more meaningful as it is based on real personal contact and knowledge. In any study pathway where e-learning is used significantly to supplement more traditional methods of study, tutors are expected to comply with a series of guidelines that place individual attention and responsiveness at the centre of their work.

Hope's mission to value the individual is not in any way at odds with electronic and distance learning. Indeed, students may well prefer to be involved in a course that enables them to have both genuine human interaction and a high quality electronic learning experience.

The recently published White Paper gives some indication of the way that higher education might be expected to develop in the UK over the next few years. It will be a time of increased participation, growing heterogeneity and diversity. Students will study part-time while engaged in full-time employment, and there will be more distance and electronic learning. But the experience of personal contact will continue to be vital in embedding a truly student-focused culture into the deeper structures, processes and expressions of an institution; that is, learning from a real understanding of the students' vision and the value of that in determining a positive way forward.

If Hope can remain true to its mission of educating the whole person – the unique, individual person – in mind, body and spirit, and maintain that emphasis in an increasingly mass higher education system through innovative service development, then it can continue to thrive and make a distinctive contribution to the sector.

NOTES

1 *The Future of Higher Education*, January 2003, HMSO, 2003.
2 R. Rowley, 'Student support services', in *Higher Education Management: The Key Elements*, ed. D. Warner and D. Palfreyman, Open University Press, 1996.
3 G. Johnson and K. Scholes, *Exploring Corporate Strategy*, 5th edn, Prentice Hall, 1999, p. 415.
4 Ibid., pp. 415–17.
5 J. Kunde, *Corporate Religion*, FT Prentice Hall, 2000, pp. 109–10, 192–94.

6 Johnson and Scholes, *Exploring Corporate Strategy*, pp. 409–11.
7 M. FitzGerald and D. Arnott, *Marketing Communications Classics*, Business Press, Thomson Learning, 2000, pp. 1–14.
8 Johnson and Scholes, *Exploring Corporate Strategy*, pp. 51–87.
9 Ibid., pp. 55–57.
10 Ibid., p. 51.
11 T. G. Cummings and C. G. Worley, *Organization Development and Change*, 7th edn, South-Western College Publishing, 2001, pp. 151–52.
12 J. C. Collins and J. I. Porras, *Built to Last: Successful Habits of Visionary Companies*, Random House Business Books, 2000, pp. 7–12.
13 P. Fifield and C. Gilligan, *Strategic Marketing Management*, Butterworth Heinemann, 1999, pp. 27–49.
14 Fifield and Gilligan, *Strategic Marketing Management*, pp. 182–83.
15 Cummings and Worley, *Organization Development and Change*, pp. 326–29.
16 P. Kotler and K. Fox, *Strategic Marketing for Educational Institutions*, Pearson Education, 1995, pp. 55–60.
17 Johnson and Scholes, *Exploring Corporate Strategy*, pp. 129–33.
18 Kotler and Fox, *Strategic Marketing for Educational Institutions*, pp. 55–60.
19 Data presented to Liverpool Hope Academic Committee, November 2002.
20 *What are Graduates? Clarifying the Attributes of 'Graduateness'*, the Higher Education Quality Council Quality Enhancement Group, 1995.
21 P. Humphreys, K. Grennhan and H. McIlveen, 'Developing work-based transferable skills in a university environment', *Journal of European Industrial Training*, 21, pp. 63–99.
22 *New Climate New Curriculum*, conference at Liverpool Hope, April 2000.
23 B. P. Shapiro, V. Kasturi Rangan and J. J. Sviokla, 'Staple yourself to an order', *Harvard Business Review*, July–August 1992, pp. 113–22.
24 'Quality on the line: benchmarks for success in internet-based distance learning', March 2000, report available at http://www.ihep.com/Publications.php?parm=Pubs/Abstract?30

CHAPTER 4

Widening Participation
in Higher Education

BERNARD LONGDEN

THE church foundation of Christ's College first attracted me to what is now Liverpool Hope University College. From its inception there was an expectation that all staff should contribute to a collegiate course in general divinity. As a young lecturer in science education I made my contribution as best I could. Reflecting back to that period in the late 1960s and early 1970s there was a sense that Christ's College was a self-conscious attempt by the hierarchy to establish a Catholic university in the spirit of John Henry Newman's *The Idea of a University*.[1] The publication of the James Report in the early 1970s heralded a period of considerable uncertainty in teacher education and precipitated a merger between Christ's College and Notre Dame College, to be followed shortly afterwards by a loose federation with S. Katharine's College to form the Liverpool Institute of Higher Education (LIHE). The changes were about survival and continuity, even if in a modified form. At this time, my own career in higher education was moving increasingly into administration as I began to work with other colleagues on student admissions.

Soon after LIHE became Liverpool Hope, new opportunities opened up and my personal professional development included a study visit to several universities in the USA. Recently, I have been involved in representing Hope to external bodies, especially the Higher Education Funding Council for England and the Teacher Training Agency, at a time when we have not been afraid to challenge the quangos. This period, which could be regarded as running from the Dearing Committee's inquiry[2] through to the publication of the 2003 White Paper,[3] has been one in which widening participation has been at the forefront of government thinking. This political context, my work at Hope, my doctoral studies and my research collaboration with Professor Mantz Yorke at Liverpool John Moores University have converged to shape the latest phase of my career: my commitment to higher education through research. Whether or not this is a typical sequence of interests, it is all consistent with the foundation and mission of Hope's original three colleges.

ANTECEDENTS OF HOPE

In this chapter I shall explore some of the thinking behind these doings and relate it to the current government concerns about widening participation. The story of S. Katharine's College is well documented through the scholarship of Dr Janet Hollinshead.[4] The history of Our Lady's Training College, Mount Pleasant, later to be named Notre Dame College, deserves wider recognition, and research conducted by a Hope doctoral student Kim Lowden[5] has provided an insight into the early development of Our Lady's. The much later foundation of Christ's College and its short span as an independent institution before federation and merger mean that less is known about its philosophy. I have turned, therefore, to two former principals in order to understand what they thought was happening in the 1960s and 1970s. The story of S. Katharine's and Notre Dame can only be understood against a background that recognises the history of the church, state and education in the middle of the nineteenth century, while the story of Christ's needs to be set in the context of changes to higher education and the Catholic church in the 1960s. The whole foundation and development of Hope must then be placed within a long-standing commitment to extending opportunities for students to achieve a well-rounded higher education.

EXCLUDED GROUPS

For the purpose of this text I shall focus on three groups traditionally excluded from access to higher education – women, Roman Catholics and the poor. In the mid-nineteenth century, these people had little or no opportunity of securing access to a university or college education; a situation that has remained the case for lower socio-economic groups through to the present day.

During the Victorian period, women's access to university level education was held back by a prevailing uncertainty about whether they would benefit from the experience. To understand this issue fully requires a knowledge of the then presupposed inferiority of women in society generally. However, by the 1870s significant new opportunities had been created for women in higher education. Pressure from the incipient women's movement and from a shift in public opinion had resulted in Cambridge agreeing to the establishment of two women-only halls, Newnham and Girton. These provided about 280 places for women students. (However, it was not until 1948 that women in Cambridge were treated equally with men over admission to the university and were entitled to the award of its degrees.) The pattern at Oxford was similar. The University of London had also established a college devoted to providing university education specifically for women.[6]

The second group excluded from university in the nineteenth century were baptised Roman Catholics. Their exclusion had its authority in statute, and was clearly intended to protect the position of the established church in the political order. In his writing, McClelland demonstrates that English Catholics were effectively regarded as 'inferior citizens', but notes that

> It is true that one or two Catholics made their way to Cambridge as under-graduates prior to the 1850s, because the religious test was only exacted there upon graduation and not at matriculation as it was at Oxford.[7]

During the mid-nineteenth century Dr Cullen, Catholic Archbishop of Armagh, commissioned Fr John Henry Newman to plan and establish a new university for Ireland. Irish nationals, who were predominantly Roman Catholic, were not permitted to attend university and were consequently excluded from entering the professions. The educational principles that Newman developed in *The Idea of a University* were to inform the subsequent design of the second Roman Catholic college in Liverpool some one hundred years later.

The third excluded group were those who could not afford to pay for the select schooling that prepared candidates in the Greek and Latin required for university entrance. This was a very effective way of ensuring that only the more privileged sections of society could go to university. Rather than an out-right ban on the poor, the hurdle was, in effect, a test of who was sufficiently well-off to be able to take and pass the entrance examination. The fact of universities being the preserve of the higher echelons of the social order was thus maintained throughout the centuries of their existence. By the end of Victoria's reign only about one person in every hundred benefited from a university education and it was highly probable that the one would be male. Not until the mid-twentieth century had the number risen to about eight in every hundred, with a marginal improvement in the proportion of women benefiting.

COLLUSION AND TENSION BETWEEN CHURCH AND STATE

The relationship between university, church and state was, until the mid-nineteenth century, a collusion which effectively ensured a steady supply of clerics for the Anglican Church. The prevailing arrangement also served the best educational interests of the gentry who had emerged as the country's non-clerical ruling elite.

Towards the middle of the Victorian period, tension developed between church and state over who should control university education. Both the universities and the Anglican Church wished to retain a system that essentially perpetuated the status quo. The state, however, as it invested ever more and more funds into the system, wanted control over it. It achieved this in the new civic universities, which offered access to members of the local professional and commercial classes. When Durham University was granted its charter in 1833 it was possibly the last to be expressly founded by the church. Though the church remained determined to maintain its power and control over all education, the state now held the view that its duty was to create higher educational opportunities for far more of its citizens.

By 1850 there were also some 30 teacher training colleges. All except five were linked to the Church of England. All were residential. They were small in size, most with less than 75 students following a two-year course. An exception was the newly formed college in Warrington which advertised a five-year course.

The growing number of Church of England elementary schools, many established by the Society for Promoting Christian Knowledge (SPCK), others supported by local benefactors, were committed to providing education for a specific social purpose. SPCK, as an agent of the Church of England, had as its main aim the salvation of souls rather than the nurture of the mind. Lowden[8] suggests that the two outcomes of the 1834 Select Committee inquiry into elementary education were that the country needed more schools *worthy of the name*, and urgently needed a supply of well-trained teachers to educate the pupils in them. As John Elford has outlined in Chapter 1, it was the remit of an all-male Diocesan Board of Education, acting for the Diocese of Chester in 1839, to ensure that there were sufficient elementary schools within the diocese to 'promote a general education of the community on sound religious principles and in accordance with the Established Church'.[9]

The expansion in provision of schools also required a corresponding increase in the number of teachers. As Secretary to the Diocesan Board, Horace Powys agreed to open a college in the cathedral city of Chester. The college was established in 1839 to train masters for the diocesan schools. The decision was quickly followed by an agreement to set up a second training institution to produce women teachers to serve the diocesan elementary schools. Lowden suggests that its location in Warrington was chosen because of its good railway links[10] and its central location in the diocese. So, in 1844 the Training Institution for Elementary School Mistresses opened – the foundation that was eventually to become S. Katharine's College. The numbers attending the college were limited to those able to pay the annual fee. It is reasonable to assume that the college could ill-afford to turn candidates away, particularly if their private funding was guaranteed through a benefactor, therefore 'the selection depended on chance patronage rather than on educational merit'.[11]

At about the same time, and within twenty miles of Warrington, other plans for a training college were under active consideration. In 1848, the Catholic Poor School Committee (CPSC) had noted the large number of children without schooling in the Liverpool area, an estimated 101,930. While 38,207 children were receiving some schooling, it was not organised and not provided by trained teachers. No provision for teacher training for Roman Catholics existed at all. The challenge for the CPSC was to remedy these deficiencies. On a visit to Liverpool the CPSC found a much worse state than in any other town they visited. This had no doubt been exacerbated by the immigration following the Irish famine, which had brought into Liverpool families close to starvation and with little or no education. Lowden traces the detailed discussions and agreements that resulted in the establishment in 1856 of a training college for Catholic teachers in Liverpool, to be known as Our Lady's. Although it had been promoted and encouraged by the secretary of the CPSC, it only came into existence following the decision of the Sisters of Notre Dame in Namur, Belgium to commit themselves to a training college for women in Liverpool. Our Lady's College was charged, along with the only other Catholic college, St Leonard's,[12] with the training of all Roman Catholic women teachers for Catholic elementary schools. The first student intake comprised 21 women who started their course of study on 2 February 1856.

Lowden astutely observes that an all-male church hierarchy founded the Anglican and Nonconformist training colleges and always opted for a man, usually a clergyman, as their principal. This was certainly true of S. Katharine's College, where the Revd Horace Powys was appointed as the first principal. In contrast, the first Roman Catholic college in the North of England, Our Lady's, was independent of the Catholic hierarchy, the bishops and the cardinal, and had its trustees based in the Notre Dame community. This ensured that there would be a female principal and an all-female staff. These differences in the foundation of the two colleges gave rise to subtle differences of approach to their commitment to widening participation. Both, however, contributed strongly to the encouragement and support of women in higher education.

POSTWAR DEVELOPMENTS IN HIGHER EDUCATION

At the start of the Second World War there were about 50,000 students attending fewer than 20 higher education institutions in the UK. Today there are over 990,000 full-time students studying for undergraduate degrees in 250 institutions. After 1945, social reconstruction raised educational expectations and aspirations. The postwar 'baby boom' led to the creation of new grammar schools for both boys and girls. In greater numbers, these young people aspired to continue into higher education to gain entry to the professions and better-paid jobs. David Eccles, then Minister of Education, set up an inquiry into higher education in 1959 and appointed Lord Robbins to chair it. Its report, to Edward Boyle in 1963, marks the start of the 'binary years' in higher education. The Robbins Report famously stated that 'courses of higher education should be available for all those who are qualified by ability and attainment to pursue them and who wish to do so'.[13] This sentence became known as the 'Robbins Principle'. Government had, at this time, little direct control over the universities other than through the student grant.

Following the publication of the Robbins Report, the opportunity was taken by the incoming Labour government to establish a rival form of institution that might shift society away from its 'snobbish caste-ridden hierarchical obsession with university status'.[14] Though this radical expression of contempt for the existing university system exposed the then Secretary of State, Anthony Crosland, to considerable criticism and probably put back his agenda to democratise higher education, the colleges of advanced technology (CATs) were established as higher education institutions within the public sector, under the direct control of their local education authorities. The CATs, free of the class-ridden associations that so offended Crosland, became the launch pad for the next phase of higher education growth. They were the means through which local people might have access to higher education within easy reach of home (and without creating the need for expensive purpose-built residential accommodation). It was even possible to gain a degree from them while remaining in a job. The CATs and other regional colleges of technology offered degree-level programmes of study supplemented by London University external degree courses. These institutions later became the polytechnics, offering their sector's own degrees under the auspices of the Council for National Academic Awards (CNAA). In 1992, the polytechnics achieved full university status; for example Leeds Polytechnic became Leeds Metropolitan University. Despite all these developments, the participation rate for attendance at university remained under 10 per cent of the age cohort.

DEVELOPMENTS IN LIVERPOOL

During the frenetic period of expansion in the early 1960s, the decision to open a second Roman Catholic college in Liverpool devoted to training teachers was taken. The Department of Education and Science (DES) had calculated, wrongly as we now know, that the demand for primary school teachers indicated a need for an additional such college in the North West. Archbishop (later Cardinal) Heenan was encouraged to establish the new Catholic college in Liverpool, but it was to be a college with a difference. Sr Catherine Hughes SND, Principal of Notre Dame College in the mid-1970s, acknowledges that the college had not moved with the times despite its national reputation for preparing women for the teaching profession. She recalls that in 1961, when she herself was a lecturer on the college staff, many of the older sisters were mortified that 'their' students were now allowed to stay up until 10.00pm at night. When she left to take up a headship in Kirkby in 1964, the college still retained such strict demands, oblivious to the changing times. So, for example, the college had

> lectures on Sunday mornings in religious education, and before I left in 1964 married women were beginning to come and they had to come in on a Sunday morning. It was just totally unreasonable.[15]

This unreasonableness weakened the college's reputation. When it wanted to admit male students as well as female, this was refused by the DES. Why was Notre Dame denied the chance to expand and extend? Views differ on this point. It was possibly because of an intention on the part of both Heenan and Bishop (later Archbishop) Beck to take greater personal interest in Roman Catholic teacher training. Notre Dame College was funded totally by the Sisters of Notre Dame and therefore the Catholic Education Council (CEC) did not have the same degree of influence over its activities as it would have over a college under its own direct control.

It was against this background that the discussions about the proposed new college – the first mixed Catholic college in the UK – were taking place. This new college would be a partnership between the CEC and an order of sisters proposed by Heenan – the Ursulines. Requests from the trustees of Notre Dame College to widen its access to include male students continued but were repeatedly turned down by the CEC. When it began, therefore, the new college, Christ's College, met with a certain local resistance even from within the Roman Catholic community.

The trustees of Christ's had appointed an exceptionally able principal in Fr Louis Hanlon, a priest with a clear vision for the future of this new college. Archbishop Beck gave Hanlon several years in which to plan for the college, design it, plan the curriculum, appoint staff and recruit students. Mgr Bernard Doyle, Hanlon's successor says,

> They looked on Hanlon who had got this great name for catechetics. So that's really where he fitted in perfectly. He had a degree in ... economics at Cambridge. He was an open man – he was a modern man.[16]

It was not unimportant that he was a priest under the jurisdiction of the Bishops of England and Wales. Hanlon was able to appoint eminent Catholic theologians to the staff of the new college. The implicit mission of the college was to become the first Catholic university in Great Britain, with theology at its centre. Hanlon had visited the University of Louvain, Belgium, and was familiar with the writing of Newman and the challenging text of *The Idea of a University*. Further clues to his thinking can be gained from the design of the main college buildings on Woolton Road, where the chapel is at the heart of the site; from the academic teaching being centred on a tutorial system; and from the celebration of Mass being given centrality in the working day. All staff, irrespective of personal belief, were encouraged to contribute to the college programme of general divinity, and a willingness to encounter diversity was emphasised. It was in itself a process of widening participation for both staff and students, searching for meaning and value in an increasingly complex world. Doyle reflects,

> Brilliant lecturers, [Fr] Frank Frost, [Fr] John O'Neil, [Fr] Alex Jones, as well as [Fr] Gus Reynolds and [Fr] Kevin Nichols, were involved in it. Many people put a tremendous commitment into it. And then the Mass time. The Mass again was a Louvain style thing. It was a common act of worship and so a part of the day, I think it was 10.00am to 11.00, was sacrosanct. You didn't have to go to Mass but you couldn't do anything else. You couldn't lecture, so the college, in a sense, came to a standstill.[17]

Christ's College opened its doors to its first students in September 1964, with a large intake of both men and women from many strongly Roman Catholic areas of England and Wales, for example Birmingham, Manchester, London, Cardiff and Newcastle. But Hanlon's own gifts for the college were never to be brought to fruition. On 6 January 1965 he tragically died in a car crash. The college was without a principal at a critical time in its formation. The CEC together with the Ursuline community, acting as trustees, appointed Hanlon's close friend from Cambridge University days – Bernard Doyle. He took up the principalship, a position that he had not sought but which, as was the way within the Catholic Church of the time, he accepted in obedience to the wishes of his bishop.

THREE COLLEGES – MERGER OR CLOSURE?

Fresh problems for all three colleges of education (as they were by then designated) in Liverpool were just about to start. A committee under the chairmanship of Lord James of Rusholme was established to inquire into the provision of teacher training in the UK. This was to signal the start of a period of turmoil for the training providers. There followed the paradoxically named White Paper, *Education: a Framework for Expansion*, prepared by Margaret Thatcher, then Secretary of State for Education, which heralded expansion for higher education in general but required a contraction in teacher training. College closure was the talk of the day. Notre Dame and S. Katharine's were proposed for closure: the new Christ's was not. The rest of that story has been summarised by John Elford in Chapter 1 of this volume.

THE FOUNDATION OF HOPE

My final section covers the period from the publication in 1997 of the report of the second inquiry into higher education, the review chaired by Sir Ron (now Lord) Dearing,[18] through to the publication in January 2003 of the government's White Paper entitled *The Future of Higher Education*.[19] The Dearing inquiry was given an extensive remit. For the purposes of this chapter it is worth drawing attention to the following principle that the committee members were directed to take account of

> maximum participation in initial higher education by young and mature students and in lifetime learning by adults, having regard to the needs of individuals, the nation and the future labour market. ... [Annex A went on to direct the committee to take account of] a growing diversity of students in higher education with a growing number of mature entrants, part-timers, and women.[20]

The agenda behind this was one of increasing and widening participation and of finding a way to pay for it. The growth in the student population had remained modest until the 1960s, when the postwar rise in university aspiration resulted in a doubling of numbers. The greatest growth occurred between 1970 and 2000, with an increase from 400,000 to just over one million full-time students attending a funded higher education course in England.

The expansion in numbers reflected an increase in participation from an index of about 8 per cent around the publication of the Robbins Report to a value of about 35 per cent in 2002. As might be expected, the participation index across the socio-economic groups remains uneven, with low uptake from potential students in lower socio-economic groups. Ross[21] notes that by the time of the publication of the Dearing Report, although the population of students in higher education had reached more than 30 per cent, almost all this expansion had taken place within the middle classes. Dearing was sufficiently concerned about the apparent resistance to higher education of those from lower socio-economic groups that he commissioned a special study to inform the committee. The data it produced confirmed that these lower socio-economic groups remained under-represented in higher education. This led to the suggestion by some that student tuition fees should rest with those who benefit from higher education, rather than remain as a tax on those excluded from it.

The government responded promptly to the Dearing recommendations, and, as Ross points out, they did so in a way that showed a remarkable symmetry with the government of the day's response to Robbins more than thirty years earlier. In both cases a Labour government swiftly and firmly rejected the main recommendations of the report, and the respective Secretaries of State then set out their alternative visions for the shape of higher education. David Blunkett rejected the Dearing proposals on funding higher education and introduced legislation to bring in means-tested tuition fees and a loan system for student maintenance support. By 1998 the emphasis in funded student growth was on

> making places available to all those capable of benefiting from higher education [and] widening access into HE for full-time and part-time study rewarding high quality learning and teaching.[22]

From 1999 the agenda for widening participation extended to colleges of further education being encouraged to undertake undergraduate teaching to degree level. An analysis and description of the history and current involvement of the further education sector in the provision of higher education reveals an increased diversity of routes into higher education and a greater opportunity for local access to such provision.

There were 839,675 home-based, full-time undergraduates, funded by either the Higher Education Funding Council for England (HEFCE) or the Teacher Training Agency (TTA), engaged in degree-level study in 2000–01. In replying to a Select Committee question, Sir Howard Newby, Chief Executive of HEFCE, commented on the extent of the challenge represented by the government's target of increasing the participation rate in higher education to 50 per cent by the year 2010. He clarified that the current participation rate is indeed 34 per cent, but went on to explain:

> It [the target] is 50 per cent of 18–30-year-olds having had some experience of higher education by 2010. Given that far fewer than 34 per cent of 18–30-year-olds will currently have some experience, the increase required is not just the increase from 34 per cent to 50 per cent, it is a much more significant increase than that.[23]

All institutions committed to widening participation are confronted by the necessity to encourage those who would not normally consider higher education to begin to do so. Such young people are predominantly from working-class backgrounds and their cultural tradition means that they have to make a conscious decision to go into higher education. Recruiting them represents a daunting challenge to all those involved in working to extend access to under-represented groups. Analysis reveals that higher education is in practice a two-tier system with inbuilt subtle barriers that perpetuate a separation of the different social and cultural groups. Liverpool Hope University College was born into all this. Between 1994 and 2000, full-time home undergraduate student numbers at Hope increased by 65 per cent. This growth was a response both to national policy and to the college's own commitment, as expressed in its mission statement, to extend access and increase participation. Clear leadership reinforced the conviction that the pool of talent was significantly larger than most people believed. When asked about the idea of a 50 per cent participation rate by 2010, Professor Simon Lee suggested that:

> the upper limit is way above 50 per cent, probably not one hundred per cent, given various people with extremely special needs, but I would put it at at least two thirds, three quarters, if we have the resources and the expertise to support those people and if you want to dedicate these [resources] to them.[24]

Professor Lee established the Network of Hope, a unique form of partnership between Liverpool Hope and several sixth form colleges[25] across the region. As has been described in Chapter 2, these colleges provide learner support and teaching accommodation, thus ensuring the provision of higher education close to the homes of people from traditionally under-represented groups. The college has, of course, maintained its commitment to the education of women, but can now add to the list of under-represented groups for which it caters the categories of mature entrants, disabled people, ethnic minority communities and members of the lower socio-economic groupings. Each year since 1997, HEFCE has published performance indicators on a range of measures, one of which relates to the participation of students from socio-economic groups IIIm, IV and V for each higher education institution, the sector as a whole, and a benchmarked (virtual) institution.[26] Hope had drawn 39 per cent of its students from the lower socio-economic groups in 2000, compared to the national UK sector average of 25 per cent and to the figure of 32 per cent for those institutions against which it was benchmarked.

HEFCE, in preparing its statistical analysis, introduced a mechanism to help with the interpretation of data and to provide a level of confidence in it. This mechanism indicates that, for each of the differences between Hope's figures and those of the benchmark group, there is statistical significance. It is therefore valid to claim that Liverpool Hope is making a significant contribution to providing higher education for students from under-represented social groups, and thereby continuing its founding mission of widening participation. Data for the number of students from low-participation neighbourhoods reveals a similar story, again with statistically significant differences between Hope and its benchmarked comparators. Figures relating to characteristics of students funded by the Teacher Training Agency all show a similar positive pattern.

Encouraging students into higher education is one thing, but ensuring that they then benefit from that experience is another. Evidence derived from HEFCE's performance indicators published in 2002 shows that 94 per cent of students from Hope had successfully gained employment within six months of graduating. This compares very well with benchmarked institutions, and places Hope as one of the most successful in the sector. All this, it must be remembered, is in a college that welcomes students with low qualifications on entry. Research evidence correlating entry qualification to degree success is problematic and needs to be interpreted with considerable caution. The view taken at Hope is that many reasons can contribute to the success or failure by students in examinations prior to their entry to higher education. On the basis of this belief, many students who would not have been considered academically suited for degree-level studies have been given their opportunity, have seized it, and, often against all the initial odds, have succeeded beyond all proportion. Elsewhere in this book there are more extensive comments about the changing student experience. For me, teaching recently on a first-year course designed to help students adjust to studying at university level proved challenging, and reminded me of earlier days teaching on the general divinity course in Christ's College. Like that earlier course, *Unique Learning*, as has been described in the preceding two chapters of this book, is an attempt to build up students' skills in argument and debate, to develop their processes of critical thought, and to give them confidence where they often lack it most.

Not all efforts to widen participation have been directed to students from the UK. It cannot escape the notice of anyone walking across the campus that the college is now a broadly based, cosmopolitan community with students from all parts of the globe, notably from the Middle East, India, Sri Lanka, China, Korea and Japan. These vibrant international students, while positive in their determination to enhance their own education, contribute greatly to Hope's diversity and provide us with the opportunity to gain a better understanding of their various cultures at first hand. This is an important and often overlooked benefit of a widened participation.

By this point in the narrative, one can see that Hope can be confident in its assertion of ongoing and successful commitment to under-represented groups. Liverpool Hope will continue to identify and create higher educational opportunities for people belonging to such groups. The recent White Paper[27] reaffirms the government's intention to achieve the much-debated 50 per cent participation rate by 2010; and this through a process of expansion that should not be interpreted as being more of the same. It also reiterates the Robbins Principle that fair access should mean entry for all those who have the potential to benefit from higher education. The White Paper goes on to confirm this fundamental principle as being

> at the heart of building a more socially just society, because education is the best and most reliable route out of poverty and disadvantage.[28]

The whole of Chapter 5 of the White Paper is devoted to an exploration of widening participation and reinforces some of the arguments developed here. I have tried to show, I believe successfully, that Hope is still true to its founding principles. This commitment has served it well and will continue to do so. Professor Leslie Wagner, the retiring Vice-Chancellor of Leeds Metropolitan University, has written,

> The problems faced by higher education in the mid-1990s arise from a system which has become mass in size but which remains elite in its values.[29]

The quotation might be recast in Hope as

> Liverpool Hope has become mass in size, has rejected elitism, and has retained its founding principles of equity and social justice.

NOTES

1 J. H. Newman, *Discourses on the scope and nature of university education*, Dublin, 1852.
2 *Higher Education in the Learning Society*, Report of the National Committee of Inquiry into Higher Education, chaired by Sir Ron (now Lord) Dearing, HMSO, July 1997.
3 *The Future of Higher Education*, January 2003, HMSO, 2003.
4 J. E. Hollinshead, ed., *In Thy Light: S. Katharine's College 1844–1994*, Liverpool Institute of Higher Education, 1994.
5 K. Lowden, 'Spirited Sisters: Anglican and Catholic contributions to women's teacher training in the nineteenth century', PhD thesis, University of Liverpool, 2002.
6 Bedford College was opened in 1878 to give women access to a university education and to allow them to become full members of the University of London. This opened up to women areas of study previously the exclusive province of men, such as medicine and law.
7 V. A. McClelland, *English Roman Catholics and Higher Education 1830–1903*, Oxford, Clarendon Press, 1973.
8 Lowden, 'Spirited Sisters'.
9 Hollinshead, *In Thy Light*.
10 Warrington had a population of about 20,000. It was well connected by rail to London and to the rest of the North of England. This was seen as an important feature to attract students to study there.
11 Lowden, 'Spirited Sisters'.
12 St Leonard's College was forced to close in 1863; all their students transferred to Our Lady's Liverpool.
13 The Robbins Report. Committee on Higher Education: Report of the Committee appointed by the Prime Minister under the Chairmanship of Lord Robbins 1961–1963, HMSO, 1963.
14 A. Crosland, 'Woolwich Polytechnic Speech', paper presented to the Association of Teachers in Technical Institutions, Woolwich Polytechnic, 1965.
15 C. Hughes SND, Personal reflections on the history of Notre Dame College, conversation held at Notre Dame Convent, Woolton Road, Liverpool, 26 February 2003.
16 B. Doyle, Personal reflections on the history of Christ's College Liverpool, conversation held at Hinsley Hall, Leeds, 18 February 2003.
17 Ibid.
18 *Higher Education in the Learning Society*.

19 *The Future of Higher Education.*
20 *Higher Education in the Learning Society.*
21 A. Ross, 'Access to Higher Education: inclusion for the masses?', in *Higher Education and Social Class: issues of exclusion and inclusion*, ed. L. Archer, M. Hutchings and A. Ross, London, RoutledgeFalmer, 2003, pp. 45–74.
22 HEFCE, 'Widening participation special funding programme 1998–99', in *Circular 98/35*, Higher Education Funding Council for England, Bristol, 1998.
23 House of Commons, 'Post-16 Student Support', in *Sixth Report of Session 2001–02*, HMSO, 2002.
24 S. Lee, 'Retaining students within a widening participation agenda', conversation held in Liverpool, 21 December 2001.
25 St Mary's College, Blackburn; Holy Cross College, Bury; St John Rigby College, Wigan; Aquinas College, Stockport; Newman College, Preston; Loreto and Xaverian Colleges, Manchester.
26 Benchmarking is a mechanism that allows comparisons to be made between a specific institution and other institutions of similar type for a prescribed range of characteristics.
27 *The Future of Higher Education.*
28 Ibid.
29 L. Wagner, 'A thirty-year perspective: From the sixties to the nineties', in *The Changing University?*, ed. T. Schiller, Buckingham, The Society for Research into Higher Education and the Open University Press, 1995.

CHAPTER 5

The Art of the Spiritual Detective –
A Research Student Experience

MICHAEL FORD

IT began, not among the yellowing tomes of an ancient library, but in a modern television studio complex on London's Euston Road. At an age when many of my friends were graduating from university, I was working as a 21-year-old journalist on the set of *This is Your Life*. It was here, as one of the undercover agents secretly unearthing stories for the big red book, that my obsession for research took root. Original ideas, imaginative proposals, painstaking planning, unceasing determination and careful checking had to be matched by consistent commitment and dedication. Having spent some of my teenage years researching and presenting surprise tributes to celebrities in my home town, I found myself working with Eamonn Andrews among the national stars of the day: one programme, which saluted a famous sportsman, brought me face to face with Liverpool's George Harrison who appeared as one of the guests.

The detective skills I acquired in the world of TV showbiz later accompanied me to the realm of the roving news reporter. Whether broadcasting from Bethlehem, Belfast or Bondi Beach, I have always been energised by the intensity of research towards the final piece, almost as much as a live transmission. Integral to the journalism have been my encounters with people – religious leaders such as Rowan Williams and Basil Hume, political figures such as Mo Mowlam and Gerry Adams, sporting heroes such as Henry Cooper and Pat Cash, not to mention crime writers, among them Minette Walters and P. D. James.

But nothing in my privileged portfolio of reportage could have prepared me for my academic trail as a doctoral sleuth, a five-year investigation which began in southern England in the summer of 1997, took me across the Atlantic and back several times, came to fruition in the academic cloisters of Liverpool Hope University College, then culminated in a magnificent graduation ceremony in the Metropolitan Cathedral of Christ the King, Liverpool, on 11 July

2002. The date was extraordinarily significant, for it had been on 11 July 1993 that the BBC had broadcast a programme I had made on the very person who would become the subject of my PhD thesis: the spiritual writer and pastoral theologian, Henri J. M. Nouwen. Fortunately, I kept a copy of the raw, unedited interview. This was to yield many clues as I began to piece together a psychological profile of a man dubbed by one of his friends, 'the most tortured human being I have ever met'.

My doctoral work was effectively a study into the emotional life of a world-renowned guide of souls. Nouwen (1932–1996) was a Roman Catholic priest, clinical psychologist and Ivy League professor who became one of the world's most successful writers of popular Christian spirituality. The Dutch-American author of more than 40 books, including *The Wounded Healer*, *The Return of the Prodigal Son*, and *The Inner Voice of Love*, he built a reputation to rival that of C. S. Lewis and Thomas Merton. As a preacher, he was once said to have had even greater impact than Billy Graham. But what I found most compelling about his story was that, at the height of his career as a university professor at Harvard, he had abandoned academia in favour of a hidden ministry among the mentally disabled of L'Arche in Richmond Hill, Ontario. Nouwen's thesis – that we heal through our wounds – found resonance with many Americans who had become disillusioned with institutional religion and had sought solace in therapy. Nouwen's spirituality brought them hope. This is what he writes about the concept:

> Hope is trusting that something will be fulfilled, but fulfilled according to the promises and not just according to our wishes. Therefore, hope is always open-ended.
>
> I have found it very important in my own life to let go of my wishes and start hoping. It was only when I was willing to let go of wishes that something really new, something beyond my own expectations, could happen to me. Just imagine what Mary was actually saying in the words, 'I am the handmaid of the Lord. Let what you have said be done to me' (Luke 1:38, JB). She was saying, 'I don't know what all this means, but I trust that good things will happen.' She trusted so deeply that her waiting was open to all possibilities. And she did not want to control them. She believed that when she listened carefully, she could trust what was going to happen.
>
> To wait open-endedly is an enormously radical attitude toward life. It is trusting that something will happen to us that is far beyond our own imaginings. It is giving up control over our future and letting God define our life. It is living with the conviction that God moulds us according to God's love and not according to our fear. The spiritual life is a life in which we wait, actively present to the moment, expecting that new things will happen to us, new things that are far beyond our own imagination or prediction. That, indeed, is a very radical stance toward life in a world preoccupied with control.[1]

I have been reading Nouwen for more than twenty years and even taken his books with me on reporting assignments. I remember being sent to Hong Kong just before the handover and meeting in a hotel bar a businessman from Manila. He was missing his wife and family, and seemed eager to talk; our conversation over several hours embraced such themes as religion, philosophy and the human condition. He was wrestling with various issues and I found myself introducing him to the theology of Nouwen who had struggled and suffered much in his own life. The man seemed enthralled. Before he returned to the Philippines, I knocked on the door of his room to give him one of the paperbacks I had brought with me. I felt like an evangelist but sensed the book would mean a lot to him.

I detected in Nouwen a kindred ecumenical spirit for, although he had been a devout Roman Catholic, he had viewed the church, not as an autonomous organisation, but as an accumulation of the experiences of its members. While his own beliefs were never compromised or diluted, he had no qualms about sharing the Eucharist with non-Catholics and, in his community, was happy to receive the sacrament from an Anglican woman priest. Embracing the worlds of theology and psychology, Nouwen had quietly cut through the religious red tape to reclaim the spiritual life for the priesthood of all believers.

The interdenominational Liverpool Hope University College could not have been a more appropriate context in which to study in depth the life of a natural bridge-builder. I think I was initially attracted by its ecumenical ethos and holistic sense of mission that seemed entirely in keeping with Nouwen's own philosophy of theological education. I knew of lecturers at Hope who viewed their teaching careers as a vocation and I had heard of students whose lives had been radically changed by what it had offered them. From my initial interview, I found the staff genuinely interested in my area of research and, as a restless reporter in search of a bit of stability, I soon discovered the campus to be a friendly and welcoming community where I could put down some roots for a while and taste its academic excellence.

The guidance I received from my supervisors, Dr David Torevell and Professor Ian Markham, was second to none. They could not have been more professional or supportive. Their blend of academic rigour, teaching experience and friendship made me value the fact that I belonged to Hope, and Hope belonged to me. I shall always be grateful to David and Ian for their belief in me as a postgraduate student and their kindness to me as a person. I also felt encouraged by the smiles of an array of doctors who often passed me on the college's 'Path of Hope', among them John Elford, Mark Elliott, J'annine Jobling, Shannon Ledbetter, Kenneth Newport and Ian Sharp, while Dr Michael McGhee, from the philosophy department at the University of Liverpool, was always a calming influence at the other end of the city. I think that, at Hope, I came to understand the meaning of *community* in a new way and I especially appreciated the many opportunities I had to connect on a regular basis with its year-round climate of academic research, something the world of nomadic journalism could never have provided. Hope was undoubtedly the place to bring to birth a project that had begun that summer's day in Northampton when I had met for the first time a spiritual writer whom many claimed to be 'a prophet of hope'.

It was surprising to discover that such a charismatic figure should have lived his 64 years without becoming the subject of a major critical study. Chapters about him appear in occasional volumes but, at the time of his death, no book focusing solely on him had been published. The situation was remedied with a Dutch publication by Jurjen Beumer.[2] For people who had read Nouwen for many years, Beumer's book was useful in bringing together the varied strands of Nouwen's theological thinking. But the book did not explore the person of Nouwen or his life in any depth, thereby failing to throw much new light on Nouwen himself, especially the more ambivalent dimensions of his recollected experience. This is what my doctoral research would seek to redress.

Initially I put my plans on hold because I knew the unpredictable nature of my journalistic work would not be conducive to academic concentration. But the challenge proved irresistible. In the end I decided to give up my staff job at the BBC and work in a freelance capacity so I could devote as much time as possible to the project. It was certainly a professional and financial risk but I knew that, as a full-time radio producer, I would never have found the energy or the time for such a study. I have never regretted the decision.

Having read theology at the University of Bristol, I was able to draw on both my academic and journalistic training as I plotted my doctoral research with all the precision of a *Panorama* production. I re-read all Nouwen's books, devising a card index to file all his key themes. I then studied the little that had been published about Nouwen and made a few preliminary telephone calls. Suddenly realising I was the first person on the scent of the *real* Nouwen, I decided to sound out a publisher who signed me up for a biography and helped finance the research. I drew up a list of potential interviewees, an inventory which grew longer and longer. Some would be questioned about Nouwen for the biography; others for the thesis which would have a different emphasis.

The acknowledgements in Nouwen's books were a useful starting point and the Henri Nouwen Literary Centre near Toronto supplied me with a number of addresses and telephone numbers. Over the course of a year I travelled across Northern Europe and North America to meet Nouwen's friends, colleagues, rivals and family members. My primary methodology was through journalistic-style interviews. Between June 1997 and May 2001, I met 125 people, most of whom had known Nouwen for many years. On most occasions, interviews were recorded in person but a number were also carried out by telephone or e-mail. Eighty per cent of those interviewed were male. Most were aged over 50. A fifth were Roman Catholic priests, Anglican priests and Protestant ministers. The majority of the 20 per cent of female interviewees comprised religious sisters or women who had spent some time living in community. The majority of interviewees were practising Roman Catholics. Others represented Orthodox, Episcopal and Baptist traditions. A small sample were Jewish. All represented key areas of Nouwen's life and ministry. I travelled to the places where Nouwen had lived, worked and visited – or to places where his associates then resided.

I remember my first doctoral scoop taking place at the University of Oxford. I was there, microphone in hand, reporting for Radio 4's *Sunday* programme on the visit of a controversial American bishop. After an interview, I asked if, by chance, he had ever met Henri Nouwen. 'Oh yes,' he said, 'I certainly have.' So I switched the tape-recorder back on and heard how Nouwen's texts had helped seminarians in the bishop's diocese. I was off to a promising start. From Britain, I travelled to such places as Rotterdam to meet the author's family, followed by a day at the University of Nijmegen scouring notice-boards and administrative records to try to track down Nouwen's former professors. I didn't know if they were even still alive. I knocked on almost every door in one department to see if the staff remembered anything about Nouwen's studying there forty years before. No joy. Few seemed to have heard of him. Then, just when I thought it was a fruitless quest, I decided to try one more door. Success! The lecturer had not only heard of Henri Nouwen, he knew the names of two of his teachers. Within an hour, one of them was eagerly cycling across to meet me and by dusk I was having tea in the home of the other.

I flew to Berlin to meet a pastor whom Nouwen had helped through a family tragedy and travelled to Brussels to see a publisher. Then it was on to the forests of Northern France to interview the founder of L'Arche, Jean Vanier, and meet members of his remarkable community among whom Nouwen had made many friends. After each encounter, another piece of the Nouwen jigsaw seemed to fall into place. From Europe I headed across the Atlantic to Boston and on to Harvard, where Nouwen had lectured; then to New York to meet more publishers and friends; to Nashville, Tennessee, to spend a weekend with his former teaching assistant; then to the deserts of New Mexico where a conference on Nouwen was taking place. Each exotic location yielded more information, more contacts, more layers of a complex personality.

I flew back to the east coast and booked in for several days at Yale Divinity School which Nouwen had joined in 1971 and where the Nouwen Archives were then located. Here I learned much about Nouwen's theological method and began to think about my own. I discovered that his had been one of the first Roman Catholic appointments to the Protestant faculty and that he had climbed the academic ladder without a formal doctorate, becoming a tenured professor of pastoral theology. Many of his lectures were turned into paperbacks, but at Yale I learned that, as his popularity and fame had grown, his colleagues had become irritated by his successful engagement with the wider public. Each year faculty members were expected to present a list of their publications and, where possible, indicate how their work was being received in their field. But it was always Nouwen who outshone his colleagues, not only by writing a book a year, but also by being footnoted in so many texts of pastoral theology. Some staff had even resented the fact that students (many of whom were training for ministry) were coming to the faculty precisely because he was teaching there.

Nouwen seemed to have offered them a vision of ministry grounded in and flowing out of contemplative life. Physical space had a significant influence on the quality of his personal relationships with students, so he always sought out the most inviting classrooms. To teach was to 'create a space in which obedience to the truth was practised'.[3] There was also a prayerful dimension to his classes, which began with biblical readings, silence and intercessions. Not only did this cultivate an inner quietude, but it was also a conscious acknowledgement of the gospel text: 'When two or three meet in my name, I shall be there with them' (Matthew 18:20). This discipline created a space in which attention was directed to Christ, in whose name the students were to minister. His former teaching assistant explained that Nouwen had sought to make visible the often unnoticed points of contact between typical human experiences and the deeper reality of God's spirit at work in the world:

> Just as the early Christian writers could appeal to a common fund of philosophical categories, methods of thought and cultural ideals to introduce the educated person of their day to the truths of Christianity, so Henri was able to use such daily experiences as loneliness, anger, joy, friendship and business to instruct his students in the ways of the Spirit, and to persuade them of the essential relation between spirituality and ministry. Henri himself most often described this effort as an attempt to see the connections between their own life stories and the one great story of God's redemption of the world in and through Jesus Christ. The many pastoral examples, personal anecdotes, psychological observations and theological analyses that went into building the floor, walls and ceiling of Henri's lectures were aimed at helping students gain a new vision of their vocation as Christians.[4]

Nouwen did not believe that intellectual formation could be separated from spiritual formation. No methods, skills, techniques, films or field trips, he argued, could replace the influence of the teacher because the essence of all religious teaching was witness, proclaiming 'something which has existed from the beginning, which we have heard, which we have seen with our own eyes, which we have watched and touched with our own hands, the Word of Life – this is our theme' (1 John 1:1–2).[5] It was hardly a philosophy to endear him to traditional academic approaches in theology, but Nouwen never wavered:

> We are not asked to teach a discipline like mathematics, physics, history or languages, but we are called to make our own faith available to others as the source of learning. To be a teacher means indeed to lay down your life for your friends, to become a 'martyr' in the original sense of witness. To be a teacher means to offer your own faith experience, your loneliness and intimacy, your doubts and hopes, your failures and successes to your students as a context in which they can struggle with their own quest for meaning.[6]

In the spirit of many Eastern Orthodox thinkers, Nouwen believed that true theology was done on the knees. While never downplaying the importance of critical analysis, he felt it could bear fruit only in the context of obedience – attentive listening – to the truth. If biblical criticism were no longer practised as part of 'true obedience', theology quickly lost its doxological character – praising God in the present moment – and generated into a 'value-free' science subjected to unproductive disputes and arguments. Nouwen reminded his students that the first usage of the word *theologia* within the Christian tradition had referred to the highest level of prayer. The Desert Fathers had spoken about three stages of prayer: the *praktike* (the discipline of bringing the whole person with all thoughts, feelings and passions into the presence of God); the *theoria physike* (the contemplation of God's creation and providential plan as it becomes visible in nature and history); and the *theologia* (a direct intimate communion with God). Only since the Enlightenment had 'theology' developed into one academic discipline among many, increasingly involving analysis and synthesis, rather than its original objective of 'union with God'. Nouwen argued that the original connection between *theologia* and prayer should never be lost – nor could theology be undertaken outside a community of faith. I felt the PhD starting to take shape in my mind but I wasn't clear which area of his life I should specialise in. Doctorates have to be focused and I knew that, whatever approach I eventually opted for, I would have to be disciplined.

From Yale I flew to Rochester, upstate New York, where Nouwen had once tested his vocation in a Trappist monastery. After a weekend with the Cistercians, I took a bus over the border into Canada to meet old friends of Nouwen, into Toronto to quiz academics at Regis College and on to the L'Arche Community at Daybreak where Nouwen had been pastor. The tape-recorder was red hot. From there it was on to South Bend, Indiana, where Nouwen's teaching career had begun and then a flight to California where he had been involved in AIDS ministry. After six weeks non-stop research in the States, I returned to England for a month or so before heading off on the trail of a South African trapeze troupe touring Germany, with whom Nouwen had spent some of his later years and among whom he had devised some highly original theology. In the New Year I drove to Surrey to speak with the British couple who had guided him through a breakdown. I was put up in a cottage where Nouwen had penned some of his books. February saw me on a visit to Washington to meet more of Nouwen's pals and then it was back to Liverpool for an Ash Wednesday interview with a Jesuit peace activist who had read Nouwen's work in jail. Later in the year I returned to Toronto and New York for further research. I must have filled more than 40 cassettes.

Although I had questions in mind for each interviewee, I did not have a specific list in front of me; therefore I did not disclose my questions before the interviews. As well as accruing information about Nouwen's ministry and career, I was also interested in the development of his inner life. I crafted the thesis from a predominantly psycho-spiritual perspective. This technique, an exercise in what I termed 'a spirituality of journalism', enabled me to address and examine a number of ambiguous and repetitive statements in Nouwen's writings on the themes of fear, loneliness and the search for love, while at the same time allowing me to put to the test rumours about the precise nature and intensity of his emotional struggles. In many respects the methodology was devised in such a way as to glean, truthfully but sensitively, 'the inner story' of a best-selling spiritual writer and its implications for the wider church.

It seemed to me that such an open-ended style of methodology and the direct involvement of people from so many different worlds would give me a certain academic equilibrium, from which I would be able to extricate fact from fantasy and make more informed and balanced judgements. My detective-like methodology, merging journalistic praxis with theological investigation, seemed pertinent and apposite. But there was also a distinctly spiritual dimension to my work. After interviewing a priest friend of Nouwen at the University of Notre Dame in Indiana, I was presented with a multicoloured Mexican stole, similar in design and fabric to the ones Nouwen used to wear. The donning of a stole always reminded Nouwen of his responsibilities to the priesthood; for me the gift came to symbolise the responsibilities of my own endeavour. The Latin word, *pontifex*, bridge-builder, is often associated with priesthood: the priest is the intermediary of divine–human encounter, a person who makes connections between the spiritual and material worlds. Back at my writing-desk in England, I found the stole a great inspiration as I tried to weave the text of Nouwen's spirituality into the story of his life. Could the two be bridged?

I published my initial research as *Wounded Prophet* in 1999.[7] As the first major portrait of Nouwen to emerge in the immediate years after his death, inevitably the recollections have the 'feel' of a community trying to make sense of a somewhat mysterious figure who has disappeared from their midst. A difficulty for some interviewees was that, even though they had genuinely admired Nouwen, they had nonetheless put him on a pedestal. This had caused them to spiritualise him to such an extent that they had tended to overlook his flaws and were often frightened of criticising him. Nouwen's spiritual presence was certainly powerful but it seemed also to create an aura that sometimes deflected any lingering doubts or questions people might have had about what he said or how he behaved in certain situations. A year after his death, an inquisitive journalist, starting his doctoral research, travelled the world asking questions and hearing more than he had anticipated. For many friends it was an opportunity to grieve openly for Nouwen for the first time and share their thoughts about him. A number of interviews ended in tears, becoming part of the process of bereavement. Other people spoke confidentially about their time with Nouwen – conversations that continued into the early hours and sometimes so confessional in intensity that I did indeed feel like a priest.

Wounded Prophet was intended to be a study in personal woundedness and its healing power for others, a recurrent theme in all Nouwen's writings. Very early in the research period, a number of people disclosed to me that Henri Nouwen had, in fact, been gay – a truth I knew would not be easy to reveal. Although I had the support of Nouwen's family and community in bringing this fact to public attention, I knew that finding the right balance of expression would be difficult. Moreover, I had been privately shown Nouwen's final journal in which he had written:

> The idea of people posthumously exploring the details of my personal life frightens me, but I am reassured by the knowledge of having friends who know me intimately and will guard me not only in life but also in memory.[8]

However, I also noticed that the journal, compiled during the last year of his life, contained more references to homosexuality than any other diary he had written. As I read again ambiguous passages from his previous works, I concluded that the author's preoccupation with loneliness and the search for love, familiar themes in all his writings, were almost certainly related to his struggles as a priest who was also gay. There was nothing to suggest that he had been living a double life and I was acutely aware that I was treading on sacred ground. Researching the life of your spiritual hero when you are a journalist schooled in objectivity is a risk-laden business. But the more I wore the stole during times of prayer, the more I sensed that it was right to explore carefully this area of his life. It was evident that Nouwen's struggles with his sexuality had been integral to his spirituality, probably even inspiring his many reflections on loneliness, love and alienation. I concluded that, while it was understandable that Nouwen had chosen not to disclose his sexuality during his lifetime for fear of rejection by readers, there was both a spiritual and an academic honesty in respectfully acknowledging the fact and sensitively examining the implications.

I realised that Henri Nouwen's readers might find parts of his story surprising, even unsettling, for he had many devotees in both the evangelical and conservative Catholic worlds. I did not care to surmise how they might react. After the book was published, I braced myself for a backlash – but instead received letters of gratitude. A 77-year-old Roman Catholic priest, writing from Australia, said no author had inspired him more than Nouwen, 'But now he inspires me even more'. A woman writing from Arizona commented that 'Henri's vulnerability only increases his credibility'. His story had given her the courage to move from what was familiar and safe, and to venture into the unknown. A former head teacher in Somerset thanked me for 'keeping him by and with us', adding that Nouwen seemed to him like a Shakespearean character, an ideal subject for a stage play. A woman reader from another part of Britain said Nouwen's struggles had spoken so profoundly that she now felt the spiritual guide to millions had become her personal friend. A Lutheran pastor, writing from Switzerland, remarked that his hope and prayer were that the church would learn from Nouwen's life 'about acceptance and affirmation of all God's people created in the image of God'.

It was also humbling to receive, from a married Anglican priest in South Africa, a confidential tape-recording of his own struggles. He had never felt able to share them with anyone before but, after reading about Nouwen, wanted to offer them to me. After listening to the cassette (only the once), I placed it beside the stole in what seemed a sacramental act.

By the time I came to write up my PhD, I had gained sufficient knowledge and confidence to argue that Nouwen's spirituality could not be fully understood in isolation from the emotional vicissitudes of his own life. The study of a particular set of spiritual writings, I surmised, could never be separated from what is known – or could be known – about the life of their author. The connection was indissoluble, too valuable to be overlooked. My journalistic instincts spurred me to hunt for theological clues. The thesis became an investigation, a piece of spiritual detective work, into the hidden life of a man described to me as 'a saint with wounds'. In this respect, the research was both a theological and journalistic exercise.

While the church and the media are sometimes regarded institutionally as arch-enemies (mutually suspicious), their offspring, spirituality and journalism, are more like siblings (mutually seeking). A comparison may be made here between monasticism and journalism. The monk is called to perceive 'what eye has not seen, nor ear heard'.[9] The journalist is trained to see what other people do not, to make connections, to hear what is not being said. My study of Nouwen owed as much to my journalistic training as it did to my spiritual formation. It therefore seemed appropriate to filter his life and work through these different lenses.

The approach was biographical in the spirit of Richard Holmes for whom biography became

> a kind of pursuit, a tracking of the physical trail of someone's path through the past, a following of footsteps. You would never quite catch them; no, you would never quite catch them. But maybe, if you were lucky, you might write about the pursuit of that fleeting figure in such a way as to bring it alive in the present.[10]

For Holmes, the essential process of biography has two main elements or 'closely entwined strands'. The first is the gathering of the factual materials; the second is the creation of a fictional or imaginary relationship between the biographer and his subject, an ongoing dialogue between the two as they move over the same historical ground and trail of events: 'There is between them a ceaseless discussion, a reviewing and questioning of motives and actions and consequences, a steady if subliminal exchange of attitudes, judgements and conclusions'.[11]

My relationship with Nouwen was not so different from Nouwen's own association with the American Trappist monk, Thomas Merton:

> I met him only once... Yet thereafter, his person and work had such an impact on me, that his sudden death stirred me as if it were the death of one of my closest friends. It therefore seems natural for me to write for others about the man who has inspired me most in recent years.[12]

The recollection of my one encounter with Nouwen (an interview) and the content of our subsequent correspondence had to merge with my earlier impressions of him as a reader of his books and the varying perspectives of him as conveyed to me by his friends. As Holmes notes, hero-worship can develop into a love affair as one more or less consciously identifies with the subject:

> If you are not in love with them you will not follow them — not very far, anyway. But the true biographic process begins precisely at the moment, at the places, where this naïve form of love and identification breaks down. The moment of personal disillusion is the moment of impersonal, objective re-creation.[13]

This was certainly true as I absorbed the less flattering stories about Nouwen and then stood back more objectively to reflect on what I had heard. Initially, I had not been too comfortable subjecting Nouwen to even my own journalistic scrutiny: as an enthusiast, I had constructed an image of him which I was reluctant to discard. But I also knew that, if I were going to take Nouwen's work seriously, I had to let go of him as a spiritual hero and evaluate from a distance his place in modern Christian spirituality. It was essential to dig, to detect, as Holmes puts it, 'a more complicated and subtle pattern'. Through its uncovering of personal suffering, biography can find creative force and human nobility.[14] Because Nouwen had never written an autobiography and there were no detailed accounts of his life, I found myself working with a tabula rasa, without any powerfully received impressions of Nouwen's character or inner identity, except through his own pen and my one encounter.

Those who have also written about Nouwen seem to warn others against delving too deeply, as though researchers should not ask too many questions. Durback, quoting Nouwen, says he is 'aware of the author's sober warning' that the mystery of one man is too immense and too profound to be explained by another person. 'Biographers beware.'[15] Beumer is also cautious:

> The biographer has an eager desire to know more and more, as gradually he does. He is like a voyeur who silently stalks the person and his environment, seeking more data and facts... Nevertheless, at a certain moment he must stop, because he may not violate the secret of the person he is writing about.[16]

While I would agree that a sensitive approach to another's life is a pre-requisite, this should not prevent a researcher from asking questions or following leads.

It was during the summer of 2001 that the academic structure began to form and the argument crystallised. I laboured every day, trying to lose as many calories in the gym in the afternoon as I had written words in the morning. Body, mind and spirit had to function with some degree of synchronicity if the thesis were to mature! I had heard stories of postgraduates casting their notes from bridges because they could not integrate or make sense of their research. But, although the pressure was relentless and at times overwhelming, I was determined to see it through.

Then September 11 happened – and a most extraordinary sequel unfolded. When friends of Fr Mychal Judge – the New York fire chaplain who perished in the atrocities – entered his friary room the following day, they discovered that he had already cleared his shelves of his books, almost as though he had experienced a premonition of death. But there, alone on the dresser, lay a solitary volume – my book on Henri Nouwen. Fr Judge's friends spent a week tracking me down. I was staggered to learn that the priest had been reading *Wounded Prophet* shortly before he died and had so identified with Nouwen's struggles that he had wanted to write his autobiography. A few weeks later, a New York publisher telephoned me and asked if I would do the honours. 'I'm flattered but I have a PhD to complete,' I spluttered. 'You can have until the end of May,' the editor pleaded. It was obviously a professional opportunity difficult to turn down but, at the same time, I did not want it to jeopardise my academic work, which was reaching its most critical stage. While agreeing to undertake some preliminary research on Judge in Britain, I continued to work on my thesis. I knew that the doctoral thesis would have to be completed before I set off for the States again and immersed myself in somebody else's life. In November 2001 I handed in a final draft to David Torevell, who had always been so patient, good-humoured and painstaking in his supervision in spite of all the other demands on his time as Head of Subject. I then went off to Scotland to record a programme for BBC World Service. It was typical of David to call me on my mobile, while I was there, to say that he'd read the manuscript from cover to cover and felt it had reached the required standard. I eventually submitted the thesis in February 2002, flew to New York to interview 50 or so people for the Mychal Judge book, and got back just in time for my viva in April. I felt sure that I would confuse the two priests during the oral examination, making references to Mychal Judge instead of Henri Nouwen. But, in the end, all was well and I was relieved and delighted to be awarded the degree. Then, encouraged by the outcome, it was straight back to the study to write another spiritual biography which was published a few months later.[17]

The graduation ceremony was one of the most memorable experiences of my life. Hope was celebrating a record number of doctorates. As I sat a little nervously in the sacred setting, double-checking my mortarboard, I glanced across at Catherine Griffiths, Gareth Lloyd, Melanie Phillips, Kim Wallace and Christopher James Williams, who would follow me on to the podium. It was the climax of a long journey for all of us. But, for me, there was an unexpected dimension to the occasion. I had always appreciated the fact that Professor Simon Lee had taken an interest in my doctoral progress but I was completely taken aback when his speech began to focus on the theology of Henri Nouwen. I was even more wide-eyed, and not a little touched, when a photograph of my biography of Henri Nouwen was beamed onto a screen with all the synchronicity of a BBC outside broadcast. The research had reached a remarkable completion.

'The mission of Hope is to open up opportunities for a well-rounded education of the whole person in mind, body and spirit,' said Professor Lee. 'Graduands are rightly proud of their University of Liverpool degrees but they also take away much more from this city of Liverpool and from their rounded experience of Hope.' I could not have agreed more. As I adjusted my cap again, pulled my shoulders back and walked towards the rostrum, I knew I would always have cause to be grateful to a unique college where high hopes and academic expectations had been complemented by quality supervision and personal encouragement.

I do not think it is possible to study for a PhD and not be changed in and by the process. It has certainly made me a much more rigorous and meticulous writer, especially in terms of research and style. But a more subtle, inner transformation has also taken place, a deeper vocation yet to be revealed, a mystery still to be solved. As the Rector put it on the day: 'Graduates are a work in progress'. When I cast my mind back to my days as a researcher on *This is Your Life*, it is hard to believe that the art of the spiritual detective was somehow taking shape through my secret investigations for the big red book. That the experience would one day lead to my receiving a doctorate in the city of Liverpool (in a big red gown) would have been unimaginable. But, with gratitude to the community of Hope and all those who form it, I feel I have gained so much more than a doctorate.

NOTES

1 H. J. M. Nouwen, *The Path of Waiting*, London, Darton, Longman and Todd, 1995, pp. 19–22.

2 J. Beumer, *Onrustig zoeken naar God: De spiritualiteit van Henri Nouwen*, Tielt, Uitgeverij Lannoo, 1997.

3 J. Mogabgab, 'The Spiritual Pedagogy of Henri Nouwen', *Reflection*, Vol. 78, No. 2, January 1981.

4 Ibid.

5 Ibid.

6 Ibid.

7 M. Ford, *Wounded Prophet, A Portrait of Henri J. M. Nouwen*, London, Darton, Longman and Todd, 1999.

8 H. J. M. Nouwen, *Sabbatical Journey, The Diary of his Final Year*, London, Darton, Longman and Todd, 1998, p. 17.

9 D. Steindl Rast OSB, with S. Lebell, *The Music of Silence, Entering the Sacred Space of Monastic Experience*, New York, HarperCollins, 1995, p. 28.

10 R. Holmes, *Footsteps, Adventures of a Romantic Biographer*, London, Flamingo, 1986, p. 27.

11 Ibid., p. 66.

12 H. J. M. Nouwen, *Thomas Merton: Contemplative Critic*, New York, Triumph Books, 1991, p. 3.

13 Holmes, *Footsteps*, p. 67.

14 Ibid., p. 130.

15 R. Durback, ed., *Seeds of Hope, a Henri Nouwen Reader*, London, Darton, Longman and Todd, 1998, p. 21.

16 J. Beumer, *Henri Nouwen, A Restless Seeking for God*, New York, Crossroad, 1997, p. 7.

17 M. Ford, *Father Mychal Judge, An Authentic American Hero*, Mahwah, Paulist Press, 2002.

CHAPTER 6

Chaplaincy Presence
and Activity

IAN C. STUART

O NE challenge for Christian educational institutions, according to
Kleinschmidt,[1] is 'to keep alive the rumour of God'. This challenge
underpins our approach to chaplaincy at Liverpool Hope – to create an awareness of a spiritual dimension in life, a vague recognition of the numinous, even
a flickering possibility of a real being who knows and cares about us. We sow
seeds for the future and perhaps some day the rumour which we have spread
may grow to a conviction, fed by experience and memory, and set afire by the
work of the Holy Spirit.

Fifty years ago, outside Oxbridge, there were just eight university chaplains
in England. Today chaplaincies of one model or another are established in
almost every institution of higher education in the country. Current statistics
indicate that there are in excess of 400 chaplains working in higher education.
This expansion of the church's involvement in this field has of course paralleled the major expansion of higher education itself since the war.[2]

The chaplaincy at Liverpool Hope University College has its origins in the
mid-nineteenth century when two of the three constituent colleges, S. Katharine's and Notre Dame, were founded. Chaplaincy responsibilities were exer-
cised by male clergy, often in conjunction with a teaching role. In Christ's
College, established in 1964, priests on the staff shared the liturgical and
pastoral functions. Although federation in 1979 under the title of the Liverpool
Institute of Higher Education brought co-operation between the Anglican and
Roman Catholic chaplaincies, they continued to function as two separate entities.
It was not until 1995 that a covenant to work together as one team was agreed,
and in 1996 the current chaplaincy centre was established.

The college's Memorandum and Articles of Association and Instrument of
Government provide for an ecumenical chaplaincy team, including at least one
Anglican Chaplain and at least one Roman Catholic Chaplain. This is a direct
reflection of the importance of the college mission to every aspect of its life.

The team currently includes an Anglican bishop, a Roman Catholic sister of the Community of the Faithful Companions of Jesus, a Methodist minister and lay assistant, a Jesuit brother and an Anglican layman in an internship. This internship is an annual appointment which provides a formation experience for men or women testing their vocation to the ordained ministry or to lay chaplaincy.

Chaplaincy is one of the many kinds of ministry offered by the church and is an expression of the abundance of God's grace and love. Chaplaincy in higher education is concerned with all aspects of the corporate life of the institution, including the pastoral care and spiritual growth of students and staff. The report, *The Way Ahead: Church of England schools in the new millennium*,[3] emphasises that chaplaincy has at its centre the question of how people and their organisational structures reflect God's purpose for humanity – the realising in human beings of the image of God through the gift of Christ's spirit, in the conviction that the gospel shows us an understanding of that fullness of life revealed in the ministry, death and resurrection of Jesus.

In considering the relationship of the institutional churches to the university, David Ford[4] identifies five areas of engagement for chaplains. These are: mission and ministry to the institution, pastoral care, worship, alertness to God, and ecumenism. These areas will be helpful in describing the variety and extent of the ministry offered by Liverpool Hope's ecumenical chaplaincy.

The chaplaincy is a support service and a resource which is at the very heart of college life, with the chaplaincy base symbolically located at the centre of the Hope Park campus. This service is a fundamental expression of the college's mission and witness and is dedicated to the well-being of all members of the college community, students as well as academic and support staff. The chaplains and the chaplaincy are there for all who embrace the Christian faith, for those of other faiths and beliefs, and for anyone in search of spirituality and meaning in life.

The chaplaincy base is a comfortable and functional suite that provides a warm and welcoming environment. The provision of networked IT equipment and a photocopier, as well as drinks and snack facilities, meets the needs of those who visit to socialise and also of those who wish to study. Members of the chaplaincy team have their offices here, and there are private rooms for confidential interviews. The design and operation of the area makes for its easy and unobtrusive use.

The chaplains are committed to supporting the spiritual, social and personal needs and aspirations of everyone. They encourage and foster the faith-life of individuals who desire such support, minister to the sacramental and liturgical needs of the college, and are always available to help with spiritual direction or counselling. They will be with students at times of sublime happiness and profound sadness, from graduations to hospital visits and at times of bereavement.

At student and staff inductions in particular, the Hope campus is sometimes likened to a village. This is to emphasise that its parts fit together and are accessible. Continuing this metaphor, the chaplaincy can be perceived as its parish church, with experienced personnel readily available for all manner of functions that centre on its worshipping life. The chaplains also promote and organise the celebrations of the regular Christian festivals, as well as significant multi-faith occasions. A recent initiative has been the increased use of the college's electronic newspaper, *Hope Virtually Daily*, to provide succinct explanations of the major Christian feasts and saints' days, as well as the important festivals of other world religions. This is an opportunity to raise awareness in the college community of those days in the calendar which are important to the main living religions. Students and staff who would not necessarily participate in worship arranged on these days frequently comment that they value this information. Another important role for the chaplaincy at Hope is marking key events in the academic calendar such as at the Start of Session and Graduation Days. These are times of celebration and thanksgiving that require carefully planned and executed liturgy relevant to the occasion. These liturgies create privileged opportunities for thoughtful preaching, by either visiting preachers or members of the chaplaincy team.

More widely, the chaplains co-ordinate initiatives and activities relating to social justice awareness, community service, leadership formation and personal development. They contribute to institutional debate on ethical questions and to reducing tensions between church and academy, if they arise. They also assist in building links with the local and wider communities. A successful example of this is the annual project with the Mothers Union (MU) during the autumn Freshers' Week. MU representatives in the 16 deaneries in the Diocese of Liverpool co-ordinate an appeal for dry and tinned foodstuffs, toiletries and other items which are subsequently collected and stored at the college. These are later packed in more than 1,000 bags, which are then distributed, by MU representatives in the chaplaincy base, to new students. A specially prepared MU cookbook and information about the chaplaincy are also included in each pack. This joint venture provides a valuable opportunity for the chaplains to meet large numbers of new students right at the start of each academic year. It also presents the MU at its practical best to students young and old who might well otherwise never have heard of it. Perhaps years later, if they come into contact with the MU again, they will remember all this and benefit from it.

It is not uncommon in higher education institutions for there to be poor working relationships between the chaplaincy and the campus branch of the Christian Union. This situation invariably arises from misunderstandings or from the fact that the two activities have different priorities: chaplaincies to provide open and extensive activities; and the Christian Union to focus on evangelical conversion and commitment. Fortunately, this is not the case at Hope. The current chaplaincy team and the Christian Union officers, like our respective predecessors, have worked hard to develop and maintain an effective partnership. The Christian Union uses the chaplaincy base for weekly meetings, which are attended from time to time by the chaplains. There is also a weekly combined Prayer and Praise service held in S. Katharine's Chapel. In addition, chaplaincy and Christian Union events in general are mutually supported, particularly in Freshers' Week.

The role of Chaplain as 'being there for others' has already been emphasised. This concept is an expression of the way Jesus interacted with those around him throughout his ministry. It recognises that the human–divine interaction is not always without difficulty. Of this, Dowling writes,

> When Jesus met, or made contact with people, he did so at the pastoral level by either contact with them where they were, involved in the ordinary tasks of life, or by demonstrating an opposition to people's misguided priorities in life. Jesus for me is an example of how pastoral care can be achieved in that he was a person being there for others.[5]

This view lies behind all the chaplaincy arrangements for the practical provision of pastoral care. The three full-time members of the chaplaincy team (Anglican and Roman Catholic) and the two part-time members (Methodist) provide an interdenominational pastoral service from the chaplaincy base. We are encouraged that, increasingly in recent years, it is evident that students and staff seeking pastoral support understand that this is ecumenical, and only rarely are requests made to see a team member of a particular denomination. This pastoral ministry to students includes listening and offering counselling, as well as explaining attitudes and policies or simply being a sounding-board. It also includes hospital visiting; baptism and marriage preparation and the conduct of these services in the college chapels; Confirmation preparation; bereavement counselling and the conduct of memorial services in the chapels, along with support of the families involved. This pastoral ministry is extended to members of all the college staff. For this reason it often acts as a timely means of communication within the wider college community.

Hope's significant growth in recent years has led the chaplaincy team to identify two groups of students with particular needs. These are the 550 international students, now from 58 countries; and the 1200 or so resident students. There are enormous challenges for students from overseas as they adjust to a new culture and community and a language in which they are not always fluent and confident. There are different, but no less daunting, challenges for those young men and women leaving home for the first time to live independently. Working closely with the college's international office and its welfare officers, the chaplains actively seek out and spend time with new students from overseas to introduce ourselves, to emphasise our availability and support, and to offer the chaplaincy base as an alternative, particularly for those seeking social opportunities which do not involve the consumption of alcohol. The location of resident students on three separate campuses around Liverpool means that effective chaplaincy provision to them has involved a review of our method of operating and our hours of work. Staffing the chaplaincy base at Hope Park from 9.00am to 5.00pm is no longer sufficient on its own. Therefore the chaplains now visit halls of residence regularly in the evening to engage with students where they live. They also identify with them in their places of study, including the Sheppard–Worlock Library. All this is part of the wider 'round the clock' emphasis on the work of the college. Chaplaincy presence in the Network of Hope, across the Irelands and the North of England, is also increasing.

Worship is, of course, central to the life of the chaplaincy. The historical legacy of the college includes two places of worship, S. Katharine's Anglican Chapel, and Christ's and Notre Dame Catholic Chapel. Hope at Everton now affords a third worship space in the restored Catholic Church of St Francis Xavier. Provision for this to be used by other Christian denominations has now been made. On weekday mornings, between 8.30 and 8.45am, Morning Prayer is said in at least one of the chapels. At Hope Park we alternate each month between Christ's and Notre Dame Chapel and S. Katharine's Chapel. At Hope at Everton, St Francis Xavier's Church is used on Tuesday mornings, with the expectation that this will extend to other days of the week. A range of ecumenical resources, including *A Prayer Book for Australia*, *The Methodist Worship Book*, and *The Roman Breviary*, are used for this morning act of worship. The service is led by a member of the chaplaincy team, and another participant reads the portion of the gospel set for the day. There is always an opportunity for offering personal prayers and intercessions and for periods of silence. On any particular day, our prayers might focus on relevant college, local, national or international issues and on students or staff experiencing illness, bereavement or some other pastoral need. As well as this intercessory prayer, there will also be prayers of thanksgiving. Staff and students who are not able or who do not wish to participate are encouraged to make their specific prayer requests through a member of the chaplaincy team, who then prays on their behalf. This is a much appreciated and growing custom. During Advent and Lent the usual rhythm of this liturgy is varied by using more meditative and reflective models, sometimes accompanied by appropriate music. A small number of people make their regular attendance at this Morning Prayer a priority. These include the Rector and other senior members of staff. They are an encouragement to the chaplains and create a nucleus which is joined by others. This, again, functions much like a parish church. It provides a regular focus of daily prayer almost throughout the calendar year; the very fact of its regularity is important to everything else that happens in the life of the college. It is a simple focus of prayerful spirituality and Christian unity.

Sharing the Eucharist in the college chapels is, sadly, not so rewarding, as John Elford has already discussed in Chapter 1. Sensitivity has to be shown to the discipline of the Roman Catholic Bishops' Conferences. Separate Eucharistic services during each week are held according to the rites of the Church of England and the Roman Catholic Church, the former attended by students and staff of other Christian denominations. Following the events of 11 September 2001 and their impact on interfaith relationships, members of the chaplaincy at Hope have sought new opportunities for interfaith worship and inter-religious dialogue, to help us explore what we have in common with our brothers and sisters of other faiths. A prayer room is provided for Muslim students, and lectures, seminars and small discussion groups are convened regularly. This programme is vital to the wider spiritual common good of the college. Not unnaturally, it is currently (Spring 2003) preoccupied with issues of war and peace in the international community.

David Johnstone[6] argues that the chaplain represents to an institution the possibility that there is a 'text for life' in its doings. This raises the questions: 'what is this text?' and 'how is life to be understood in such a context?' The institutional context of chaplaincy is dictated by many things which are, of course, far beyond its control. This has to be respected and responded to at every possible opportunity. It is, importantly, a two-way process. Chaplaincy learns just as much as it teaches. The manner of its learning, moreover, in the service of the institution, should at its best be exemplary. This is a tall order for the simple reason that it is not always possible for chaplaincy to rise above the realpolitik of everyday institutional life. The maintenance of regular, dignified and quality worship is again crucial here. It is the principal means whereby the 'text' of the faith maintains its profile. Chaplains bring their learned institutional experience to bear upon this and, in so doing, perhaps enable others around them to do the same. In action, such a view of the role of chaplaincy in the life of an institution helps to create the so-called 'hermeneutic circle' within which there is a continuing and dynamic enrichment of the faith in relation to the lived constraints and opportunities of institutional life. In this context, it is inevitably the institution that sets the agenda and, thereby, prescribes the function of the chaplaincy. For this reason, it is important that expectations of chaplaincy are regularly assessed and updated by institutional leaders. Working in a church college, where it is a condition of appointment of such leaders that they be persons with faith commitment, makes this so much more a vibrant possibility.

All this will be familiar territory to anyone versed in theological discussion about the relationship of the gospel to culture. Richard Niebuhr[7] famously proposed five understandings of this. They are paradigms in the sense that no one of them at any time can ever be seen to encapsulate everything which might or might not be happening to that relationship. They can, however, be used as what sociologists call 'ideal types' to throw light on what is, and what ought to be, happening. Niebuhr's typologies range from ones in which Christ is against culture to ones in which Christ is identified totally with culture. While he does not actually argue a preference for any of these, Niebuhr's indicated preference is for a relationship in which Christ is the 'transformer' of culture. Given, however, that the relationship of chaplaincy to an institution needs to be one of reciprocity if it is to do its job, it becomes necessary to add to Niebuhr's analysis that the Christ too be vulnerable to transformation. Here, of course, we are close to the heart of the Christian 'text' for life. New birth and being, regeneration and hope are all fundamentals of the faith that a Christian institution needs to embrace if it is to thrive in God's sight.

No one chaplain can ever achieve, day-in, day-out, all that there is to be achieved in chaplaincy, so understood. Legood observes that inevitably chaplains will emphasise some particular aspect of ministry, depending on their theology and gifts. He writes,

> Some will have talents which point them towards a ministry with individuals, while others will have talents which equip them for specific work with groups or structures. A ministry which fails to work for the salvation of the individual and for the world in which she lives will fall short of being a fully adequate Christian ministry.[8]

Legood's point emphasises the advantage which a diverse team ministry can offer to an institution. The continual challenge, of course, is to achieve a right balance between individuals doing their own thing and matching the gifts of the team members with the particular needs which exist at the time. This is why, as explained above, the chaplaincy team at Hope is carefully constructed as it is.

Cultural engagement of the sort described above requires hard work. This is why chaplains at Hope are encouraged to teach in subject areas where they have the necessary expertise. This is seen as an important opportunity to engage with students and staff in a core college activity. It helps to create a spontaneous personal interaction which spills over into the life of the chaplaincy. A significant proportion of those who regularly seek it for help and support are first encountered in a seminar or lecture.

Other chaplaincy activities which are integrated with wider college life also enable this. For example, I have had the opportunity and satisfaction during the last two years of serving the college in the dual roles of Anglican Chaplain and Provost of Hope Park. The work of the Provost is very much mission-related and therefore complements the work of the chaplaincy. In developing the role, I have reflected on Paul's advice to the Romans about hospitality (Romans 12:9–13). The core elements involve helping to ensure that those who use Hope Park are appropriately welcomed, assisted and supported; facilitating the further opening up of Hope Park to church, school and local community use; and developing ideas for improving the environment. My work as Assistant Bishop in the diocese has in turn enhanced and facilitated what I have been trying to achieve in my other roles. It is pleasing that, as time goes on, I find that there is an inevitable blurring of the boundaries between all these related activities.

Given that the history of Liverpool Hope is what it is, its mission requires it to be fully Anglican, fully Roman Catholic, fully ecumenical and fully open to those of other faiths and secular beliefs. This is just another of the tall orders the chaplaincy has to face. Whereas there is a great deal that can be achieved ecumenically in college life, it remains constrained by the wider state of the relationships between the churches. This, as is mentioned elsewhere in this volume, can be a cause of frustration. It is necessary for the chaplaincy to respect this, yet also to rise above it. In this way it can help to create something of a dignified poise while, at the same time, always seeking opportunities to improve the nature and extent of college ecumenical life. Here, again, maintaining attention to the appropriate biblical traditions is of central importance. Jesus prayed that his disciples might be one so that the world may believe (John 17:21). Unity of the church is inseparable from mission and is a sign of the reconciling love which God offers to all people. The call to be one is a call to live out the unity which God already gives us. It is a call for the sake of a divided world rather than a divided church. It is a call towards something the shape of which we cannot yet fully see. 'They continued steadfastly in the apostles' teaching and fellowship, in the breaking of bread and prayers.' In these words, Luke describes the life of the first Christians (Acts 2:42). The New Testament uses the term *koinonia* for the communion, fellowship or mutual participation that baptised believers share with the Holy Trinity and with one another in the Body of Christ. The theology of *koinonia* helps us to recognise the many bonds of communion that Christian churches share. We are called to *koinonia* because God has made us in the divine image for a life of relationship and mutual giving and receiving, patterned on his own life. We are constituted as persons and discover ourselves as such within our developing relationships with God and with one another.

God calls us together to learn with one another and from one another, to share together and to work for him together, to be – in our togetherness and love for one another – a sign of his love for the world. *Koinonia* is about responsible, accountable sharing, as we journey on together, responsible to God and responsible to and for one another. For all these reasons, the chaplaincy team is encouraged by the currently proposed Anglican–Methodist Covenant.[9] We also remain optimistic about Anglican–Roman Catholic relations at the national level, despite what some regard as the setbacks caused by *One Bread One Body*[10] and *Dominus Iesus*.[11] Though difficulties remain, we always need to remember, as Deborah Jones[12] reminds us, that true ecumenism demands rigour, commitment and the will to keep making fresh starts. However, while we continue to work, talk and pray together, share meals and socialise, we are confident that the momentum can be maintained. With Jones, we remain hopeful that the God of surprises will fulfil our vision of ultimate unity.

The members of the chaplaincy team at Liverpool Hope are keen to work in collaboration with colleagues, and we participate in our various local, national and international networks. These provide opportunities for theological reflection, mutual support, fellowship and sharing best practice. At the local level there are regular meetings with chaplains in other higher and further education institutions. Valuable support is also offered by the chaplaincy committees of the Church of England's Board of Education and the Catholic Bishops' Conferences, through their advisors, annual conferences and regular communications. As a church college, Liverpool Hope belongs to the Colleges and Universities of the Anglican Communion (CUAC), which is an association of over 120 higher education institutions that were founded by, or retain ties with, a branch of the Anglican communion. With institutions on five continents, CUAC was founded for the exchange of ideas, for the development of programmes among member institutions, and for our mutual support that we might better serve our students, our societies and the world. An exciting CUAC initiative in promoting world understanding is the International Partnership for Service-Learning which links academic study and volunteer service. IPS-L offers programmes in 13 nations, where students study at an accredited university and spend 15–20 hours per week volunteering in a community service agency.

The ecumenical chaplaincy at Liverpool Hope is well resourced and it is used, supported and affirmed by the Rector and members of the senior management. Other members of staff also use it regularly and there are many more who identify with it on formal occasions. All this is part of the wider example the chaplaincy tries to set for students. One third of young adults undertake higher education and many of them will be tomorrow's thinkers and creators. The presence of such an example in their higher education institution might just therefore rub off on them and serve them well as they enter their professions. This gives something of a lie to the view, held by some, that such chaplaincy is but a specialism at the margins rather than in the mainstream of Christian ministries. There is a reluctance on the part of some church leaders to value the role of chaplain or to see this area of ministry as anything more than a temporary aberration in the professional life of the person involved. Such views might well be the reason why some chaplains, in secular institutions in particular, often feel misunderstood and unsupported by their sponsoring churches. To mitigate this, the Church of England's Board of Education[13] has identified five prerequisites for effective chaplaincy: good structure, adequate resourcing, clear channels of formal communication, accountability and support. To these I would add a sixth essential – the careful recruitment, training and formation of those who feel called to the ministry of chaplain in an educational institution. Chaplaincy is a vocation requiring particular gifts, insights and experience and above all respect for and ease with people of all ages, particularly the young.

The ecumenical chaplaincy at Liverpool Hope stands as a sign of Christian unity. As, that is, an indication that we can work together as Christians of different denominations, as people of different yet essentially similar faith-journeys and understandings of God. It is our privilege to be alongside students and staff who either need us for some such reason, or simply want to share companionship at a particular stage of their life's journey. There is no better inspiration for all this than Jesus' reminder: 'Just as you did it to one of the least of these who are members of my family, you did it to me' (Matthew 25:40). For this reason, on the occasion of my Licensing by the Bishop of Liverpool in S. Katharine's Chapel on 21 April 1999, I concluded my sermon with these words:

> My prayer today is that I may assist members of our community to make all the varied, unknown, exciting, challenging, bewildering experiences which we will encounter together, meeting points with the Living God. When the time comes for students to leave and begin another stage in their life's journey, I would hope that they can say that, in coming to Hope, they not only collected a degree but also encountered on the paths and in the corridors of this place the God who is the same 'yesterday, today and forever' (Hebrews 13:8).

NOTES

1 R. Kleinschmidt, *The 2000 Reuther Oration*, distributed by the Board for Lutheran Schools, Adelaide.

2 S. Giliat-Ray, *Religion in Higher Education*, Aldershot, Ashgate, 2000, p. 28.

3 The Church Schools Review Group, *The Way Ahead: Church of England schools in the new millennium*, London, Church House Publishing, 2001, p. 71.

4 D. F. Ford, *God in the University*, lecture given at the University of Nottingham in 1999 and published by the University of Nottingham Chaplaincy Team, pp. 13–15.

5 D. Dowling, 'Chaplain to the Whole Community', in *Managing The Ministry*, Adelaide, AARE, 1997.

6 D. Johnstone, 'A Theology for School Ministry', in *Managing The Ministry*, Adelaide, AARE, 1997.
7 H. R. Niebuhr, *Christ and Culture*, New York, Harper & Bros Publishers, 1951.
8 G. Legood, *Chaplaincy*, London, Cassell, 1999, p. 135.
9 Methodist Church of Great Britain and the Church of England, *An Anglican–Methodist Covenant*, London, Methodist Publishing House and Church House Publishing, 2001.
10 Catholic Bishops' Conferences of England and Wales, Ireland, and Scotland, *One Bread One Body*, London, CTS, 1998.
11 The House of Bishops of the Church of England, *The Eucharist: sacrament of unity*, London, Church House Publishing, 2001.
12 D. Jones, *Priests and People*, London, The Tablet Publishing Company Limited, 2001, p. 2.
13 *Pillars of the Church*, London, Church House Publishing, p. viii.

CHAPTER 7

The Foundation Deanery
and the Mission

IAN SHARP

L IVERPOOL Hope University College is probably unique among higher education establishments in publicly acknowledging and celebrating its foundation in its structures. The Foundation Deanery was established in 1995 as one of the four 'pillars' of the college, and since then it has been integral to the workings of academic and communal life. By foundation we mean, in this context, the original church college foundations of S. Katharine's (Warrington Training College), Notre Dame at Mount Pleasant, and Christ's, which together evolved into Liverpool Institute of Higher Education and later Liverpool Hope University College. The story of some of these exciting developments has been summarised in Chapter 1, and is more fully written elsewhere.[1] It is significant that, when in 1995 the new name of Liverpool Hope University College was agreed by the Governing Council, it was felt desirable to set up a Foundation Deanery which unashamedly proclaimed our indebtedness to our foundations. The constituent colleges all had title deeds, and the intentions of the original founders undoubtedly reflected the various interpretations of principle and expediency of their own times, whether the Victorian era or the second Elizabethan one. The names of the three colleges — and their mottoes, their governing bodies, their intakes and curricula, their reputation in local and national communities — all proclaimed that they were church colleges, or (depending on the time) more specifically Anglican or Catholic training colleges, or colleges of education. Everything that they did and were seen to do was both implicitly and explicitly foundation-driven.

The term foundation can have several meanings. In schools, 'foundation governors' represent the founding body, often a church. In higher education today, 'foundation degrees' are initial, two-year degrees, closely related to the world of work. At Hope, the 'foundations' are clearly those of our Christian heritage as exemplified by the traditions of the founding colleges and typified by our mission statement.[2] Our mission derives from our Anglican, Catholic and (more recently) ecumenical traditions, and draws attention to the fact that we are fully committed to 'educating the whole person in mind, body and spirit'. The Foundation Deanery exists, then, to promote all activity immediately related to the church foundation and the mission.

The nature of the Foundation Deanery is best revealed by the activities that it promotes; yet in the eight years since its inception there have been significant changes. Currently, there are two main dimensions to the deanery – academic and pastoral. On the academic side, the Foundation Deanery is home to the disciplines of theology and religious studies. The undergraduate courses (certificate of HE, BA combined subjects degrees, BA theology and religious studies, and BA QTS with a specialism in theology and religious studies) are taught at Hope Park and in three colleges of the Network of Hope. The annual intake is around 110 students. The postgraduate programmes (MA in theology and religious studies, MPhil and PhD) are well subscribed, with some 35 research students currently registered in theology and religious studies. There are three professors, including the Revd Professor Nicholas Sagovsky, holder of the Liverpool Chair of Theology and Public Life – the first such chair to be established in this country. New academic developments include, at under-graduate level, a minor pathway in philosophy and ethics and, at taught postgraduate level, additional pathways in Anglican and Catholic studies. Hope's research in theology and religious studies has been much developed over the last seven years and the college is rightly proud to have achieved a grading of 4 in the latest Research Assessment Exercise. Much of the detail of this story is written up later in this book, but it is no exaggeration to claim that the department is now among the strongest in the country, serving local, national and international needs. Allied to this success is the secondary PGCE teacher training course in religious education, which is organised by the Education Deanery and recruits well. All religious education courses, at whatever level, are the concern of Hope's Religious Education Board which also deals with the teaching of the Anglican and Catholic church certificates [see the *Church Certificates* section below]. The Foundation Deanery also feeds into the Church and Community Connections Board (CCCB), which exists to support our strong partnership with churches and other faith communities. Hope's connection with the Anglican, Catholic and Methodist churches is long-standing and is one of mutual respect and co-operation. The CCCB is also instrumental in developing links with organisations such as Habitat for Humanity, as well as with other community groups in the region. As far as we know, Hope's approach, fusing both church and community, is, yet again, a pioneering concept.

The second element of the Foundation Deanery is student support. At the present time this consists of a range of services under the umbrella of the 'one-start-shop' of COMPASS, which has been described fully in Chapter 3. So, in a meeting of Foundation Deanery managers you will find, typically, many areas represented – residential services, chaplaincy, counselling and health, college events, alumni relations, church and community connections – alongside the taught and research aspects of theology and religious studies. The Foundation Deanery is, then, much more than another name for the department of theology, and Foundation Deans have not always been theologians. Since 1995 the post has been held by the Revd Canon Dr John Elford (Canon Theologian of Liverpool Cathedral and Pro-Rector of Hope), Professor Ian Markham (Liverpool Professor of Theology and Public Life), and Dr Ian Sharp (former Associate Foundation Dean and a lecturer in music and education). The fourth Foundation Dean, from September 2003, is to be Professor John Sullivan (Professor of Christian Education).

Something of the transformation which has taken place in the organisation of college life in a relatively short period can be seen from the various titles of the posts of senior managers in the area of student support. In 1995 there were still two 'halls', Christ's and Notre Dame and S. Katharine's, each of which had a Senior Tutor (Mr Michael Seddon and Mr Jeffrey Brache). Senior Tutors then became Deans of Hall (Sr Anne McDowell SND and Mrs Doreen Heraty). The two halls were the successors of the two colleges of the same names. What had been distinct colleges had by now become, in effect, halls of residence, although some traces of former, independent, existence still survived. Some students, and very few staff, had some kind of allegiance to this older tradition. The allocation of students to personal tutors was still arranged by the halls, but this way of organising personal tutoring was seen to be anachronistic. For, as the students resident at Childwall now only accounted for under a quarter of the Hope community, it was inevitable that the halls, as separate entities, ceased to have validity. This meant that the Foundation Deanery, as the successor to the halls, was charged with preserving the best of their traditions (and, in effect, of what remained of the founding colleges' communities).

Readers of this narrative might, at this point, be excused for thinking that this account is extraordinarily parochial and only of marginal interest even to those who lived through the changes. True, the majority of students were probably totally unaware of the sequence of events. Colleges, halls or deaneries were of little consequence to them. But what happened at Hope in the late 1990s reflected developments that all institutions have to face as they grow. The structures that had served the training of teachers for (in the main) church schools over a period of 150 years were no longer appropriate to a modern higher education institution. Size alone meant that it was not possible for a Rector to walk along a corridor and greet everyone, staff and students alike, by name, as it had been for a college principal in the 1960s. The curriculum, too, had expanded to encompass a range of degree programmes, and students themselves came from a wide variety of backgrounds and ages. The college was growing rapidly and what had formerly been open spaces now became car parks (though the gracious lawns remained). The old concept of a small, closely knit residential college for the training of teachers was well and truly gone: it was now timely to review how to put the mission into practice in the modern Liverpool Hope University College.

The most effective way of doing this must always be through the daily work undertaken by all staff, and it is not insignificant that every applicant for a job at Liverpool Hope is asked to explain how they would see themselves as a channel for making the mission work. They are asked to reflect on what 'body, mind and spirit' means in the context of their particular academic, admin-istrative or domestic specialism. As a result, we have staff across the college, and certainly not restricted to the Foundation Deanery, who deliver the mission of Hope, day-in, day-out. The particular illustrations that are taken up in the sections that follow are all examples of mission-related activity within the ambit of the Foundation Deanery. Not all of them could be regarded as mainstream, given the small number of students who are involved. But even if the various enterprises reach only a fraction of the members of the college community at any one time, they are still worthwhile.

FOUNDATION HOUR

Foundation Hour is the occasion in the week when Liverpool Hope pauses for a while to celebrate the values of its foundation. Every Wednesday from 12.00 to 1.00pm, this special time is observed. Foundation Hour sometimes takes the form of a talk or presentation, sometimes a service; and it is always followed by an opportunity for people to chat and enjoy light refreshments. Foundation Hour is, in some respects, a cross between an extended school assembly, collective worship and a current affairs programme. But it is much more than these, and we like to think that there's nothing else quite like it! Thanks to the regular publicity given by *Hope Virtually Daily* (the electronic newspaper), staff and students are able to plan ahead to see what is coming up, and over the last few years the numbers attending Foundation Hour have been steadily increasing. Some would say, too, that its quality has been improving all the time. We consider Foundation Hour to be an arena for exploration of the mission of the college. Few restrictions are put on contributors – apart from the standard exhortation to keep to time – as long as they relate their theme to some aspect of the mission.

The roots of Foundation Hour can be traced back to the original colleges. Regular acts of worship have always been a feature of life in a church college.

Notre Dame College and Christ's College had daily Mass, and attendance was a high priority for many staff and students. Sunday Masses at college were happy, communal occasions, often supported by many families and friends from the neighbourhood. S. Katharine's College, too, had liturgical traditions, with the main service of the week being held not on a Sunday but during the week in a timetabled morning slot, first on Tuesdays and then on Wednesdays. The services were well organised and varied, and all teaching stopped at this time. These traditions were continued by the federated Liverpool Institute of Higher Education, but the complexities of working life impinged upon the time allotted. Making space for chapel time was increasingly honoured more in the breach than the observance. And so, fairly soon after the establishment of the Foundation Deanery, there came into being what was termed Foundation Hour, the middle hour of the middle day of the week, every month of the year apart from August. It was expected that all members of the college would refrain from all work activities during that time, even if, in practice, most of them did not attend at all regularly. Foundation Hour took some time to become established and there was a period when the chaplains struggled valiantly to organise ecumenical services and other events. By 1999 an Associate Foundation Dean was appointed who was responsible for the Foundation Hour arrangements, along with a small working party that gave invaluable advice. One semester's set of programmes was formalised at a time and suggested topics would often come from the Rector, who is a committed supporter of Foundation Hour.

Foundation Hour as an institution has been subjected to an in-depth analysis by a colleague, Ruth Price, in a recent dissertation.[3] She observes that Foundation Hour can be seen as an instrument for the operation of the mission statement, and that it has become 'a ritual to reproduce and confirm common organisational traditions'.[4] This might well be true, yet it is undoubtedly the case that there are mixed reactions to Foundation Hour. There are those staff who find it irrelevant and even an intrusion into their busy schedules; there are others who would like to see more religious services being included. But most staff are pleased to know that Foundation Hour exists, even if they attend infrequently. It is harder to judge student reaction, and unless students are actually taking part in a presentation their presence is less apparent. This remains a cause for concern but is probably part of a broader pattern of student reaction, or perhaps indifference, to any activities immediately outside formal academic commitments. Numbers attending Foundation Hour range from 20 or so in the quietest time of the year to over 200 on big occasions. Speaking as the organiser of Foundation Hour over a four-year period, I can say that I receive many requests from staff, and from some student groups, to be included in the programme. Naturally, I tend to pick up the more positive responses to Foundation Hour, but, in my judgement, its disappearance would deprive the college of an opportunity for self-reflection, instruction, celebration, and the sharing of values and practices – in short, all those things which make communities worth living in. There are issues to address as the college's work expands to more locations – do we keep to the one Foundation Hour, or do we attempt to replicate it on other sites? Whatever, Foundation Hour is one tradition that Hope would do well to retain.

It is tempting for me, as the current Foundation Dean, to extol events at the most recent Foundation Hours, but permit me to offer a few illustrations. The month of February 2003 has been typically varied. Starting with a talk by the chief executive of the Royal Liverpool Philharmonic Society, the series continued with an interview with Rita Lewis, a long-serving member of the domestic services team whose experience extends from Mount Pleasant in the 1970s to Hope Park today. Alice Bennett and her team gave a presentation on student volunteering at Hope, and, to finish off the month, John Patterson and a host of supporters gave us 'Closing the digital divide; the Schools Inter-Generational Nurturing and Learning (SIGNAL) project'. Even that catalogue of topics in one four-week period does not do full justice to the extent of the programme; so, to give a fuller picture, in the next paragraphs I shall rehearse the highlights of Foundation Hour during the 'millennium' academic year 2000–01.

Ecumenical services and events are always held to mark significant days in the life of the college. Some reflect the rhythms of the liturgical year, such as Christmas, New Year, Epiphany, Christian Unity Week and Ash Wednesday. In the year 2000 Christ's and Notre Dame Chapel was the venue for Hope at Christmas, at which, to the great delight of all those present, we were joined by our friends from Hope Park Nursery. Other ecumenical services traditionally commemorate significant moments in the academic year, commencing with the Start of Session service held, in 2000, in S. Katharine's Chapel when the visiting preacher was the Revd Eric Bramhall, vicar of All Saints', Childwall. As always, the musicians gave resounding support. In October the college community assembled to endorse the ministry of the Revd Dr Kenneth Newport (then Reader in Christian Thought, now a professor), recently ordained deacon in the Anglican communion.

We welcomed several visitors to the college during that year: in September, tutors from Hope College in Michigan came; in February 2001, Sr Anne Burke SND described the educational work of the Sisters of Notre Dame in Liverpool over the last 150 years; and in March, Siobhan Garrighan, from Galway, delivered an evocative presentation on Celtic spirituality, as part of Irish week in college. Hope One World gave a flavour of the fascinating and varied projects undertaken in India and Africa by Hope students and staff during the year. The Community Deanery's contribution was on the important theme of valuing diversity. The international students' presentation was magnificently varied, including an original Hope Anthem on the piano! 'Songs of Praise' (old and new) was an innovation, and was well supported by students.

The varied programme included individual contributions from members of our own community. The Revd Dr Andrew Fox, Methodist Chaplain, drew some fascinating parallels with achievements in the recent Olympics. Laura Cockram, the then Student President, interviewed Luke McFarlane from the students' union. Professor Simon Lee spoke about 'Law, ethics and morality and the case of the Siamese twins'. Lewis Ayres, of the theology and religious studies team, took on the role of Thomas Aquinas, answering questions put to him by the audience. Peter Lawman challenged us to consider what we understand by collegiality. Liz Powell, Methodist Chaplain, introduced the topic of 'Faith, law and charity'; while Liz Ramsey co-ordinated a moving and personal session on 'Remembering the Holocaust'. We moved to Hope at Everton for an introduction to the work of Stanley Spencer, given by Matthew Stibbe and Fiona Ward. John Phillips's talk on 'Gods, mortals and garbage cans' was an intriguing critique of modern management techniques as they can be applied to higher educational models. Frank Lennon developed a challenging subject: 'Known only to god; the historian's quest for truth'. David Moulton's session on folk tradition and music in the UK had to be heard to be fully appreciated; and, in a practical session, Sabine Isaac presented a meditation based on Indian head massage. In the year 2000–01 much invaluable assistance was given by our chaplains, Bishop Ian Stuart and Fr Vladimir Nikiforov, and we were particularly grateful, as always, for the meticulous preparation and presentation of acts of worship. Until January 2001, the administration of Foundation Hour was undertaken by Alma Whitfield, and after that by Margaret Harwood. A cheerful welcome and a plentiful supply of sandwiches always work wonders for the spirit of collegiality! And that, as they say, concludes the account of Foundation Hour 2000–01.

COLLEGE EVENTS

A vital element of the Foundation Deanery is to preserve the best of our traditions, some of which go back for many years. As the reader will by now be familiar, there are several strands in the history of the present college, and each generation of students should be given the opportunity to re-engage with this heritage. One date has been firmly fixed in the calendar for many years: 25 November, S. Katharine's Day. It was customary for S. Katharine's College to celebrate with a day free of lectures, a service and a formal dinner with invited guests. Traditionally, Notre Dame College had celebratory events in December, February and May, and Christ's College made much of Christmas and the Going Down Day. In 2000–01 the decision was taken to have two college feast

days, S. Katharine's Day and 2 February, the feast of Candlemas (the Presentation of Christ in the Temple), which was styled Christ's and Notre Dame
Day. Both events were successful, but the following year we (that is the
Foundation Deanery organising committee) decided to promote just the one
College Foundation Day, on the nearest Thursday to 25 November. Not only
are there strong historical connections with the month of November, but this
period is sufficiently far away from Christmas and formal examinations (which
is the problem with a May celebration) to be a time of year which stands out in
the college calendar. And so, within just two years, a new tradition has been
born, of a College Foundation (Feast) Day in November, consisting of lunch-
time exhibitions and events, an afternoon karaoke 'singathon' in the students'
union building, an ecumenical chapel service, a sherry reception and a formal
dinner. Proceeds of a raffle go to Hope One World. The Hope Park refectory
is laid out for 250 guests and there is a real feeling of festivity and celebration,
enjoyed by governors, staff and students. It would be unrealistic to open up the
meal to more people, and one could argue that to cater for under 4 per cent of
the Hope community amounts to tokenism. Still, Foundation Day is a symbol
of what the college stands for, and as tickets are available on a first-come-first-
served basis, no one is disadvantaged.[5]

The college arranges other events during the year. All first-year students
are given a welcome meal, personal tutor lunches are laid on during the first
semester, and there are Christmas celebrations, including the staff Christmas
brunch. And special groups, such as international students and Irish students,
meet together for meals. Added to all this, the students' union puts on a varied
programme of sporting and social events, including Christmas and Graduation
balls. And Graduation at Hope is the biggest celebration of them all! Each year
has its own flavour, and from time to time there have been inter-collegiate
church college events, such as the Church Colleges Choir Festivals of 1990 and
2002.[6] We like to claim that Liverpool Hope offers a 'village in the city' experience, where individuals really matter. And so, within the financial constraints
of today's higher education budget, the Foundation Deanery continues to
sustain and encourage this vital social side of community life, without which
students' experience of education would be featureless and unmemorable.

CHURCH CERTIFICATES

One of the distinguishing features of Liverpool Hope is the provision of
courses for teachers in church schools, Catholic and Anglican. The Catholic
Certificate in Religious Studies has always been crucial for those intending to
teach in Catholic schools, and numbers for this certificate have been high. The
Anglican certificates, while not mandatory for teachers in Church of England

schools, have attracted a steady, but modest following. These qualifications have always been additional to degrees and other qualifications taken, and have been outside the formal timetable and course arrangements. It follows that their teaching, too, has been outside the standard timetable, and this has caused several administrative problems, for tutors as well as for students. By the late 1990s it was becoming increasingly difficult to timetable and staff the church certificates, and so it was decided to integrate them into Hope's curriculum. A simple enough task, one might think.

The process was twofold. Internally, the due processes of consultation had to be undertaken, and externally, there were the national bodies to consult. At pretty well every stage of the negotiations there were differences in content, emphasis and level to be ironed out. It was essential to preserve the professional standing of the awards. After several months of detailed work a solution was found. Each of the national certificates would be drafted as two elective 15-credit modules, thus enabling students to gain academic credit for their work. Nothing in the existing content of the national certificates needed to be changed, and titles of the Hope modules reflecting this content were agreed. For the Catholic Certificate in Religious Studies, the two modules were entitled *Christianity in the Roman Catholic Tradition: exploring the Church, Sacraments and Christian Morality*; and *Christianity in the Roman Catholic Tradition: exploring the Old and New Testaments and the Person of Christ*. For the Church Colleges Certificate in Church School Studies, the respective modules were *Collective Worship and Ethos in Anglican Schools*; and *Religious Education and Ethos in Anglican Schools*.

Now that both these church certificates are in the second year of operation as modules within Hope's undergraduate and PGCE courses, it is encouraging to note that numbers are increasing and students now take it for granted that these modules will be offered within their actual degree programme. People are now asking if some of the content of the two denominational modules could be shared, and a 'chaplaincy' module is being proposed which will have full ecumenical support. Such questions would not have been asked a few years ago, and one would like to think that Hope's ecumenical stance on such issues will continue to have an impact on those student teachers who take these certificates as a vital element of their professional training.

ALUMNI

The story of the old students' associations connected with Liverpool Hope and its former constituent colleges reflects the rich tapestry of our diverse traditions and heritage. People are strongly attached to buildings and places[7] and, inevitably, some of the links with former parts of the Hope ancestry are less strong than they were. Warrington, Keswick, Scarisbrick and even Mount Pleasant are names from the past. Sadly, the Old Warringtonians, who used to assemble for their annual festival in S. Katharine's, no longer function as a separate entity. But former students of Mount Pleasant are still going strong, and in September 2002 it was a pleasure to welcome to Hope Park a group celebrating their fiftieth anniversary. Similarly, several groups of former students keep up their old friendships, often in informal gatherings. The college maintains a register of alumni/alumnae and is always willing to facilitate reunions for special groups of any size. At the present time there are plans for a S. Katharine's reunion of students from the 1970s in the summer of 2003; and a massive reunion for that cohort of students who enrolled in Christ's College in its very first year is expected to take place in the summer of 2004. If previous reunions are anything to go by, those of 2003 and 2004 will be equally poignant and memorable.

The college has, in recent years, organised an annual reunion in June or July for any former students who wish to attend. We provide a day of eating and meeting, culminating in a formal dinner with a speaker. Holding the day together are the memories, the photographs and the tales of then and now. And at such a reunion, the former (we daren't call them 'old'!) students across more than fifty years and from three colleges, from LIHE and from Liverpool Hope renew their connection with the college of today – and, incidentally, often make new friends. It must be recalled that in earlier generations it would have been most unusual for Catholic students, either in college or within the school system, to have met Protestant students, and vice versa. But times have changed, and emphatically so for the better.

Links with all alumni and alumnae are, according to the government White Paper of January 2003,[8] to be encouraged. Here at Hope we have a somewhat fragmented set of traditions, and the signs are that recent and younger graduates are less likely to want to participate in formal reunions. Indeed, it might be that as higher education establishments get larger, so students actually get to know fewer people during their time at university: when a whole college could eat or pray together, then it was that the foundations of lasting friendships were made. But all former students can be assured that Hope will not forget them, for they are among our best ambassadors of all that we offered – and still have to offer – as a higher education establishment.

PROGRESS CRITIQUE

How far is the Foundation Deanery able to live up to its claim to promote 'all activity immediately related to the church foundation and the mission'? Does it really, in the words of the Corporate Plan, help people to 'take faith seriously, being fully Anglican, fully Catholic, fully ecumenical, fully open to those of all faiths and beliefs'? Does it help to sustain a college which is 'hospitable, welcoming, cheerful, professional; creating collegial, aesthetically pleasing environments and supportive communities'? No-one could ever claim 100 per cent success in meeting such challenging aims, and the promulgation of the mission is not the exclusive preserve of those who work in the Foundation Deanery. Yet the very use of the word 'foundation', as in Foundation Deanery and Foundation Hour, helps to focus the mind on why the college was founded and why it has continued to develop in the way that it has.

There are still close links with the founding churches: in the composition of the Governing Council; in the work of the chaplaincy; in the training of teachers; in the teaching of the church certificates; in teaching and research in a vibrant and developing curriculum that includes theology, religious studies, philosophy and ethics; in community outreach; and in lifelong learning. Equally, the college is open to those of all faiths and none. Hope means what it says when it strives to be a collegial establishment where people matter and where the mission is lived out in the daily lives of all who work and study there. All these claims might seem unbelievably idealistic, but looking back over 150 years, we can sense that those who established the original colleges must have struggled against the odds; they must have had a vision. The task of those who are charged with leading the college in the first years of the twenty-first century is no less daunting. The values encapsulated in Hope's Foundation are integral to the success of our educational enterprise. One might even dare to venture that: 'Without Foundations there can be no Hope'.

NOTES

1 See, e.g., R. J. Elford, 'S. Katharine's College, Liverpool: Impressions on Arrival', in *150 Years: the Church Colleges in Higher Education*, ed. T. Brighton, West Sussex Institute of Higher Education, 1989; J. E. Hollinshead, ed., *In thy Light: S. Katharine's College, 1844–1944*, Liverpool Institute of Higher Education, 1994; K. Lowden, 'Spirited Sisters: Anglican and Catholic contributions to women's teacher training in the nineteenth century', PhD thesis, University of Liverpool, 2002; 'About Liverpool Hope', Staff Handbook, Liverpool Hope University College, published annually.

2 The use of such a term, 'mission statement', is illustrative of the self-consciousness of late twentieth-century institutions; previous generations were content with Latin mottoes. The motto of S. Katharine's College, for instance, is taken from Psalm 36, verse 9: 'et in lumine tuo videbimus lumen', 'and in thy light we shall see light'.

3 R. Price, 'A study of two aspects of a college mission and corporate plan, to investigate the degree to which they were manifest in the college, and the extent to which they impacted on the day-to-day activities and events of the college community', BPhil thesis, University of Liverpool, 2001.

4 Price, 'A college mission and corporate plan', p. 65.

5 Where and how we eat matters. In *The Art of Learning: a personal journey*, The Book

Guild Ltd, 2000, p. 90, Patrick Nuttgens, formerly Director of Leeds Polytechnic, writes about his experience as a founder member of the University of York in the early 1960s. His comments about the optimum size of a college community are based on the realities of the numbers of those who can sit down to eat together.

> It was thought... that 150 residents would economically support a kitchen and dining room which could also cater for 150 outsiders. It was decided that every member of the University (staff as well as students) should be a member of a college. Each college would have a dining-room big enough for 300, common rooms, study bedrooms, a library and, of course, a bar.

It is worth recalling that a 'companion' is, literally, 'one who eats bread with another'.

6 In 2002 nine choirs took part, from Birmingham, Canterbury, Chester, Chichester, Lancaster, Lincoln, Liverpool, Winchester and York.

7 *Whither now?*, a report of a working party set up by the Institute Governing Council in 1982 became notorious for its reference to the scent of gilly-flowers (p. 13). One can detect the hand of Bishop Michael Henshall in this passage:

> Collegiality ultimately is about a commendable form of patriotism, about loyalty, about symbols, even about the shape of bricks and mortar and the way the clock chimes. It is about the way grace is said over bread and the way in which the laundry is collected and about the smell of disinfectant from a lavatory and the scent of gilly-flowers in the quad. These are the things that haunt the years and encourage College loyalty in middle age!

8 *The Future of Higher Education*, January 2003, HMSO, 2003.

Dr John Elford, Mrs Patricia Lee, Mr Raymond Semple and Professor Simon Lee.

Ms Janet Ireland, Mr Sean Gallagher, Mr Abdul Sallam, Ms Brenda Ashton and others with students from Korea and Japan.

Bishop Ian Stuart and Mrs Alison Duerden of the Mothers Union presenting a new student with a welcome pack.

The entrance to the Sheppard–Worlock Library.

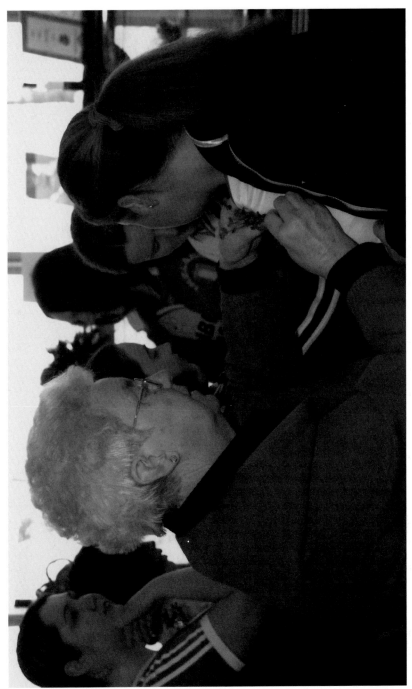

Sr Eileen Kelleher SND and students from across the Irish Sea on St Patrick's Day.

The students' union bar.

Graduation in the round, Metropolitan Cathedral of Christ the King.

Graduation at Liverpool Cathedral.

Hope at Everton on Graduation Day, the atrium and Great Hall beyond.

Ms Manie Markar, a postgraduate student, training to teach mathematics at secondary level.

The Cornerstone, Hope at Everton, with reflections of St Francis Xavier's Church.

Professor Kenneth Newport (centre) with Professor Leslie Houlden (left) and the Revd Canon Dr John Newton (right).

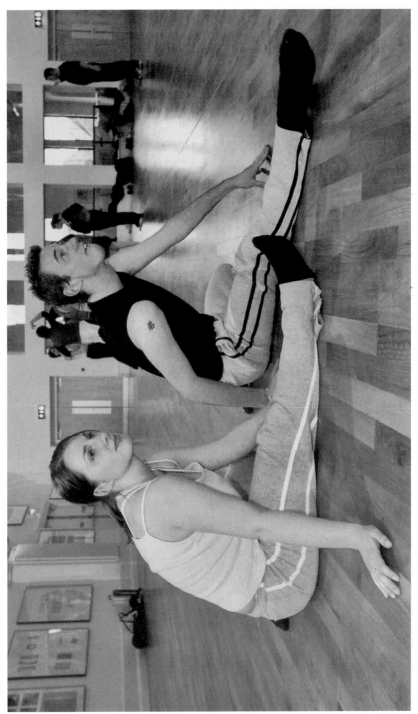

Dance class in the Great Hall, Hope at Everton.

First day on the pathway at Hope Park.

Professor Gerald J. Pillay, Rector and Chief Executive designate.

Mgr Alexander Jones, translator of the Jerusalem Bible.

CHAPTER 8

The Reconstruction
of Theology

IAN S. MARKHAM

THEOLOGY depends on institutions. When Rowan Williams explained that his methodological starting point was always in the middle, he was drawing attention to this dependency on institutions. Williams writes,

> I assume that the theologian is always beginning in the middle of things. There is a practice of common life and language already there, a practice that defines a specific shared way of interpreting human life as lived in relation to God.[1]

So the primary institution for the theologian is the church. If the church did not exist, then Christian theology would not exist. It is on that living community of the church, carrying the life-blood of faith from the first century to the present, that the theologian is entirely parasitic. The church does not simply supply the 'content' of theology but also provides the community that ultimately will listen – the 'hearers'. It supplies the 'content' in that it provides the vocabulary and the texts that extend the discussion; it provides the 'hearers' of theology because ultimately the task of making sense of God and God's relations with the world is a primary concern of the church. This does not deny that the cultural setting of the church can become part of the content, but even when this happens, it is still the church that absorbs the content. Likewise, although non-Christians outside the church might be curious about the theological task (in much the same way that an English-speaking person can be interested in the Spanish language), curiosity does not involve the same commitment as living and thinking within language.

A church college is a distinctive institution. It is the creation of the church: Christian men and women created the institution. Christians dominate the governing body, which often includes, as in the case of Liverpool Hope's Governing Council, several senior prelates. Yet it is also part of the academy. To be effective in the modern academy, it must accept that many students are non-Christians; it must teach a vast range of subjects and provide an inclusive setting for study.

In this chapter, I shall explore how one church college, Liverpool Hope University College, thought through its institutional commitment to theology. The chapter divides into four sections: first, I briefly examine the institutional commitments to theology that shaped the period from 1996 to 2000 and the position that Hope wanted to take. Second, I shall look at the *Engaging the Curriculum* project, a national attempt to think through mission distinctiveness. Third, I shall look at the content and impact of the so-called Liverpool Statement. And finally, I shall comment on the institutional commitment to making a contribution to the academy by investing in projects that will not see an immediate return.

Perhaps right at the outset, it is worth stating that this text is illustrative of theology at Hope. There has also been a substantial religious studies provision in the department, led by the distinguished specialist on Chinese religions, Stewart McFarlane, and ably supported by Victoria La'Porte and Tinu Ruparell; while others have been closely identified with religious education, for example, Elizabeth Ramsey, David Torevell and Geoffrey Chorley. Furthermore it is important to recognise that theology has always been strong at Hope; when I arrived in 1996, there were 13 specialists in theology and religious studies, led by Andrew Bebb. However, my selection in what follows is intended to stress the 'reconstitution of theology' – the task of building up a selfconsciously theologically orientated team in the 1990s in an urban and ecumenical setting. Others who lived through these years with me would not necessarily concur or affirm my rationale or perspective.

A SURVEY OF INSTITUTIONAL ATTITUDES TO THEOLOGY

In 1996 John Major was prime minister, although the signs were there that the Tories, after 17 uninterrupted years in office, were due for a spell in opposition. The Archbishop of Canterbury was George Carey; he was preoccupied with the plans for the millennium, but was giving indications that he would then step down. Cardinal Basil Hume was still at Westminster. By the year 2002, all these key players were going to have changed.

However, unlike these offices, the theological academy has been much more static. The theological conservatives were in control in 1996, and still are in 2001. A quick survey of professorial positions revealed the Barthians in the ascendancy. David Ford had moved to Cambridge; Timothy Gorringe (the Barthian socialist) moved to Exeter; Haddon Wilmer (a conservative ethicist) was replaced by the evangelical Nigel Biggar at the University of Leeds; Colin Gunton used the period to create a centre of like-minded theologians at King's

College London; and Anthony Thiselton (another who can own the label evangelical) was replaced by Alan Ford (a conservative church historian).

Naturally there were institutions with a different emphasis. Bristol and Lancaster continued to develop the religious studies track, with a strong interest in comparative religions or with a particular emphasis on 'study zones' in, say, Japanese religions or Buddhism. Keith Ward, at Oxford, was busy attracting funding for comparative theology and building up a faculty with a significant Islamic and Hindu presence; although despite this, the best-known theologian in Oxford is the Principal of Wycliffe Hall, Alister McGrath. But sophisticated conservatives held the majority of positions during this period.

In addition, Cambridge was becoming strongly identified with the movement started by John Milbank. Milbank had moved from Lancaster and with enthusiastic support from Nicholas Lash was encouraged to develop his movement in Cambridge. Building on his substantial study *Theology and Social Theory*,[2] Milbank found key allies in his project in Catherine Pickstock and Graham Ward. Although Radical Orthodoxy has a radical political and sexual agenda, the dominant and best-known themes tend towards a conservative account of the relationship of faith to the world. Although they want to see themselves differently (a fusion of the pre-modern – classics and renaissance – and the postmodern),[3] in actual fact the corollary of their world-view is that one sees the community of the church in resolute opposition to secular society.

Using the language of the postmodern, Milbank called for the distinctive ethos of the church to witness to a different way of living and thinking within the church. There was no doubt that in 1996, Radical Orthodoxy was the most exciting vision of the theological task that Britain had produced for several generations. It was not surprising that the American Academy of Religion devoted two sessions in 1997 to this new movement.

One should not be surprised that institutions go through periods when a certain approach to theology dominates. The modern day King's College, with Gunton, Banner, Helm and Burridge, is only a conservative version of the 1970s King's of Houlden, Nineham, Sutherland and Dunstan. It is the dynamic of institutions that a few key appointments can end up shaping an institution. Theologians tend to admire others who are like-minded in terms of task and approach. They then appoint each other onto the faculty. In addition, the holders of the senior chairs will be responsible for the growth of the next generation of theologians. It is the senior chairs at British universities that attract the funding from the British Academy and therefore produce the finest research students, who then get the next available positions. Conservative supervisors often end up producing conservative research students.

To many in the church, the theological academy looked very conservative. For the clergy, life on the front line of parish work tends to make theology more messy and complicated. It was my view at Liverpool Hope that we had a duty to put the church and the academy into rather more effective conversation.

Three strategies emerged to facilitate this conversation. The first was that the church college itself had to be rather more self-consciously mission-specific. This was the *Engaging the Curriculum* project. The second was that theologians of a liberal disposition needed a support group. This was the Liverpool Statement. And the third, described elsewhere in this volume but to be mentioned here, was the institutional commitment to projects that do not promise an immediate return.

ENGAGING THE CURRICULUM

Engaging the Curriculum was a project of the Council of Church and Associated Colleges (CCAC), an organisation representing the senior administrators of the 19 church colleges in England and Wales. It was set up in 1993 under the chairmanship of Dr John Elford, and having Adrian Thatcher as its first Director. The goal was to reflect on the curriculum of a church college and see what difference mission distinctiveness might make to the content. In other words, the task of its bulletin and conferences was to think through the relationship of theology to such subjects as sociology, psychology and education.

Fairly rapidly, it became apparent that the interpretation of this task took two different and contrasting forms. For some, it was simply a 'content' issue: the religious aspects of these subjects needed to be made more explicit. For example, in English Literature it would be vitally important to stress that one cannot fully understand the plays of Shakespeare without appreciating the world of the Bible. For others, it was an 'approach' issue. Being a Christian means having a distinctive set of values that contrast markedly with a secular approach. On this view, one might stress the 'ends' of teaching English Literature should include the moral dimension of literature appreciation.

The first Director was responsible for the consultations on sociology and on science education. The latter ran into what was to prove a perpetual problem: the church colleges themselves were not very supportive of the consultations, and as a result the science education project was cancelled. Ultimately, a booklet outlining the vision of Michael Poole was printed privately.

The directorship then moved to Liverpool Hope. Shannon Ledbetter became Assistant Director, a post that was funded by Hope and which provided the much-needed administrative attention the programme had lacked. It was during this period that a further three consultations were organised: 'Theology and English Literature' was hosted at Chester; 'Theology and Spirituality' was held at Southampton; and 'Theology and Sociology' at St Deiniol's in Hawarden, North Wales. Three publications emerged during this period.

Under the series title *Theology in Dialogue*, Adrian Thatcher edited the 'Theology and Spirituality' volume,[4] Liam Gearon edited the 'Theology and English Literature' book[5] and Leslie Francis edited the 'Theology and Sociology' volume.[6]

These consultations were very worthwhile. The exchange between David Jasper and Terence R. Wright about the problem of reading the Bible, which was reproduced in the 'Theology and English Literature' volume, was both interesting and profound. Both Jasper, from the University of Glasgow, and Wright, from Newcastle, seemed to appreciate the opportunity to explore in a creative exchange some of the issues upon which they disagree. The format of the consultation, made possible by the funding provided by the CCAC, proved very congenial towards concentrated theological exchange.

As with many of these projects, the main beneficiaries were those who participated in the programme. The initial hope that this would create a mission-distinctive approach to education in the church colleges was probably not realised. The government's emphasis on its 'Teaching Quality Assessment' had a much greater impact on the sector. The threat that these institutions would be refused degree-awarding powers for at least five years if a score of less than 3 were awarded in any one of the six categories of assessment meant that the church colleges poured considerable resources into making sure that they performed satisfactorily in these inspections. Yet the *Engaging the Curriculum* programme did demonstrate that the church college sector wanted to think more selfconsciously about their approach to higher education.

In 1999 the programme moved to King Alfred's College, Winchester. At this point the programme simply disappeared; no further activities were produced and the *Engaging the Curriculum Journal* ceased to be published. There was a possibility of a partnership with the Bible Society, but, ultimately, this was not realised. Though there is still talk of creating a successor to the project, probably the best way forward would be a set of prizes (for example, of research income) for the department that provides the best set of mission-related courses, which could then be widely published as an example of good practice that other departments might emulate. The future needs to be different from the past, but it should build on the hard work that has been done.

Ultimately, however, the *Engaging the Curriculum* project reflects a wider concern for the church colleges. If the sector is going to survive in an increasingly homogeneous higher education scene in the United Kingdom, it is important that the sector strives for mission distinctiveness. Church colleges must be that: colleges that are shaped by a church ethos. To that end, they must be institutions deeply committed to the theological enterprise. It is in this context that the Liverpool Statement should be placed.

THE LIVERPOOL STATEMENT

We have already noted how conservatives dominate the theological scene in Britain. Interestingly they are conservatives of a particular type. Both the Barthians and the Radical Orthodox agree that there is nothing to be learned from 'non-Christian' sources (save, perhaps, for understanding the nature of the opposition). Although there is nothing intrinsic to a conservative theology that entails such antagonism to the role of the theological task as involving conversation and learning from others, the particular brand of Protestant conservatism that dominates the English academy has taken this position.

From a church college perspective, this looked especially unwise. The churches, ironically, did not see the theological task in those ways. This was the period of *Unemployment and the Future of Work*,[7] which was a commission, supported by Bishop David Sheppard, convened to provide a Christian critique of the social and economic costs of unemployment. This commission needed theologians in conversation with economists; a task that John Milbank, among others, had pronounced as impossible.[8] It is not surprising that the only theologian who served on the commission was located midway between church and academy, namely Bishop Peter Selby.

There were also dangers for the academy. A theological task that sees itself as completely self-referring might well have a problem in justifying its continued existence in a secular universe of ideas (that is, the modern university). The question was there waiting to be asked: why should the academy continue to support a subject that sees itself disconnected from the rest of the institution? In addition, compared to the United States, it seems that English theology was turning in on itself. The Society for the Study of Theology, for example, almost seems to take some pride in the fact that it has never had a woman president. Feminist theology, let alone gay and lesbian theologies, is not taken seriously in the departments of theology.[9]

The topic of the meeting that ultimately produced the Liverpool Statement was the 'State of British Theology'. The co-convener was Gareth Jones – then at Birmingham, but later at a sister church college, namely Canterbury Christ Church University College. To help focus the discussion Dr Christopher Williams had produced an interesting study of American attitudes to English theology. Rachael Penketh helpfully summarises the results of the study:

> During the period August to September 1997, 340 questionnaires were sent out to various individuals in the United States of America... The results were quite startling. Thirty-three per cent thought that there was nothing significant about British theology; 22 per cent could not name someone whom they thought was the most important British theologian; arguably, 60 per cent saw British theological trends to be irrelevant to their work; and

overall, the impression was that British theology is 'insular' and 'staid'. It would appear that the 'widely held view' that 'American theologians know little about British theology and so do not use it' was justified.[10]

Twelve scholars made the journey to Liverpool to discuss the state of British theology on 26–27 September 1997. In addition to the two conveners (Gareth Jones and myself) there were Jim Byrne, Mark Chapman, David Horrell, David Law, Shannon Ledbetter, Clive Marsh, George Newlands, Kenneth Newport, Martyn Percy and Linda Woodhead. The resulting statement attracted many signatories, including Keith Ward, John Elford, Leslie Houlden and Sean Gill. The statement started by setting out the scene:

> As we approach the new millennium, it is a good time to take stock theologically. For those of us in the West, this century has seen a constant shift of emphasis between more 'conservative' and more 'liberal' approaches to theology. Emerging from the nineteenth century, a classical liberal theology was in the ascendant. The optimism and naiveté of such theology was challenged by conservative theologians. The late fifties and sixties saw a new liberalism emerge, one which suggested a new morality and a new theology for a newly self-confident age. Since the seventies, the conservatives have returned to the fray. In this battle there is no obvious winner. The agenda seems stale and the in-fighting futile. Theology seems too often a minority interest which has failed to keep pace with new scholarship and a rapidly changing world.[11]

Five proposals to bring about a more engaged theology transcending the traditional liberal and conservative divide were made. These were:

> First, we must engage openly with our contemporary culture... Second, we need to be much more international in our vision... Third, the neglect of other faith traditions is wilful... Fourth, a plurality of approaches in theological method and formulation needs to be encouraged, in order that, in a time of undeniable change, the better may be seen to stand out from the worse. Departments of theology and religious studies should encourage a plurality of perspectives among the staff... Fifth, there is a need for structural change... We are a group which hopes that some sort of umbrella organisation shall emerge that can encourage the creation of a British equivalent to the American Academy of Religion.[12]

For a short period of time, there was a flurry of press interest (*The Guardian*, *The Independent*, and *The Church Times* all carried the story). But, perhaps more importantly, it did encourage a number of British theologians to use the word 'liberal' again. The form this took varied considerably. As the follow-up book, edited by J'annine Jobling and myself and called *Theological Liberalism: Creative and Critical*, revealed, the term was being used differently by different writers. For some 'liberal' meant a critical engagement with the Enlightenment. So, for example, Leslie Houlden was part of that 1970s brand of liberals characterised by the collection of essays called *The Myth of God Incarnate*.[13] And it has been interesting to see a revival in this approach to theology. John Elford's two most recent books, *The Pastoral Nature of Theology*[14] and *The Ethics of Uncertainty*,[15] are very much in this tradition. For others, 'liberal' meant recognition of the epistemological limitations of the theological discourse. This is very much the approach of Gareth Jones and is shared, perhaps to a lesser extent, by David Law. Jones provides an eloquent description of his understanding of the theological task in *Critical Theology*.[16] For others again, 'liberal' represents the need for engagement, whether with science, other religious traditions, or culture more broadly. This is perhaps where Clive Marsh's delightful book *Christianity in a Post-Atheist Age*[17] or Martyn Percy's substantial analysis of culture in *The Salt of the Earth: Religious Resilience in a Secular Age*[18] should be placed. However, the strongest representative of this form of liberalism is Keith Ward in Oxford. His four-part series setting out an approach to systematic theology that takes into account the insights of other faith traditions stands as a model for this approach to liberal theology.[19] Finally, we have those who want to weave liberal theology with postmodernism and liberation theologies. Probably the best representative of this is Hope's own J'annine Jobling. Reviewers, almost unanimously, acclaimed the two chapters written by Jobling in *Theological Liberalism* as the most striking and original.[20] Her dialogue with Catherine Pickstock is especially illuminating.[21]

Even though, the term 'liberal' was being used in four different and contrasting ways, the good thing was that at least the term *was* being used. It is not healthy when an entire approach to theology disappears, to be replaced by those only comfortable with the label 'conservative'. Simon Lee understood precisely what the Liverpool Statement was trying to do, when he picked up on the Henri Nouwen image about 'clowns' and suggested that we were 'clowning in Liverpool'.[22] The clowns, Nouwen had explained, are the light relief that exposes absurdity and conceit and uses humour as a way of engaging with the crowd. They unmask tragedy or, in the tradition of the court jesters, they are the revealers or usurpers (as in Shakespeare's *King Lear*). So, by analogy, the statement was intended to provoke, tease and question. We might not be on the high wire, but the task of asking the questions and providing the interludes that place everything else in context is important.

There are obvious dangers in having an institution so clearly identified with a certain label in theology, especially given the explicit call in the Statement for a range of different approaches in any department. So it was especially pleasing to see that two opponents of the Statement were both at Liverpool Hope when they offered their critique in *Theological Liberalism*. Lewis Ayres and Mark

Elliott both saw the Liverpool Statement as misguided and mistaken. Many of their trenchant criticisms were both thoughtful and insightful. Yet the task of ensuring that Liverpool Hope was not confined to the 'clowning' of the Liverpool Statement brings us to the third and final aspect of Hope's programme in theology and religious studies.

SPECIALISED RESEARCH

One important, and perhaps the most enduring, aspect of Liverpool Hope's approach to theological research is the emphasis, described elsewhere in this book, on major research projects. The pressures on British higher education are not quite making the major research project an impossibility to deliver. To retain research funding, there is an obligation to make sure that every five or six years a major monograph is published. Yet many projects in the humanities take longer than this. The best Hope illustration is the Charles Wesley Letters Project. Oxford University Press has committed to publishing the two resulting volumes that will run to 750,000 words. Professor Kenneth Newport's commitment to such a specialised research project requires an institution that is willing to underpin the work. There is no doubt that Newport's terms and conditions would be the envy of many an Oxbridge professor. To accompany the various grants he has managed to bring into the institution, he has over the last few years had resource for several overseas trips and the services of a research assistant. Newport is a worthy successor to Alexander Jones, the renowned translator of the *Jerusalem Bible*, who taught at Christ's College in the 1960s.

The church colleges are some of the oldest institutions of higher education in Britain today. To commit to such long-term projects is completely appropriate for institutions that know their origins and value the judgement of history. With a growing culture in higher education of being preoccupied with the immediate and fashionable, we do need some institutions willing to challenge the barbarians currently in control in the new dark ages already upon us (to borrow freely from the conclusion to *After Virtue* by Alasdair MacIntyre).[23] The privilege of working at Liverpool Hope, under Professor Lee and Dr Elford, was that it afforded me the space to support such projects which do not promise an immediate return, but which many of our academic successors will value and appreciate.

CONCLUSION

As I move on to Hartford Seminary, it is pleasing to see the continued strength of the team at Liverpool Hope. The appointment of Revd Professor Nicholas Sagovsky as my successor has brought to Hope the country's leading specialist in ecumenism and social ethics. With Sagovsky alongside Professor Newport and Professor Hinnells, Hope now has an outstanding professorial team to progress the Hope project. In addition to the professors, Drs Torevell, Elliott and Jobling provide a research-rich environment for students. Theology at Hope should go from strength to strength.

To be at Liverpool Hope at the turn of the millennium was an undoubted privilege for me and for my career. To be granted the gift and honour to shape an institution and help it live its mission is both a responsibility and a thrill. It is a responsibility because one has those years to make appointments and cultivate colleagues; it is a thrill because one has, for a short period of time, the gift of opportunity to make a small difference. Liverpool Hope taught me what the 'vocation of institutional care' involves. To lead a department of theology is not simply an opportunity to promote one's own writing, but to cultivate and support a team, within the context of an institution, and promote that team both nationally and internationally. In practice this might mean 'sitting in numerous meetings', but to fail to recognise that this is what the vocation involves is a failure to grasp the significance of the task that has been entrusted to one.[24]

There is no doubt that the leadership of Professor Simon Lee during this period was crucial. He understood exactly what was being attempted. He was willing to take risks, think imaginatively, and pioneer a distinctive approach to the institutional position of theology. For his leadership, I am truly grateful.

NOTES

1 R. D. Williams, *On Christian Theology*, Oxford, Blackwell, 2000, p. xii.
2 J. Milbank, *Theology and Social Theory*, Oxford, Blackwell, 1993.
3 I am grateful for discussions with Martyn Percy on Radical Orthodoxy for this insight.
4 A. Thatcher, ed., *Spirituality and the Curriculum*, London, Cassell, 1999.
5 L. Gearon, ed., *English Literature, Theology and the Curriculum*, London, Cassell, 1999.
6 L. J. Francis, ed., *Sociology, Theology and the Curriculum*, London, Cassell, 1999.
7 This was published by the Council of Churches for Britain and Ireland (CCBI) in April 1997.
8 See Milbank, *Theology and Social Theory*. In this book, he argues that the social sciences as conceived in modernity assume an 'ontology of violence'. The task of the church is to oppose this mode of thinking. For a fuller critique see R. J. Elford and I. S. Markham, eds, *The Middle Way*, London, SCM Press, 2000, pp. 257–66.
9 There are, of course, significant exceptions to this: Manchester and St Andrews are probably the best illustrations.
10 R. Penketh, 'The Liverpool Statement: An Overview', in *Theological Liberalism: Creative and Critical*, ed. J. Jobling and I. Markham, London, SPCK, 2000, pp. 177–78.
11 'A New Theological Vision: A Call to Join the Forum for Religion and Theology', in Jobling and Markham, eds, *Theological Liberalism*, p. ix.
12 Ibid. pp. x–xi.

13 J. Hick, ed., *The Myth of God Incarnate*, London, SCM Press, 1977.

14 R. J. Elford, *The Pastoral Nature of Theology*, London, Cassell, 1999.

15 R. J. Elford, *The Ethics of Uncertainty: A New Christian Approach to Moral Decision-Making*, Oxford, Oneworld, 2000.

16 G. Jones, *Critical Theology*, Cambridge, Polity Press, 1995.

17 C. Marsh, *Christianity in a Post-Atheist Age*, London, SCM Press, 2002.

18 M. Percy, *The Salt of the Earth: Religious Resilience in a Secular Age*, Sheffield Academic Press, 2002.

19 See Keith Ward's *Religion and Revelation*; *Religion and Creation*; *Religion and Community*; and *Religion and Human Nature*. All published by Oxford University Press.

20 See, for example, Timothy Gorringe in *Theology*.

21 J. Jobling, 'On the Liberal Consummation of Theology: A Dialogue with Catherine Pickstock', in Jobling and Markham, eds, *Theological Liberalism*. Jobling's other chapter was co-written with Hannah Bacon and is entitled 'Why Feminists Should Still be Liberals'.

22 See Simon Lee, Graduation Address 2002, unpublished. Go to *www.hope.ac.uk* , click news, then graduation. For Henri Nouwen, see *Clowning in Rome: Reflections on Solitude, Celibacy, Prayer and Contemplation*, London, Hodder and Stoughton, 2001.

23 See Alasdair MacIntyre, *After Virtue*, London, Duckworth, 1981. The actual quote reads: 'What matters at this stage is the construction of local forms of community within which civility and the intellectual and moral life can be sustained through the new dark ages which are already upon us. And if the tradition of the virtues was able to survive the horrors of the last dark ages, we are not entirely without grounds for hope. This time however the barbarians are not waiting beyond the frontiers; they have already been governing us for quite some time' (p. 263).

24 It is perhaps worth noting that the Hope theology department was awarded a score of 23 (out of a maximum of 24) in the Teaching Quality Assessment, and a 4 (a significant improvement on the 3b of 1996) in the Research Assessment Exercise. The credit for this achievement should go to the college and the team, who all worked so hard on both the teaching and research fronts.

—◆—

Theology, Ecumenism
and Public Life[1]

NICHOLAS SAGOVSKY

—◆—

ITHIN a tradition of teaching and learning, the wisdom of former
generations all too easily becomes absolutised. When young people are
taught 'what Plato said' or 'what Aristotle said' rather than learning to enter
into a Socratic or a Platonic or an Aristotelian style of questioning, this is a
huge loss. They have not learned the most important lesson they could take
from the great thinkers: how to ask questions, how to enter into dialogue. This
is hugely disabling for the practice of any discipline, but the focus in this
chapter will be specifically on theology. I shall be contending that the Western
tradition of theological learning, as taught at Liverpool Hope, is a tradition in
which the dialogical questioning of Scripture and the dialogical questioning of
Greek philosophy were brought together. It is an open tradition of dialogical
wisdom, and in an age when the opinions of 'the experts' all too easily pass
unchallenged, one key task of theology as practised within this tradition is to
draw on that ancient wisdom to foster the critical questioning which needs to
be addressed to the issues of today.

THE UNIVERSITY AS A PLACE OF DIALOGUE

The place, above all, where the practice of such critical questioning has, in the
Western tradition, been developed is the university. The university has a dual
role. It is, of course, a place where up-to-date knowledge is transmitted: young
people have to become competent in the knowledge that is conveyed by the
study of mathematics, or business studies, or information technology, or
whatever may be their chosen discipline. This is a huge task, which can all too
easily consume the entire energies of teachers and learners. However, if the
body of knowledge is to grow and change to meet the needs of new generations, it has constantly to be relativised, questioned and reassessed. The point
about this taking place within a *university* is that, traditionally, the university is

a place which reflects in its identity a belief in the *unity* of knowing and the *unity* of what there is to know.[2] What it teaches and what it explores is not adventitious: it is concerned with the whole corpus of all that constitutes human being-in-the-world. Dr Johnson defined a university as 'a school, where all the arts and faculties are taught and studied', though its earlier meaning may have been looser and referred more to an institution in which there was 'a body' of teachers and learners bound together as one society.[3]

Traditionally, it has been the place of theology within the university to make explicit the pre-conscious intuition of the wholeness of all that is (of the *cosmos*), and of the possible knowledge of the cosmos, which has been held to be a reflection of the creative activity of the one God.[4] Where there has been responsible intellectual and scientific exploration it has been seen theologically as 'exploration into God' because it is exploration of the universe created by God. The research agenda, driven by the asking of new questions and the positing of new answers, has been seen as integral to the enterprise. The university, understood in this theological light, is inalienably a place of question and answer, of dialogue and of continuing growth in critically appropriated understanding.

THEOLOGY AS DIALOGUE

There is a popular misconception that the learning of theology is nothing more than the learning of the tenets of the Christian faith. This is to absolutise the tradition, to reduce 'tradition' to 'the things which are handed on' (*tradita*) rather than the dynamic process of 'handing on' (*traditio*), or of critical appropriation. The parallel with learning in other disciplines will be obvious: the kind of history which absolutises the learning of 'what really happened' or 'what certain historians have said really happened' is utterly different from the openness of fresh historical enquiry and the fresh insight which comes through the clash of competing interpretations. In all disciplines there is a need to master the basic data, and there is bound to be a strong element of such learning in both school and university curricula, but where the teaching and learning goes no further, where is it not subjected to critical scrutiny, it is appropriate to speak of the work of a 'technical college' (a college where practical skills are transmitted) rather than that of a university.

This is very clear in the teaching and learning of law. It is vital that future legal practitioners understand legal procedures and know how to give, wherever possible, correct legal advice. This is all that is necessary for the conveyancer or the lawyer who draws up a will. However, where there is likely to be a 'clash of interpretations', whether in civil or criminal law, it is vital that the lawyer learns how to deploy argument and counter-argument in debate, to be competent in arguing a case when the issue is being seen from more than one perspective. More than that, the creative lawyer needs to be able to understand the law itself in new perspectives, quite possibly perspectives that have not been explored before.[5]

The analogy with theology is close. At a first level, theology consists in the handing on of the accumulated wisdom of the Christian tradition. At a second level, it consists in the deployment of that wisdom in the 'clash of interpretations' about current situations and events: our focus in this chapter will be on the way it is deployed in critique of issues in public life. At a third level, the process of critique is turned upon the tradition itself, so that it is seen to be formed by an 'open dynamic', a continuing, evolving dialogue. The practice of theology in the university must, then, include an induction into the disciplined practice of this dialogue: this is what 'doing theology' is really about.[6]

At the centre of this dialogue is the practice of the interpretation of Scripture: theology, as it were, continues the dialogue, or dialogues, to be found in Scripture. These are both dialogues with God (as conducted by Adam and Eve, Abraham, Moses, and so on) and dialogues about how to interpret the action of God in the world (as in the Deuteronomic literature). The practice of theology can thus be seen as the disciplined practice of dialogue *coram deo* (in the presence of God), in which that presence may be made explicit as the very focus of the dialogue, or may be implicit as the 'horizon' of a dialogue which focuses on things, events or possible courses of action-in-the-world. Thus, Thomas Aquinas says, of *sacra doctrina* (his term for Christian theology): 'In *sacra doctrina* all things are dealt with in the light of God (*sub ratione dei*) either because they are God himself or because they are related to God as their origin and end.'[7]

Thomas's term for the ground-rules of the dialogue is *ratio dei*: 'the reason, or the rationality, of God'; God's logic, we might say. What does it mean to see 'all things *sub ratione dei*'? That is at the core of the dialogue which is taken up in Christian theology. What it means is not simple. In the Scriptures of the Old and New Testaments we have a canonical collection of explorations, in various styles and from various viewpoints, of what it meant in the past to see 'all things *sub ratione dei*'. In the New Testament, it is made clear that the key to seeing things from or in the divine perspective is, quite simply, Christ: 'No one has ever seen God; the only Son, who is in the bosom of the Father, he has made him known' (John 1:18).[8] It is also made clear that the continuing practice of such Christocentric 'exegesis' is a matter of the Spirit: 'I am the truth' (John 14:6), says the Jesus of the Fourth Gospel, and 'When the Spirit of truth comes, he will guide you into all the truth' (John 16:13). The practice of theology is thus the continuing practice of interpretation 'in the spirit' of the practice of interpretation that is evident in the Scriptures of the Old and New Testaments.

What must be taught in the (Christian) university is both the accumulated store of past interpretations and the disciplined practice of interpretation itself. The implications of this for contemporary theology are profound.

Characteristic of modernity has been a sharp awareness of the historicity of the biblical texts. The text of Scripture, which was in medieval times, for example in the work of Thomas Aquinas, seen as two-dimensional (a stable, revealed, authoritative text) began at the time of the Enlightenment to be seen from a wholly new perspective — as an historical product. First there was a recognition of traditions within the text itself, and then of disciplined selection of traditions by both Jewish editors and by the early church to produce the texts recognised by the church as canonical.[9] Characteristic of late modernity (after Marx) has been a determination to uncover the ideological use of the biblical texts (the texts now seen from a perspective of power[10]) and a rejection of hegemonic strategies of interpretation, whether by a powerful, patriarchal church or a supposedly Christian state. The approaches of liberation theologians and other critics from outside the Western world, of feminist biblical critics, and of gay critics have all sought to re-read Scripture from new perspectives that reject the ideological uses to which Scripture has been put in the past. They have thus found themselves in dialogue with mainstream ecclesiastical traditions, much as earlier critical readers from early Protestant groups did.

All of this makes for a rich, continuing tradition of dialogue, in which the boundaries and the disciplines are by no means clear. This is why there needs to be a provisional distinction between the exploratory work of theology and the authoritative teaching of the Christian church or churches. The question of the identity of the church must remain, for theological reasons, ultimately open (cf. Matthew 7:21–23), but for the existence of the church as a coherent body in the world, whose primary function is the worship of God, it is vital that the church itself is able authoritatively to identify that which is explicitly 'Christian', explicitly 'of the church'. It is the task of theologians constantly to probe the identity of the church in the light of Scripture, but it is the prerogative of the church to receive or not to receive the insights of theologians as recognisably in conformity with, or as responsible interpretations of, the Scriptures which the church receives. It is because of the dynamic nature of this interaction that there needs to be a critical distance between the theologian and the authority-structures of the church. Only if such a critical distance is maintained can there be genuine dialogue. If it is absent, the theologian runs the danger of becoming merely a church ideologue, and the church itself runs the danger of losing its distinctiveness as an institution constantly open to challenge by new theological questions and insights.

ECUMENISM AS DIALOGUE

Just as the question of the responsible reading of Scripture is central to the practice of theology, so is the question of the identity of the church. Debates over who has authority within the church, over the meaning of law-keeping for Christians, over who can be baptised and when, over who may be said to have the Spirit of Christ, over the implications of wrongdoing for continuing membership of the church, over the need for public identification as a follower of Christ, about the unity of the actual churches visible on earth, and of the relation between them and the eschatological church constituted by all those definitively 'redeemed', are all present within the New Testament. Such debates have continued within and between the Christian churches.

The ecumenical movement of the twentieth century shifted attention from a mythical past in which the church existed as a unity before it fell into divisions to a future in which the unity of the church is assured by the promise of God (cf. Ephesians 1:22–23). The question for the ecumenical movement at the end of the twentieth century has been how to grow into that unity which God desires for the church, how to be the one, differentiated Body of Christ in the world.[11]

The implications of this question have been understood differently within the Roman Catholic church, the Orthodox churches, the Anglican communion, and the Protestant churches in general. Here I shall comment only on the situation with respect to Roman Catholicism and Anglicanism, as these are the two partners committed to working together at Liverpool Hope. The situation is obviously one of asymmetry as the Roman Catholic church believes that it presently lacks nothing of that which will constitute the unity of the eschatological Church of the future,[12] whereas the Anglican churches believe they are 'part of the one, holy, catholic and apostolic Church, worshipping the one true God, Father, Son and Holy Spirit'[13] and, since they are not currently in eucharistic communion with other major parts of the church, what they lack is precisely the benefits of this communion. Nevertheless, each is committed to a continuing dialogue with the other in the search for 'visible unity'. This continuing commitment to dialogue is vital to the identity of Liverpool Hope.

I do not propose here to sketch the current state of Anglican–Roman Catholic dialogue, especially as it has developed through the work of the Anglican–Roman Catholic International Commission (ARCIC). However, I do wish to say something about how the existence of this dialogue at a formal and official level impinges on Liverpool Hope as a place in which to study Theology and Public Life. It would be possible to take a negative view of the differences between Roman Catholic and Anglican theology, and to see them not so much as complementary but as competing: if the approach of one is right, the other must be wrong. Nevertheless, the main fruit of the work of ARCIC, which has, as yet, been only partially received by the churches, has been to emphasise and to restate vigorously all that there is in common between the two traditions. However different certain presentations of Christian teaching or practice may be at the surface level, there is a common fund of shared biblical interpretation, of shared tradition and shared practice which binds the two traditions together, and this ARCIC has sought to illuminate. Only in this context of what can be said together has ARCIC addressed outstanding differences.

The document that does this most clearly with reference to public life (and even then not as a primary focus) is *Life in Christ, Morals, Communion and the Church*,[14] perhaps the least-known and the most underestimated of the ARCIC agreed statements. Here ARCIC has sought to address the field of morals, one area where the teaching of the two traditions is seen to be obviously divergent. What the statement brings out is that, though there is indeed divergent teaching on marriage after divorce, contraception and, to some extent, abortion and homosexual practice, behind these divergences 'Anglicans and Roman Catholics derive from Scriptures and Tradition the same controlling vision of the nature and destiny of humanity and share the same fundamental moral values' (*LC* 1). Anglicans and Roman Catholics, it claims (*LC* 11), are concerned with the same fundamental questions, questions such as 'What are persons called to be, as individuals and as members one of another in the human family?' or 'What constitutes human dignity, and what are the social as well as the individual dimensions of human dignity and responsibility?' or 'How are the conditions and structures of human life related to the goal of human fulfilment?' The kinds of answers that might be given to each of these questions are, of course, of profound importance for what the churches may wish to say on issues of public life.

In the final section of *Life in Christ*, the question of the extent to which Anglicans and Roman Catholics can address ethical questions together is looked at again in the light of communion. Once more it is claimed that 'their deep desire to find an honest and faithful resolution of their disagreements is itself evidence of a continuing communion at a more profound level than that on which disagreement has occurred' (*LC* 96). In other words, it is *because of the existing communion* between the two traditions that they are inalienably bound to continue their dialogue on issues where there is misunderstanding or divergent teaching. The fact that the church itself is seen as 'a communion'[15] means that its continuing life is seen as one of dialogue: the example is given of the consultation that preceded pastoral letters by Bishops' Conferences, principally in the United States: 'One such example of ... the interaction of communion and authority, we suggest, is the careful and sustained process of listening and public consultation which has preceded the publication of some of the pastoral letters of Bishops' Conferences of the Roman Catholic Church in different parts of the world.' The subjects of the two best known of these pastoral letters were the possession of nuclear weapons,[16] and the management of the US economy,[17] in each case major issues in public life. What the church was doing was formulating its own mind and teaching in a process of internal discussion. *Life in Christ* suggests explicitly that, because of the communion that is already shared, there must be continuing dialogue between the two traditions not only to promote mutual understanding and unity, but for the promotion of the contribution that they can together make in the public arena: 'We are convinced, therefore, that further exchange between our two traditions on moral questions will serve both the cause of Christian unity and the good of that larger society of which we are all part' (*LC* 102).

The point I wish to make here is that the church characteristically does not speak with one voice. It has, from the beginning, contained within it a variety of voices that must, to be church, continue to speak to and to learn from one another. In this process, all parties to the dialogue are changed by the very act of remaining within the dialogue. In *Life in Christ*, there is the merest hint as to how this process of dialogue can be widened to take in voices from the public domain. The statement does, however, clearly argue that the manner in which the churches conduct their mutual dialogue is of profound significance for their contribution to public life. This contribution is sure to be most effective where the churches speak *as much as possible* with one voice, though the very ability of the churches to hold within themselves a variety of positions in some sort of harmony must – where it happens – be seen as an effective prophetic witness in defence of plurality and of respect for minority points of view.

THE CHURCHES, DIALOGUE AND PUBLIC LIFE

I tried in an earlier section to distinguish between the activity of theologians which is offered to the churches to be received or rejected, and the authoritative teaching of the churches. It is, of course, perfectly possible for theologians to make their contribution to public discussion of issues as individual theologians and to make no claim to be the authentic voice of a church. It is also possible for their teaching and insights to be taken up by the churches and incorporated within the authoritative teaching of the churches on issues of public concern. It is these two possibilities that I wish to review in the final sections of this chapter.

In a country such as Britain, the churches are, of course, publicly recognisable institutions that play their part in debate of major issues of public life. The Church of England made a major contribution to public discussion with its reports *The Church and the Bomb* (1982)[18] and *Faith in the City* (1985),[19] the latter being addressed to both the church and the nation. The Roman Catholic

Bishops of England and Wales produced a broad critique of social and political issues in *The Common Good* (1996)[20] and the Council of Churches for Britain and Ireland contributed to the new agenda adopted by the incoming Labour government, when, shortly before the 1997 election, it published *Unemployment and the Future of Work* (1997).[21] In each of these reports the church either made a claim on the way its own adherents were to participate in public life, or directly addressed those involved in public life.

There is a marked difference in theological method between *The Common Good* and the other three documents. *The Common Good* draws on a tradition of Roman Catholic social teaching which goes back to the encyclical *Rerum Novarum* (1891). It brings together in brief summary, and in critique of prevailing economic and social practices, teaching which has been carefully developed out of the Aristotelian–Thomist tradition and is heavily dependent upon a Thomist construal of natural law. This provides a strong base for criticism of market liberalism, but it does depend upon a mediating Aristotelian framework, a framework which may to some extent be admired but is not generally shared by the Protestant churches. Protestant critiques in the social and political realm have tended to appeal more directly to Scripture, but the difficulties of doing this well have often been pointed out.[22] The kinds of problems addressed in the reports (nuclear weapons, inner-city decay, long-term unemployment) were simply not dreamt of in the time of the Scriptures, so that to extrapolate from the very broad principles of Scripture to the complexities of modern society in, say, banking or biotechnology is to risk making banal or tendentious comments.

The strength of the Roman Catholic position is that it holds to a well-developed view of human flourishing which represents an adventurous extrapolation from Scripture. It privileges the 'common good' over the good of individuals, while at the same time affirming certain inalienable rights for individuals, principally the right to life. The way this right is deployed – as the right to adequacy of provision for human flourishing – turns out to be very radical in its social and political implications. Anglican social teaching has tended to be far less specific in its induction from natural law and therefore runs the risk of reflecting a liberal consensus as opposed to adopting tenets with a clear scriptural resonance. The question about how churches can develop theologically grounded teaching in the political and social domain, especially as new issues arise through hitherto undreamt-of technologies, remains.

What the churches can do is continually to promote public debate about difficult and controverted issues. Though the reports I have mentioned were in each case criticised for generality of approach and for lack of specific expertise, they were each major, interrogative contributions to public debate, asking and probing as to whether there could not be other ways of shaping policy and ordering affairs. In the case of *Unemployment and the Future of Work*, which argued vigorously that 'good work' contributed to human flourishing and that 'enough good work for all' was a proper and achievable social goal, this ran directly counter to the dominant model of the Thatcher years, in which unemployment was seen as a price worth paying for restoring the competitiveness of British industry. The churches, acting together, saw it as their role to challenge the dominance of this position. They were contributing to the discussion about public policy on the basis of a kind of accounting different from the dominant economic model. For the churches, trying to see all things 'in the light of God', the ruination of individual lives and the destruction of communities through long-term unemployment could not be 'a price worth paying' for greater overall prosperity. The report came as a timely intervention, offering a sketch of a totally new direction in employment policy, one founded on the infinite value of each human being scandalously deprived of 'good work'. This striking shift in priorities was, in the event, endorsed by the incoming Labour government and swiftly enacted through the New Deal programmes. The point I am making here is that the churches had contributed significantly to public debate by suggesting an alternative basis and direction for public policy, based on Christian principles. *Unemployment and the Future of Work* represented a timely and effective, and theologically grounded, contribution to the setting of new priorities on a major issue in public life.

LIVERPOOL HOPE, THEOLOGY AND PUBLIC LIFE

If there is a vital role for the churches, acting corporately, to challenge public policy and to point in alternative directions which might better ensure human flourishing, there is also a vital role for the individual theologian, or the theological think-tank, suggesting and exploring new directions of theological interpretation and questioning. This, I take it, is why Liverpool Hope has a Professor of Theology and Public Life. If so, there are particular structural reasons why Liverpool Hope must be a good base from which to operate.

The first of these reasons is the position of Liverpool Hope on the outskirts of Liverpool. It is strategically placed within a region that has experienced massive changes through industrial prosperity and decline, through successive waves of immigration, through urban unrest and the struggle to build a multi-ethnic and inclusive society. According to its mission statement,[23] Liverpool Hope is committed to contributing to 'the educational, religious, cultural, social and economic life of Liverpool, Merseyside, the North West and beyond'. It is also committed to the inclusion of 'those who might otherwise not have had an opportunity to enter higher education'. These two public commitments within its mission statement ensure that Liverpool Hope must strive to play a creative part in public life both at a local and at a national level. The question is how.

A second pointer in the mission statement to the involvement of Liverpool Hope in public life is the emphasis placed upon its commitment to education. As the fruit of the amalgamation of teacher training colleges, Liverpool Hope retains a strong emphasis on 'the education, training and professional development of teachers for church and state schools', and on teaching and learning about education. This emphasis on education picks up the long-standing commitment of the Christian churches in this field, a commitment which has followed from their belief in the importance of the healthy formation of the minds of the young. Since the state has now become by far the major national funder of education, in both schools and universities, the commitment of Liverpool Hope to education means that it is bound, once more, in every aspect of its life, to engage with issues of public policy.

A third pointer in the mission statement to the engagement of Liverpool Hope with issues of public life is the commitment to 'sustain an academic community, as a sign of hope, enriched by Christian values and worship, which supports teaching and learning, scholarship and research, encourages the understanding of Christian and other faiths and beliefs and promotes religious and social harmony'. What I have been arguing throughout this chapter is that the theological contribution to the pursuit of this commitment does not lie in the realm of the didactic. It lies in the realm of the dialogical, for it is by promoting serious questioning, serious engagement with 'the other', and serious dialogue that minds and hearts are enlarged, and there begins to be a sense of the place of a particular enterprise within a wider scheme of things.

I do not myself believe that a Professor of Theology and Public Life, who asks questions of public policy and proposes new ways of looking at issues in the public domain, need constantly be relating this questioning back to Scripture and the Christian tradition. I do, however, believe that to be Christian, such questioning ought demonstrably to arise from engagement with the Christian tradition, and this means at its most fundamental the struggle to interpret Scripture. If Liverpool Hope is to be truly inclusive, there is the chance that students and staff from economically poor backgrounds, from overseas, from marginalised groups, or ethnic minorities, or of other faiths, will in turn find new ways of bringing their experience to the questioning of received Christian teaching and of Scripture. This is a profoundly exciting prospect.

What Liverpool Hope offers as an environment in which to do the kind of theology which may make a difference in public life is a range of students and staff, and of concerns, that is extremely rich. It also offers a living experience of the struggle for ecumenical reconciliation. The theology which is done at Liverpool Hope comes out of the dialogical experience of ecumenism, an experience of the struggle to understand, of frustration at slow and tentative progress, of the joy of day-to-day working and praying with Christians of differing faith traditions and experiences. Here, the daily prayer of Liverpool Hope is of enormous importance. It provides a space in which, for an all-too-brief moment at the beginning of each working day, to glimpse 'all things *sub ratione dei*'. The twin facts that the lens by which we see – the church – is cracked, but that the issues with which we have to deal in teaching and learning thrust us into the public domain, are a profound stimulus to serious theological reflection.

In the secular arena, Christian engagement is rightly to be seen, as I have argued, in the interrogative mode: 'Could not', the theologian asks, 'this issue or problem or activity be approached in this or that way which would better promote human flourishing?' Simply to ask the question is to suggest the hope of a positive answer and simply to suggest the hope of a positive answer is to be unwilling to rest with anything less than continuing engagement and continuing dialogue until the struggle for God's justice has its God-given fulfilment. To enter into dialogue in this spirit is to take seriously the promise of Jesus: 'When the Spirit of truth comes, he will guide you into all the truth' (John 16:13); it is to live in hope of that guidance not only for God's church but also for God's world.

NOTES

1 An earlier version of this chapter was read at the Hope Theological Society on 27 February 2003. I am very grateful for the constructive criticism of the participants at that seminar.
2 Thus, Newman writes, 'A University should teach universal knowledge' (I. T. Ker (ed.), John Henry Newman, *The Idea of a University*, Oxford, Oxford University Press, 1976, p. 34). Alan Cobban takes issue with this when he writes, 'The word "university" has nothing to do with the universality of learning, and it is only by accident that the Latin term *universitas* has given rise to the established nomenclature' (A. B. Cobban, *The Medieval Universities: Their Development and Organisation*, London, Methuen, 1975, p. 22).
3 Only in the late fourteenth century did 'university' begin to be used as 'a convenient shorthand label applied especially to academic corporations'. See Cobban, *The Medieval Universities*, pp. 22–23.
4 It was along these broad lines of 'wholeness' that Newman argued for the inclusion of theology within 'the idea of a university': 'To withdraw Theology from the public schools is to *impair the completeness* ... of all that is actually taught in them' (*The Idea of a University*, p. 71, my emphasis).
5 This is magnificently illustrated in Ronald Dworkin's *Law's Empire*, Oxford, Hart, 1986. Dworkin argues for a principle of 'law as integrity', asserting that 'the imperatives of integrity always challenge today's law with the possibilities of tomorrow's' (p. 410).
6 In using the term 'practice' here, and setting it in the context of an understanding of 'tradition', I am consciously alluding to Alasdair MacIntyre's *After Virtue* (2nd edn, London, Duckworth, 1985).

7 '*Omnia autem tractantur in sacra doctrina sub ratione Dei, vel quia sunt ipse Deus vel quia habent ordinem ad Deum ut ad principium et finem.*' (*ST* Ia.I.7) I have translated '*sub ratione dei*' as 'in the light of God' because the modern notion of 'reason' is not that of Thomas; but Thomas would not object to an emphasis on the doing of theology as a 'reflective' activity (cf. Ps 36:9).

8 Literally: 'he has been his exegete'.

9 It is important to note that, though the received canonical text may be regarded as *relatively* stable, it has in various places been modified as the outcome of historical scholarship, and of new textual discoveries (especially the Dead Sea Scrolls).

10 Hence the importance of secular critics such as Marx, Nietzsche and Foucault for theology.

11 This question is addressed in *The Unity We Have and The Unity We Seek*, ed. J. Morris and N. Sagovsky, Edinburgh, T. & T. Clark, 2003.

12 'This unity, we believe, *subsists* in the Catholic Church as something she can never lose' (*Unitatis Redintegratio* [*The Decree on Ecumenism* from *The Documents of Vatican II*] 4).

13 These words are taken from the Preface to the Declaration of Assent, as, for example, in the service for the ordination of a Bishop (*Alternative Service Book 1980*, Cambridge, Cambridge University Press, Colchester, Clowes/London, SPCK, 1980, p. 387).

14 London, Church House Publishing/Catholic Truth Society, 1994.

15 Cf. *Church as Communion, An Agreed Statement by the Second Anglican–Roman Catholic International Commission*, London, Church House Publishing/Catholic Truth Society, 1991, which sets out the ecclesiology underlying the work of ARCIC.

16 American Episcopal Conference, *War and Peace in the Nuclear Age*, London, CTS/SPCK, 1983.

17 American Episcopal Conference, *Economic Justice for All: Catholic Social Teaching and the US Economy*, London, CTS, 1986.

18 *The Church and The Bomb: Nuclear Weapons and the Christian Conscience*, London, Hodder and Stoughton and CIO, 1982.

19 Archbishop's Commission on Urban Priority Areas, *Faith in the City: A Call for Action by Church and Nation*, London, Church House Publishing, 1985.

20 Bishops' Conference for England and Wales, *The Common Good*, Manchester, Gabriel Communications, 1996.

21 Council of Churches for Britain and Ireland, *Unemployment and the Future of Work: an Enquiry for the Churches*, London, CCBI, 1997.

22 For example, by A. E. Harvey in *By What Authority?, The Churches and Social Concern*, London, SCM, 2001; see, e.g., pp. 6–9.

23 The full mission statement reads: 'Liverpool Hope is an ecumenical Christian foundation which strives to provide opportunities for the well-rounded development of Christians and students from other faiths and beliefs, educating the whole person in mind, body and spirit, irrespective of age, social or ethnic origins or physical capacity, including in particular those who might otherwise not have had an opportunity to enter higher education; to be a national provider of a wide range of high quality programmes responsive to the needs of students, including the education, training and professional development of teachers for church and state schools; to sustain an academic community, as a sign of hope, enriched by Christian values and worship, which supports teaching and learning, scholarship and research, encourages the understanding of Christian and other faiths and beliefs and promotes religious and social harmony; to contribute to the educational, religious, cultural, social and economic life of Liverpool, Merseyside, the North West and beyond.'

CHAPTER 10

Research in Theology and Religious Studies

KENNETH G. C. NEWPORT

I T is perhaps particularly fitting that in a building named after one of the great Bible translators of the twentieth century, Mgr Alexander Jones (died 1970), the teaching of the biblical languages is once again being undertaken: New Testament Greek has been taught at Hope since 2000, while biblical Hebrew has been run on a trial basis for the first time during the academic year 2002–03. Both have proved attractive to students. While biblical languages have been taught at Hope and the former constituent colleges before, this present move towards making both Greek and Hebrew (and perhaps later Aramaic) fully available to undergraduates who may pursue such studies as part of their degree is a relatively new (or at least revitalised) development. So too is the proposed Postgraduate Certificate in Biblical Languages, which should be available within the next two years.

To those involved in both the teaching and learning of the biblical languages at Hope, the photograph of Mgr Jones, which hangs just inside the main entrance of the building that now bears his name, ought to be an inspiration. He was formerly Head of Theology at Christ's College and as such played a central part in laying the foundations of what would later become (though he did not live to see it) the ecumenical institution of Liverpool Hope University College. He is more widely known for the central role he played in the production of a text that was to become of great importance and influence in the English-speaking Roman Catholic world: the *Jerusalem Bible* (1966). In fact, as general editor, Jones was without doubt the single most important individual in bringing that vast work of scholarship to completion. The achievement should not be forgotten.

The idea behind the *Jerusalem Bible* was simple enough when it was first conceived in the world of mainly French-speaking Roman Catholics. In 1943 Pope Pius XII had issued the encyclical letter *Divino Afflante Spiritu* which enabled Roman Catholic scholars seriously to consider a departure from tradition and the preparation of a 'Catholic' Bible that was not based upon Jerome's Latin Vulgate.[1] The challenge was quickly taken up by French scholars, who determined to produce a translation of the Bible based on the very best Greek, Hebrew and Aramaic manuscripts that twentieth-century textual critics were able to deliver.[2] The Bible translation would contain also extensive scholarly notes. The task of producing this new (French) translation was undertaken mainly by scholars based at the immensely prestigious École Biblique in Jerusalem headed by Fr Roland de Vaux.[3] It was appropriate, then, that the Bible became known as *La Bible de Jérusalem* (1956, revised 1961).[4]

What the scholars of the École Biblique did for French-speaking Catholics Mgr Jones and his team undertook to apply in an English context: they would produce the first ever complete and fully authorised 'Catholic' edition of the Bible in English, together with all the scholarly apparatus and annotation found in the French edition.[5] Although the work of the French translators would not be ignored, the English version would not be a simple translation of the French, but rather of the original manuscripts, with reference being made to the earlier work that had been done in Jerusalem. (Jones had in fact himself studied at the École Biblique and was much influenced by the work that was going on there.) The task was huge and the team of 27 scholars over which Jones had editorial oversight impressive.[6]

In 1966 the English *Jerusalem Bible* appeared. The translation is still in wide circulation and still in print – no mean feat in these days of such rapid change. (Some of the extensive apparatus and annotation prepared for the French edition and the first English edition of 1966 was much condensed in later editions, beginning with that of 1968.) The *Jerusalem Bible* still provokes response and inevitably one will find criticism of the work as well as praise. For example, a few years ago a letter came to Hope for the attention of Mgr Jones, in his role as Head of Theology (a post he had long since vacated) and editor of the *Jerusalem Bible*. In particular the letter raised the question of the translation of a small portion of Matthew's gospel, the *Jerusalem Bible* version of which, according to the writer, 'contained an error'. While it would be foolish in the extreme to suggest that errors are entirely absent from the work, in this particular case the arguments against the rendering of the Greek given in the *Jerusalem Bible* seemed entirely threadbare. What appeared at first sight to be a mistake, was in fact the result of allowance being made for Semitic syntax underlying the surface Greek. Seen as a whole, the translation given indicated clearly enough that the translator of the Matthean passage was well aware of the fact (as many New Testament scholars would now be so bold as to call it) that the Greek of the New Testament reflects the fundamentally Semitic context in which Christianity was born. As a part of that legacy one has to allow for the presence of a distinctive 'Semitic Greek' in much of the New Testament. In 1966 that argument was still to be won. In 2003 it largely has been.[7] On this point at least the *Jerusalem Bible* was somewhat ahead of its time.

In the photographic portrait in the Alexander Jones Building (AJB) mentioned earlier, Mgr Jones is holding a copy of the edition of the Bible over which he had oversight and so much influence. The production of such a volume is a huge responsibility, both academically and pastorally: academically since it would be subjected to so much scrutiny and must reflect the very best linguistic and textual studies then available; and pastorally since, for millions of English-speaking Roman Catholics not themselves academics, the *Jerusalem Bible* would become not just the translation of some ancient texts, but 'the Bible' itself. (As Jones's remarks in the editor's preface to the 1968 edition clearly indicate, this somewhat shorter version was prepared with this latter readership specifically in view.) As such it would be depended upon for the very revelation of God. Nevertheless, how easy it would be to forget the work of those involved in the production of the English *Jerusalem Bible*. How easy it would be to forget also just what a scholarly figure Mgr Jones was, and to overlook the really quite exceptional contribution that a former 'Hope' scholar has made to the world of biblical studies in general and Catholic biblical studies in particular.

Jones's contribution was as appropriate as it was important. It was appropriate in the obvious sense that here was a senior Roman Catholic biblical scholar working at a Catholic college undertaking a task that would be of benefit to the Catholic community (both the academy and the congregation) to which he himself so centrally belonged. But it was appropriate too in the sense that what he did was to put his scholarly weight, and that of the team he headed, to the service of not just the narrow academic constituency, important as that was, but also the much wider ecclesial community. What he did may not have been about educating the 'body' very much, but it was certainly about both the 'mind' and the 'spirit'. It was scholarship not just for scholarship's sake, but scholarship undertaken in the direct and very obvious interests of community.

Perhaps just as significantly, however, the magnitude of the task which Jones undertook, the importance of what he did and the uncompromising academic standards he brought to bear were entirely appropriate given his context at Christ's. A college such as Christ's was then, as Hope is now, is a visible, tangible expression of the church's place in the world of tertiary education. Such a standing brings with it certain responsibilities. Some of these are of course shared with 'secular' institutions (for example, a commitment to what Christians might call the 'social gospel' – widening access, equality of opportunity, and so forth), but some are not. It could and should be argued, for example, that a church college must also fulfil a role as a visible sign of the engagement of the church with the society within which it exists and which it seeks to serve. In this sense a church college has a near sacramental role to play: it is a visible sign of God's activity and engagement with the world. This is not a recipe for arrogance and we must be realistic about the day-to-day reality of the life and work of the Hope community 'warts and all'. However, undergirding the very institution of any church college is the fundamental belief of its founders that a part of God's work is education. Not necessarily instruction in the Christian faith, though that may be a part of it, but education in any or all of the forms it takes – the growth of the mind, the exploration of creation, the exploration of human creativity and so on. Some would want to argue, therefore, that the task which Hope and like institutions are about must be undertaken with a particular seriousness, integrity and determination of intent. For theological reasons, as well as for all sorts of others, what goes on at Hope cannot afford to be thought of as second-rate. An institution such as Hope cannot be in the position of being an also-ran in the context of British higher education. If the church is to continue to be a player in such a world (and unless one is prepared to give way to the forces of secularisation and the constituent increased marginalisation of the church from society, it must) then it has to be a serious one. God is not served by halves. And so, to return to the work of Mgr Jones, the task he undertook and the scholarly expertise and diligence he brought to bear were appropriate. The scholarly contribution he made was worthy of the context out of which it came.

It would be a mistake then to imagine that the relatively 'new kids on the block' who now inhabit the Alexander Jones Building at Liverpool Hope University College are pushing forward the frontiers of theological and religious studies research where before no such efforts were being made. On the contrary, Mgr Jones was very much at the forefront of his discipline. He set an exceptionally high standard both in terms of personal achievement and, no less significantly perhaps, in his leadership of a research team. Those who have come after him will be aware of how difficult an act they have to follow. However, as Hope now enters a new phase of its institutional life, one would like to think that he would not be disappointed with the research efforts of those who inhabit that bit of the Hope campus that now bears his name.

Closest perhaps to Mgr Jones's heart would be the current and ongoing work in biblical studies. This was an important area of the Hope curriculum for many years, with Revd Alex Smith and Sr Eileen Cassidy SND teaching Old and New Testament studies respectively. More recently this long-standing commitment has been built upon and represented in the research as well as in the teaching work of the subject area. Central here has been the contribution of Dr Mark Elliott. Elliott came to Hope in 1999 after graduating from the Universities of Aberdeen, Oxford and Cambridge. Among his many publications is the volume *The Song of Songs and Christology in the Early Church 381–451.*[8]

This account of how a portion of the Old Testament was reflected upon by early church theologians in the light of developing Christologies would no doubt have appealed to Mgr Jones, who similarly had a broad interest in the Christian scriptures, both Old and New Testaments.

Elliott's book touches upon an area of biblical studies that others in the Hope community have explored. Of particular interest to me have been two closely related questions: how the text of the Bible impacts on society and how in the interpretation of the Bible the dynamic between reader and text is balanced. Both questions are taken up in my *Apocalypse and Millennium: Studies in Biblical Eisegesis*,[9] where it is argued that meaning is often 'read into' rather than 'out of' a biblical text, hence the interpretative process might better be described as *ei*segesis rather than *ex*egesis. Such a view is, of course, not radically new. However, two further arguments were then advanced: first that studying the *ei*segesis of an individual or group is a useful way into the thought world they inhabit; and second that *ei*segesis can be a very dangerous thing, at worst appearing to give divine sanction to what are very obviously human prejudices and fears.[10] As a development of this, I proposed that programme space be allocated to a discussion of this area at the 2002 international meeting of the Society of Biblical Literature, held in Berlin. It was. A second meeting of that group is due to be held in Cambridge in 2003. My work was supported financially both by Hope and the Arts and Humanities Research Board. Further, Elliott's continued work in biblical studies received a significant external mark of recognition through the award of a Humboldt Stipendium in 2002. This award enabled Elliott to spend a full six months at Heidelberg working on his next major book, a study of Old Testament theologies.

Much of the work of Dr J'annine Jobling similarly falls into the general area of biblical studies, though from a rather different (and very fresh) perspective. In *Feminist Biblical Interpretation in Theological Context: Restless Readings*,[11] Jobling presented a new model for biblical interpretation, through the exploration of the intersecting perspectives of feminism, postmodern philosophies and Christian theology. Again, the whole question of the balance between texts and readers comes into focus.

Biblical studies at Hope, then, have developed in directions that Mgr Jones himself might well have found rather contrary to the thoroughgoing historical–critical context in which the discipline was conducted in his own day. But the discipline has moved on and it is unsurprising that some of these newer areas of biblical studies are now central to the Hope research agenda, while more traditional approaches continue to be of importance. This variety is reflected both in staff activity and also in the topics of interest of current research students.[12]

Before moving on to other areas that are important to the established, present and developing research profile of Liverpool Hope, a few words in general regarding theology and religious studies research students seem appropriate. At the time of writing there are 30 or more students either pursuing or just about to begin research degrees in theology and religious studies at the college. This has been an enormous growth area within the past few years and those who have been accepted are by no means all who have applied. The research degree programme is quite properly focused upon areas of expertise represented among the Hope staff. As research has become ever more central to the workings of the subject area, so the number and range of research students has increased.

Research students in theology and religious studies at Hope are registered as students in the department of philosophy at the University of Liverpool (which awards either the MPhil or PhD degree). This throws up some interesting anomalies: why, for example, would a person writing a PhD degree on Islamic Education in Britain, Zoroastrian Communities, or the origin and function of the 1933 *Methodist Hymn Book* be registered as a student in philosophy? More important is the question of the supervision of such students. In this context it is significant that a number of Hope staff now have sole supervisor status at the University of Liverpool, which means that the supervision of their students takes place entirely at Hope rather than jointly by a Hope and a university supervisor. This is significant for two reasons. First, because it speaks volumes about the perception by the university of the quality of supervision students at Hope can expect. Further, and perhaps even more importantly, because it is a clear indication that here is an area that could not be covered elsewhere in Merseyside. The philosophy department at the University of Liverpool is excellent and has an international reputation, but it is not a theology department (though there are some staff whose interests overlap somewhat). In this area at least, as in education also, Hope is clearly supplying a need that is not otherwise being met. The increasing number of applications indicates that the need is a significant one.

It is extremely important that Hope maintains good research student numbers in theology and religious studies (others will make the argument for other subject areas). This is because research students really are the future of the discipline. Not all of those graduating with MPhil or PhD degrees will of course go into the profession, but nevertheless those who do graduate with advanced degrees make up the scholarly guild within the parameters of which the discipline develops. Further, by definition a PhD degree, and to a lesser extent an MPhil, must be an 'original' and 'significant' contribution to learning – a pushing back, however slightly, of the borders. At some indefinite point in the production of a PhD, a metamorphosis should take place. The 'student' becomes the 'teacher' as he or she now has something 'original and significant' to contribute and to plough back into the discipline. Any scholarly community that wishes as a community to make a contribution to the furtherance of the discipline, then, ought to be promoting research activity at the MPhil and PhD level. It is a symbiotic relationship whereby the supervisor, the supervisee, the community of scholars at the institution and the discipline in general work together to make progress. One might of course counter-argue one, the other or both of two things: that the progress of this discipline is a bad thing, or that Hope should not be involved in making it. Such arguments may appeal to some; Mgr Jones would not have been among them.

It was noted above that biblical studies, a subject dear to Mgr Jones's heart, is currently alive and well at Liverpool Hope. In the context of Liverpool, of course, this cannot but be a good thing for this is an area not taught (let alone researched) at either the University of Liverpool or Liverpool John Moores University. It is true that Manchester has a superb standing in biblical studies and that biblical studies can also be taken at Chester College. Hope nevertheless provides the only opportunity on Merseyside for the scholarly study of the Bible. This is important both in terms of the Christian community and also more generally, for even if one does not believe that the Bible is a part of the self-revelation of God, the book remains a singularly important text. None has made a more significant contribution to the development of Western society. (In this context it is a pleasure to recall the contribution made to the Johannine Literature course by a mature Jewish student some years ago.)

Just as it is appropriate that biblical studies is still an important part of the research profile of the community of scholars now resident in the Alexander Jones Building, so it is appropriate that there is a discernible and growing emphasis on Roman Catholic studies. Again it would be a mistake to view the work that is currently going on at Hope as an entirely new development. Roman Catholic studies have been important for some considerable time, which is hardly surprising given the origins of the institution. Mgr Jones himself has already been noted. We could note too Andrew Bebb, the former head of department at Liverpool Hope, now retired, whose interest in Catholic studies was, and still is, very strong. And mention certainly needs to be made of the Revd Dr Kevin T. Kelly. Kelly, who still serves the Hope community in the role of Research Fellow Emeritus, has had a very distinguished career indeed in the field of Catholic moral theology, a subject area in which he taught for many years at Heythrop College, London before coming to Hope in 1993. Among Kelly's several books and numerous articles are *Divorce and Second Marriage*, *New Directions in Moral Theology*, and *New Directions in Sexual Ethics: The Challenge of Aids*.[13]

However, there is much more that Hope can do in the field of Catholic studies, especially so given the recent acquisition of a major Roman Catholic library collection, the Gradwell collection, of which more will be said shortly.

There have been major recent developments. Central in this regard is the work of Dr David Torevell, whose volume *Losing the Sacred: Ritual, Modernity and Liturgical Reform*[14] is a particularly provocative analysis of recent trends in Roman Catholic liturgy. One of Torevell's current research students is also looking into this general area, conducting this time an in-depth, local analysis of just why it is that attendance at Mass in Warrington is in such obvious decline, despite what appears to be a fairly static (and high) sense of 'the spiritual' among the UK population in general.[15] Dr Michael Ford, the author of another chapter in this volume, was also one of Dr Torevell's students.[16]

Professor Simon Lee, Rector and Chief Executive of Liverpool Hope, has similarly played an important role in promoting a distinctively Roman Catholic focus within the broader concerns of the theology and religious studies team. Lee's work in the legal aspects of Catholic ethics and public policy (particularly the abortion debate) are well-known, and it is surely as much a mark of Lee's industry as it is an indication of the level of institutional support given to theology and religious studies at Hope to note that he was entered in the theology unit of assessment in the 2001 Research Assessment Exercise (RAE).

Roman Catholic studies at Hope have recently received a major boost through the appointments of Professors Nicholas Sagovsky and John Sullivan. Professor Sagovsky, an Anglican priest whose current research interests lie in the area of ecumenism and social justice,[17] is a well-known expert also on the work of the Roman Catholic modernist George Tyrrell.[18] Professor Sullivan, also an expert in the area of Roman Catholic modernism as witnessed by his current project, a book on Maurice Blondel, has developed a national profile in the area of Roman Catholic educational practice and leadership.[19] It is a particular pleasure to note the attraction of Hope to those wishing to pursue research in these areas.[20]

In 2000, Hope's interest in developing a national, indeed international, research profile in Roman Catholic Studies received a major boost through the acquisition of the Gradwell Library.[21] This collection was housed at St Joseph's seminary in Upholland, one of the places where Alexander Jones had himself studied; it is now in the Sheppard–Worlock library at Hope. Most of the 40,000 or so volumes that came from St Joseph's to Hope were located on the main reading floor at the old seminary building. However, several hundred were found in an upper attic, access to which was possible only by means of a some-what wobbly spiral staircase. How long they had been in that attic is anyone's guess and it is unfortunate that the nesting activities of a number of pigeons and other vermin had caused irreparable damage to a number of items. On inspection it quickly became apparent that some of these materials went back several hundred years, with some volumes being dated as early as the sixteenth century. What could be rescued was, and the fate that had otherwise awaited them (a rubbish skip) was averted. There is much to be done to conserve that which has now been secured.

Even a cursory examination of the holdings reveals something of the collection's potential. The main working library speaks for itself. Here we have a good, very precisely focused collection that was built up over nearly a hundred years to serve the needs of Roman Catholic seminarians. Alongside that material are the several hundred very old volumes such as those found in the attic. However, in a research context, what might well prove to be the most valuable of all are not the really old volumes nor yet the comparatively new, but rather the many thousands of books, pamphlets and other printed materials that are illustrative in particular of recusancy (especially recusancy in the North West). In this area the materials may well prove to be world-class. Some, but not by any means all, have already been listed in Blom et al.[22] A small amount of research has been done already by Hope staff using Gradwell materials, but its riches are yet to be fully explored.[23] The possibility of establishing a Robert Gradwell Research Studentship at Hope is currently being investigated, with a view to furthering this research.

The current signs then are good. The introduction of a postgraduate certificate, diploma and MA in Catholic Studies, which seek very properly both to exploit the research interests of current Hope staff and also to live up to the college's foundation, is a major step forward. The college is currently poised to become a national leader in the area. One hopes that not only Mgr Jones but Fr Gradwell too would be pleased with such developments, and certainly the preservation of those materials will prove to be a service to the wider academic guild.[24]

Somewhat outside of Mgr Jones's immediate interests, but well within the ecumenical scope of Hope, is the substantial emphasis now placed upon Wesley studies. Again there is a track record that has been built upon and enhanced. Hope staff member Geoffrey Chorley, for example, has long been involved in a detailed historical analysis of Methodism's contribution to educational theory and practice, particularly in the context of the nineteenth century, and both the present and previous chairs of the Liverpool Methodist District have been firm supporters of what is now the Hope community. The responsibility for Methodist studies at Hope now largely rests with me. Though an Anglican priest, I have a particular interest in aspects of eighteenth-century Methodism, especially the theological and literary legacy of Charles Wesley (1707–1788).

Of particular advantage in this context is the relative proximity of Hope to major Methodist archive collections. First and foremost among these is the John Rylands University Library in Manchester.[25] The Rylands University Library houses what is easily one of the finest general academic collections in the country (it is the largest library, apart from the legal-deposit libraries, in the UK). In the context of Hope's developing research profile in theology and religious studies, it is particularly fortuitous that the University of Manchester has long had a world-class department (formerly faculty) of theology. The main Rylands library building, situated on the Oxford Road campus, reflects Manchester's traditional strength in this area. Through an agreement with the University of Manchester, all of Hope's theology and religious studies research students and staff have access to all of the material held in the main library.

It is, however, the 'old' John Rylands Library, located on Deansgate in the very centre of Manchester, that has proved particularly fruitful for some members of the Hope theological community. Dr Gareth Lloyd, for example, a full-time member of staff at the Rylands and hence an employee of the University of Manchester, completed his PhD studies at Hope on the subject of Charles Wesley's place in early Methodism.[26] As a cataloguer of many of the relevant sources, Dr Lloyd was in prime position to undertake this research and his superb thesis (which was passed first time and is now out for consideration by a major academic press) reflects well both his own ability and the very fruitful relationship that has been developed between Hope and the Rylands Library, Deansgate. A further example of this co-operation is the work of the Revd Andrew Pratt, who has written his PhD thesis on aspects of Methodist hymnody; again almost all of the relevant materials were located at the Rylands.[27] Other such students include Edward Phelan (MPhil, 2003) who again worked on the Charles Wesley papers,[28] and three students currently registered to work on topics relating to Methodism as reflected almost exclusively through the materials located in the Manchester archives.[29]

Having spent considerable time at the Rylands Library, first as a research fellow of that institution and then as a member of the Hope staff with a particular research brief, I attempted in my inaugural lecture (as Hope's first internally promoted professor) to give some insight into my work in this area, showing by example how the Rylands holdings can make a real difference to the way in which, for instance, one assesses the work of Charles Wesley. Much of the work that both I and my students conduct is based upon manuscript (as opposed to published) sources, a fact that brings its own challenges, including in some cases the necessity of learning Charles Wesley's highly idiosyncratic shorthand script. Some substantial publications have resulted: the first ever complete edition of Charles Wesley's sermons appeared in 2001 and a contract is in place to produce, in two volumes, an edition of his letters.[30] In 2000 Hope hosted the eleventh annual meeting of the Charles Wesley Society, the papers of which have now appeared in published form.[31]

Neither should the St Deiniol's Residential Library at Hawarden be underestimated. This library is also only some thirty miles from Hope, and both its holdings and its residential facilities have proved attractive both to staff members and to students. The collection of Methodist materials, while being nowhere near that of the Rylands, nevertheless holds some unexpected treasures. For example one current PhD student has discovered that nineteenth-century materials on Wesley are in particularly good supply at St Deiniol's. The other strengths of that collection, especially Anglicanism, will doubtless become more apparent to Hope staff as a specialism is developed in this area, first at taught master's and then at research degree level. Again the appointment of new professors, in this context Sagovsky in particular, gives cause for some considerable optimism.

It is apparent then that Hope is particularly well placed to make use of substantial research collections in the region, and it is fortunate in the extreme that collections such as those mentioned are so obviously related to a part of the college's mission. The best collection of Methodist materials anywhere in the world, by a very substantial margin, is on Hope's doorstep, as are other Rylands sub-collections in many other areas of the Free Church tradition; the Quaker, Baptist and Unitarian collections, for example, are substantial and still largely untouched. A Roman Catholic collection of very significant proportions is on campus, and other locations in the region provide further research-rich resources. The opportunities provided ought not to be, and will not be, ignored.

The work of Fr Kevin Kelly has already been mentioned briefly above in the context of Hope's current developing profile in Roman Catholic studies. Fr Kelly's work ties in very clearly, however, with another major field of theological expertise that has been a focus for both present and past Hope staff members, namely Christian ethics. Christian ethics have long been a matter of very keen interest to a key member of the Hope Rectorate and theology team the Revd Canon Dr R. John Elford, who moved to Hope in 1988 from a post in Christian ethics at the University of Manchester. Elford's early work, written partly in conversation with the late Revd Professor Ronald Preston, concerned medical ethics and war (the latter subject being one that Elford has had the opportunity to discuss widely in recent months).[32] Since he took semi-retirement, Elford's literary output has increased several fold. In addition to co-editing a substantial volume of the work of Ronald Preston,[33] he has produced also two monographs, with a third on the way.[34]

It was a desire to have institutional expertise in this area that would command national, indeed international, respect that informed the criteria for the appointment of the first Liverpool Hope professor in 1996. That post was filled by Professor Ian S. Markham, who brought with him to Hope not only his research record, but an infectious enthusiasm for the subject. Markham's major publication upon taking up what was soon to be named the Liverpool Chair in Theology and Public Life was his book *Plurality and Christian Ethics*.[35] During his time at Hope, Markham did much to promote his subject and to encourage other members of the theology and religious studies team in bringing their own work to publication. A prime example of this is the book *Encountering Religion* published in October 2000.[36] This volume was written almost entirely by members of the Hope team, with contributions by, among others, Jobling, Ruparell, Torevell and Ramsey. A follow-up volume, *Encountering Theology*, is now well under way. Other examples of co-operative work include *Theological Liberalism* (co-edited by Jobling with contributions by several Hope scholars).[37] Markham's solo publishing career continued in tandem.[38]

Markham's arrival also greatly enhanced the possibility of research students in theology and religious studies at Hope. There was one such student when Markham arrived, and more than 20 when he left. As already noted, at the time of writing the total number is over 30. His own students included Dr Shannon Ledbetter (Hope's first theology PhD success),[39] Dr Christopher Williams and Dr Melanie Phillips.[40] Markham left Hope in 2001 to take up the post of Dean at Hartford Theological Seminary in Connecticut.

Markham's interests were distinctly theological, as opposed to the more specifically biblical, liturgical, historical, philosophical and linguistic concerns of some of the other Hope theology and religious studies team members sketched in above. The broader context of those interests, as well as some of the specifics regarding how these found expression during his years at Hope, have been indicated elsewhere in this volume, and there is no need to repeat Markham's own critical survey here. One adds only that, following Markham's departure, a concern with the liberal theological tradition has been maintained at Hope, principally through the activities of Jobling. It was she who established a liberal theology submeeting at the American Academy of Religion (the first such meeting was held in 2002 and the 2003 session is now planned). The impact of Sagovsky on the overall profile of theology and religious studies at Hope is still being established.

Although Christian theology has been very much the focus of research activity at Hope over the past several years, religious studies have also played an important part. Again this is not an entirely new development. Former colleagues Dr John Highfield and the late Elizabeth Scantlebury had a keen interest in Hinduism and Islam respectively. Torevell, noted above for his contribution to Catholic studies, has for many years been involved also in the study and teaching of the Buddhist tradition. Similarly Elizabeth Ramsey's work in Judaism has been ongoing for a number of years, and recently she brought to Hope a major conference on the Holocaust.[41]

With the arrival of Dr Tinu Ruparell in 1997 and then Dr Stewart McFarlane in 1999, however, the study of other religious traditions became an even more obvious feature of the curriculum, and increasingly of the research profile of the institution. This seems now set to continue with the appointment in 2002 of John R. Hinnells as Professor of Comparative Religion. Hinnells is a world-class scholar in the field, with a particular specialism in Zoroastrian studies. As a Parsi expert, he is virtually unrivalled.[42]

This growing emphasis upon research in non-Christian religions is entirely appropriate to an ecumenical university college. To be sure, on a practical level the question of ecumenical relations as they relate to the Anglican and Roman Catholic conversation is of more obvious day-to-day significance 'on the ground' at Hope. However, in a wider perspective interfaith dialogue is vital. This is true both in a local setting – one ought not to forget that the Chinese community in Liverpool is the oldest in Europe, nor that the Liverpool Jewish community is one of the most important in the UK – and also in a more general one, especially after September 11. Markham's work in interfaith ethics was an important contribution to getting such dialogue off the ground at Hope, while Ruparell's work in 'interstitial' theology took a radical approach to the whole question of how interfaith dialogue can best be conducted. When coupled with detailed factual and theoretical understanding of individual religions such as that possessed by Hinnells, McFarlane and Ramsey, the concern for interfaith dialogue at Hope seems likely to produce good results. Hope's commitment to this area can be seen further by the appointment of Richard King as Visiting Professor for 2002–03 and Julius Lipner for 2003–04. Both are distinguished religious studies scholars who have much to contribute to the ever-widening debate. The growing number of research students in religious studies is similarly a very welcome development.[43]

Of much narrower scope, my own work on the Branch Davidians also feeds into the ecumenical/interfaith emphasis. I am currently writing a substantial monograph on this relatively small group, whose impact on American politics and the religious liberty and 'cults' debate has far outweighed its numerical size.[44] The leader of the Branch Davidians in the early 1990s was David Koresh, and it was they who were involved in a 51-day standoff with the FBI in Waco, Texas in 1993. The crisis ended when the buildings in which the Branch Davidians lived caught fire and the end result was some 74 deaths; a further six Branch Davidians and four government agents had died earlier in the siege. I argue that both the popular media and the US government agencies seriously misunderstood the nature of the group inside 'Mount Carmel' (the name of the Branch Davidian headquarters) and that, if we are to avoid such conflicts in the future, much more understanding of how religious groups function and the nature of their beliefs will be needed.

Research in theology and religious studies at Hope is, then, an important part of the activities of the subject area. This is true now, and it has been true in the past, as Mgr Jones's *Jerusalem Bible* amply demonstrates. What has changed relatively recently, however, is that since the 1996 RAE (in which Hope scored a 3b in theology), research in this area has been made an institutional priority and the importance attached to it has been followed up with resources. A number of theology staff have enjoyed research-specific contracts enabling them to consider taking on major research projects, and all theology staff have access to research funds and sabbatical leave that match those available elsewhere. This institutional support has provided great opportunities for those privileged to enjoy them. A combination of institutional support and sheer good luck (for Hope if not for St Joseph's) has resulted in the acquisition of the Gradwell collection.

Reflecting on this from the point of view of the health of the discipline in the UK and further afield, one cannot but feel privileged to have been a part of the developments that have taken place. It is good that Christian theology as a subject area, in all of its various forms, is not just being kept alive but is positively expanding at an institution such as Hope. One might not want to agree entirely with Markham's suggestion that theology can be done only inside the church (not the sort of thing we expect this non-Barthian to say!) nor that the ability of the unchurched to converse theologically is on a level with that of a non-Spanish speaker trying to converse in Spanish; he is surely right, however, in his suggestion that the church colleges are places where one might reasonably expect theology to be done. It is good too that religious studies is so well represented at Hope. The attraction to Hope of such a major figure as Hinnells, with all the scholarly weight and management and administrative experience he brings, is a major development and a visible sign of the importance to Hope of religious studies as a subject area.

Reflection on this from the point of view of the Christian faith is similarly heartening. In this chapter the exclusive emphasis has been upon theology and religious studies research, but there are other developments at Hope, some of which are detailed elsewhere in this book. Some of these developments involve research activity, but many do not. Some are huge, for example the Everton project and the Network of Hope. Seen in this broader context, the growth in research in theology and religious studies is a small part of a much larger picture.

Liverpool Hope University College is already an important provider of tertiary education in Liverpool and, through the Network of Hope, in the North West more generally. It has reached where it is now as a result of the vision, determination and sheer hard work of all those who have been a part of the S. Katharine's, Christ's, Notre Dame, LIHE and now Hope communities over nearly 160 years. (And one must surely place on record the view that few have been possessed of such qualities to the extent evident in the contribution of the outgoing Rector and Chief Executive, Professor Simon Lee.) Hope is now sufficiently well established to move forward.

That is good. It is good not just because there is another provider of tertiary education out there seeking to provide opportunities to those in the locality and further afield to enter higher education and to pursue courses at under-graduate, postgraduate and research degree level (though that is a part of it). It is good also because in a society in which the church is being pushed increas-ingly to the margins (even if the level of religious belief evident among the individual members of that society is more or less static, perhaps even on the increase), institutions such as Hope are an important symbol. They are a symbol of the commitment of the church to education: they are a symbol of the intersection of the church and society. Theologically we could go on: such institutions are a symbol also of the integrity of creation and of God's activity in the world. (And the *Engaging the Curriculum* project outlined in Markham's chapter gives one example of how this might affect the form and content of education as it is both theorised and done in institutions such as church colleges.)[45] Hope is a symbol too, and an expression, of the faith of its founders and of the continued determination of all those that are a part of the Hope community to make a difference to individuals, to Liverpool, to Merseyside, to the region and to higher education more generally. As a part of this overall exercise, research in theology and religious studies has a part to play, as together the whole of the Hope team seeks the common good.

NOTES

1 The production of the Vulgate was commissioned by Pope Damasus in 382 CE and St Jerome worked on the task for the next twenty years. The end product was a complete Latin Bible. The text base is not entirely clear, but it is certainly the case that Jerome used Hebrew manuscripts for much of the Old Testament (rather than relying on the Septuagint). The Vulgate became the Bible of the Latin Church (hence its name 'vulgate', or 'common' Bible) and was used as the basis for the Douay-Rheims Bible (NT 1582, OT 1610 with subsequent revisions), the principal Roman Catholic Bible available in English prior to the work of Jones.

2 Almost all of the Old Testament upon which Protestants and Catholics agree has been preserved in Hebrew, with a few portions of Aramaic (the most substantial being a section of the book of Daniel). The Apocrypha, the full canonical status of which has been generally disputed by Protestants, is preserved only in Greek. The New Testament too is in Greek.

3 The École Biblique, properly the École Biblique et Archeologique Française de Jéru-salem, was founded in 1890 by Father Marie-Joseph Lagrange (1855–1938). It remains one of the foremost research centres for biblical studies in the world.

4 This move away from a tradition which had been strongly reinforced by the Council of Trent (1545–1563) was further encouraged as a result of Vatican II (1962–1965) and the push for 'aggiornamento'. This too enabled, indeed encouraged, Catholic biblical scholars to employ the modern tools of biblical and historical criticism.

5 This is not the place to get entangled in the status, manuscript-base or value of the three other 'Catholic' Bibles (or portions thereof) that appeared in English earlier in the

twentieth century. These are the *Westminster Version of the Sacred Scriptures* (NT 1935), *The New Testament of our Lord and Saviour Jesus Christ* (NT 1945) and the *RSV Catholic Edition* (1966).

6   Translators included Joseph Leo Alston, Florence M. Bennett, Joseph Blenkinsopp, David Joseph Bourke, Douglas Carter, Aldhelm Dean OSB, Illtud Evans OP, Kenelm Foster OP, Ernest Graf OSB, Prospero Grech OSA, Edmund Hill OP, Sylvester Houédard OSB, Leonard Johnston, Anthony J. Kenny, D. O. Lloyd James, James McAuley, Alan Neame, Hubert Richards, Edward Sackville-West, Ronald Senator, Walter Shewring, Robert Speaight, J. R. R. Tolkien, R. F. Trevett, Thomas Worden, John Wright, Basil Wrighton.

7   The letter was answered by Newport, who was well placed to deal with the enquiry since his own publishing career began with the publication of part of his MA thesis under the title 'Semitic Influence on Prepositions in Revelation: Some Examples', published in *Technical Papers for the Bible Translator* 37, 1986, pp. 328–34.

8   M. W. Elliott, *The Song of Songs and Christology in the Early Church 381–451*, Studien und Texte zu Antike und Christentum, vol. 7, J. C. B. Mohr (Paul Siebeck), 2000.

9   K. G. C. Newport, *Apocalypse and Millennium: Studies in Biblical Eisegesis*, Cambridge, Cambridge University Press, 2000.

10 See also K. G. C. Newport, 'The Psalms of David (Koresh): A Study into the Afterlife of a Biblical Text', in *Religious Studies News* SBL Edition, October 2001 (web published on Society of Biblical Literature website http://www.sbl-site.org/Newsletter/ 10_2001/NewportFullP.htm).

11 J. Jobling, *Feminist Biblical Interpretation in Theological Context: Restless Readings*, Ashgate New Critical Thinking in Religion, Aldershot, Ashgate, 2002.

12 D. A. Bullen, 'E. P. Sanders and Paul's "Pattern of Religion": A Critical Analysis', MPhil, University of Liverpool, 1999. Current (working) thesis titles include 'Sectarian Exegesis: A Comparative Study'.

13 K. T. Kelly, *New Directions in Moral Theology*, London, Geoffrey Chapman, 1992; *Divorce and Second Marriage: Facing the Challenge*, London, Geoffrey Chapman, 1997; *New Directions in Sexual Ethics: The Challenge of Aids*, London, Cassell Academic, 1999.

14 D. Torevell, *Losing the Sacred: Ritual, Modernity and Liturgical Reform*, Edinburgh, T. & T. Clark, 2002.

15 The working title of the thesis is 'Belief without Belonging or Secularisation? – A study of the experience of St Gregory's Deanery in the Roman Catholic Archdiocese of Liverpool'. The research is being financially sponsored by Hope through the allocation of a fees scholarship.

16 M. Ford, 'Wounded Lover: The Emotional Life and Spiritual Writings of Henri J. M. Nouwen', PhD thesis, University of Liverpool, 2002. Ford is also the author of *Wounded Prophet: A Portrait of Henri J. M. Nouwen*, New York, Doubleday, 1999.

17 See, for example, N. Sagovsky, *Ecumenism, Christian Origins and the Practice of Communion*, Cambridge, Cambridge University Press, 2001.

18 N. Sagovsky, *'On God's Side' – A Life of George Tyrrell*, Oxford, Clarendon Press, 1990.

19 J. Sullivan, *Catholic Schools in Contention*, Dublin, Veritas, 2000; *Catholic Education: Distinctive and Inclusive*, Dordrecht, Kluwer Academic Publishers, 2001.

20 Current thesis titles of students being supervised by Sullivan include 'The Nature and Effect of Postmodernism on Attitudes of Lower Secondary School Children to Religious Education'.

21 Named after Fr Robert Gradwell (1825–1906), a Roman Catholic priest who was trained at Ushaw College, Durham (ordained 1849), but who spent all of his clerical life in the Lancashire village of Claughton-on-Brock. When St Joseph's seminary was

established in the 1880s Fr Gradwell took a great interest in it and left his substantial collection of books to the seminary when he died.

22 F. Blom, J. Blom, F. Korsten and G. Scott, eds, *English Catholic Books 1701–1800: A Bibliography*, Aldershot, Scholar Press, 1996.

23 See 'Catholic Apocalypse: The Book of Revelation in Roman Catholicism from c. 1600–1800' in Newport, *Apocalypse and Millennium*, for an example. That chapter was written using materials from the Gradwell.

24 In addition to the Gradwell materials, Hope also houses the personal library of the late Archbishop Derek Worlock. While a much smaller collection, the Worlock library is a useful resource. As a potential primary collection (i.e. a collection that tells us about Archbishop Derek rather than the subject matter of the books themselves) the library may well prove to be a resource of exceptional value. A comparison is useful: Charles Wesley's library has been kept intact and is housed as 'the Charles Wesley library' at the Rylands. One can tell a great deal about Charles by looking at what he was reading (though not as much as one can tell about John Wesley from his books, for John, unlike Charles, was in the habit of making critical notes in the margins).

25 The Rylands Library was built in the 1890s and opened to the public on 1 January 1900. It was founded by Mrs Enriqueta Augustina Rylands in memory of her husband, the wealthy Manchester businessman John Rylands. From the outset the emphasis was upon theology, and the Rylands quickly built up one of the finest collections in the country. The unrivalled collection of Bibles is a legacy of those early days. In 1972 it joined with the Library of the University of Manchester, to form The John Rylands University Library of Manchester. Other collections at the Rylands include that of the Northern Baptist College, the Unitarian College, and a substantial Quaker collection.

26 G. Lloyd, 'Charles Wesley: A New Assessment, with particular reference to his relationship with his brother and role in early Methodism', PhD thesis, University of Liverpool, 2002.

27 A. E. Pratt, 'The Origin of the *Methodist Hymn Book* (1933)', PhD thesis submitted to the University of Liverpool, 2003.

28 E. Phelan, 'More Than a Hymn Writer: Charles Wesley as Evangelist, Trouble-Shooter and Theologian in his Context', MPhil thesis, University of Liverpool, 2003.

29 The titles of these three projects are 'A Man of One Book?: John Wesley and the Bible' (PhD); 'Mary Fletcher and Early Methodist Spirituality' (MPhil/PhD); and 'Methodism in Crosby' (MPhil/PhD).

30 K. G. C. Newport, ed., *The Sermons of Charles Wesley: A Critical Edition with an Introduction and Notes*, Oxford, Oxford University Press, 2000.

31 S. Kimbrough, ed., *Proceedings of the Charles Wesley Society*, Vol. 6, 1999–2000.

32 Works include R. J. Elford and R. Bauckham, eds, *The Nuclear Weapons Debate: Theological and Ethical Issues*, London, SPCK, 1989; and R. J. Elford, ed., *Medical Ethics and Elderly People*, Edinburgh, Churchill Livingstone, 1987.

33 R. J. Elford and I. S. Markham, eds, *The Middle Way: Theology, Politics and Economics in the Later Thought of R. H. Preston*, London, SCM Press, 2001.

34 These are *The Ethics of Uncertainty: A New Christian Approach to Moral Decision-Making*, Oxford, Oneworld, 2000; and *The Pastoral Nature of Theology: An Upholding Presence*, London, Cassell Academic, 2000. The new book is provisionally entitled *Beyond Belief?*

35 I. S. Markham, *Plurality and Christian Ethics*, Cambridge, Cambridge University Press, 1994.

36 I. S. Markham and T. Ruparell, eds, *Encountering Religion: An Introduction to the Religions of the World*, Oxford, Blackwell, 2000.

37 J. Jobling and I. Markham, eds, *Theological Liberalism: Creative and Critical*, London, SPCK, 2000.

38 I. S. Markham, *Truth and the Reality of God*, Edinburgh, T. & T. Clark, 1998.

39 S. C. Ledbetter, 'Providence and Vocation: Towards a Theology of Work', 2000.

40 C. Williams, 'The Creative Tension: Case-Studies in Scientific and Religious Methodologies', 2002; Melanie Phillips, 'The Genesis of the Later MacIntyre: A MacIntyrean Perspective', 2002.

41 The conference convened on 25 June 2002 and was attended by some 150 people. Speakers included the internationally renowned Holocaust scholar, Dr Carol Rittner, Distinguished Professor of Holocaust Studies at The Richard Stockton College of New Jersey. Other speakers were David Arnold, President of the Greater Manchester Jewish Community and an Associate Lecturer at Hope, and Mayer Hersh, a Holocaust survivor.

42 See, for example, *Persian Mythology*, rev. edn, London, Newnes, 1985; *Zoroastrians in Britain: The Ratanbai Katrak Lectures, University of Oxford 1985*, Oxford, Oxford University Press, 1996; and *Zoroastrian and Parsi Studies*, Aldershot, Ashgate, 2000. Hinnells's forthcoming book, *Zoroastrian Diaspora*, Oxford, Oxford University Press, is now in press.

43 Thesis titles include 'Truth and Method in the Study of Religion and Theology: A Non-Confessional Approach'; 'Taoist Elements of Chinese Religious Understanding with particular referent to the Tao Yuan Ching'; and 'Devotional Islam in Britain'.

44 K. G. C. Newport, *The Branch Davidians: The History and Beliefs of an Apocalyptic Sect*, Oxford, Oxford University Press (forthcoming).

45 See also J. Sullivan, 'University, Christian Faith and the Church', in *The Idea of a Christian University*, ed. J. Astley, L. Francis and J. Sullivan, Aldershot, Ashgate (forthcoming 2003).

CHAPTER 11

Government Policy and Research
at Liverpool Hope

JOHN R. HINNELLS

IN January 2003 the British government released a long-awaited White
Paper setting out its vision and policies for Higher Education.[1] That is taken
as a starting point for this chapter because the White Paper grew out of debates
and reviews that had been conducted over several years. I shall therefore be
reflecting on what might be seen as the culminating document of that process
and shall be mostly concerned with research and the role that it has in
Liverpool Hope, a relatively small institution new to research. By using this
specific example, my intention is to flag how such institutions in general might
be affected by these discussions and proposals.

As this is a rather personal perspective, it is important – even at the risk of
seeming egocentric – to indicate where I am 'coming from'.[2] Before joining the
staff at Liverpool Hope I had held chairs in two 'old' universities.[3] I had also
held a chair at the new University of Derby, which enlightened me about the
contrast between new and old. In the national perspective, I was a member of
the last two Research Assessment Exercise (RAE) panels in my subject; co-
chaired the benchmarking panel for this subject with regard to undergraduate
degrees; served as president of the national body for theology and religious
studies (TRS); and served on the research panels of the British Academy, of
the Arts and Humanities Research Board and of three learned societies. Clearly
my concern is with the role of research in a variety of contexts, even though I
have always enjoyed teaching.

The White Paper addresses a number of issues that have long been neglected. Up to now, research has been funded according to external review through
the RAEs. Teaching was also assessed by external review, through Teaching
Quality Assessments (TQAs), but, in contrast with research, this assessment
triggered neither financial reward nor penalty. This clearly was unjust and
prompted some universities to prioritise research at the cost of teaching. Inevitably many undergraduates suffered. The evidence is anecdotal, but compelling.

Several colleagues in different 'old' universities showed me circulars from their vice-chancellors instructing them to end small-scale seminars so that they could spend more time on their research. The White Paper rightly insists that excellence in teaching should be recognised by funding rewards and the spread of best practice.[4] It also, for the first time, takes account of the needs of part-time students, many of whom come from disadvantaged backgrounds (single parents, the disabled, the carers of the sick or elderly). It recognises the importance that higher education can have for enabling them to overcome their disadvantages, for example racial minorities facing prejudice or the disabled for whom a higher education can help to overcome some of the employment problems their disability can cause.[5] The emphasis on collaboration, with regard to both teaching and research, will be welcomed by many. The repeated assertion is that the government 'must do everything that can be done to make sure that everyone who has the potential to benefit from university education has the opportunity to do so'.[6]

One of the major features of the White Paper is that, whereas university and college staff have felt devalued by successive governments, this document emphasises the benefits that higher education provides, not only to individuals, but also to the local region and to wider society. It opens with a welcome statement that 'research pushes back the frontiers of human knowledge and is the foundation of human progress'.[7] The emphasis is heavily on economic issues – the creation of jobs in an area, wealth generation, business, equipping the labour force and supporting productivity.[8] In particular, the government calls for shorter, more work-focused courses, and for two-year foundation degrees designed particularly for training for industry and business. It calls for some (perhaps most is the implication) institutions to be involved in know-ledge transfer activities to bolster the local region.

The White Paper addresses a long-standing issue: the relationship between teaching (or training) and research. On the basis of various reports the con-clusion is that 'it is clear that good scholarship, in the sense of remaining aware of the latest research and thinking within a subject, is essential for good teaching, but not that it is necessary to be active in cutting-edge research to be an excellent teacher'. As a model it cites the California State University system which provides, across its 23 campuses, professional training to 400,000 students and is forecast to grow to 500,000 by the year 2010.

Obviously there are good teachers who are not research-active, and there are good researchers who are poor teachers, but most colleagues I have worked with will object strongly to the two activities being polarised in this way. Before addressing that subject, it is perhaps important to bring in another long-standing debate (touched on only in passing in the White Paper), that is, the common polarisation of pure and applied research, usually with the innuendo that the latter is not 'real' research or is of a less scholarly nature. It is a distinction with which I am uncomfortable. An earlier specialisation of mine was the Roman cult of Mithras. Involvement in the study of archaeological remains may seem like pure research; even here, however, there is the possibility of a practical outcome. From the city of Rome to Hadrian's Wall near the Scottish border, Roman sites fascinate many and support a tourist trade. Seeking to interpret the silent stones of shattered temples into the terms of a living religion, as Mithraism was, has provided intellectual challenges to several generations of students. My current work on Parsis in the diaspora was triggered by a deep fascination of the various communities I encountered, but its implications for education policy, health care ethics, bereavement counselling and so on are considerable. Research does not have to be conducted at a distance, even anthropological work.

Research related to the local community is a clear example of how universities can interact productively with the region and societies where they function. In my opinion, what is important is the excellence of the original research, not whether it is applied locally or based on abstract issues. This has not, of course, been the perspective of many RAE panels. The criterion for a high rating was that the research should be of 'international excellence', a phrase that was interpreted by some (maybe most) panels to indicate that the research should not simply be of local concern. I have read RAE reports where subjects such as music and fine art were criticised, and by implication marked down, for focusing on production and performance in the local region. The TRS panel explicitly stated that 'international' was understood to mean research that was of outstanding excellence, because, for example, an excavation of a medieval church in, say, Lincoln could have been conducted to the highest standards of excellence, but not have international importance or relevance. In my own opinion, the RAE approach to categorising research excellence was determined by the model of the sciences, where any outstanding work can be expected to arouse international attention. In some subjects, surely, research can be of the very highest standards and yet relate directly only to local issues. If, as the White Paper assumes, there is to be another RAE, and the importance of universities to the local region is to be stressed in evolving educational policy, then that particular criterion from previous exercises has to be changed.

What of the relationship of teaching to research? As I indicated earlier, I personally find their polarisation totally unacceptable. For teachers who are research-active, the time when their teaching becomes inspiring is when they are talking about, and sharing, the enthusiasm and excitement that they feel for their work. Although I like to think I am a competent teacher, the time my students sit on the edge of their seats is where I can say, 'well most argue so and so, but my work suggests…' Similarly, most researchers, certainly in my field, find debates with students lively and challenging; and such debates commonly make me reassess my own arguments. Few aspects of academic life are as rewarding as seeing students challenged to develop their own research, be it in an essay, dissertation or thesis. To stimulate research, it is generally important to be a researcher. That is not to devalue the teaching excellence of people who are not research-active. An educational institution is like a football team: it is important to have goalkeepers and strikers, defenders and midfield players. An educational institution equally has to be a balanced team, where each respects the concerns of the other, and each supports the other.

The career prospects for a young researcher, or someone starting an academic career, will be seriously damaged if their research interests and potential are not given support. The White Paper makes occasional passing references to ensuring that good quality research in isolated pockets should be supported.[9] It also refers to 'supporting young researchers', but when it refers to the recruitment, retention, training and career progress of junior researchers it does so only in the context of science and engineering.[10] It may be that the wider higher education field is intended for it does require that 'support for junior researchers will be expected to feature in institutions' human resources strategies'.[11] As the White Paper argues that everyone who has the potential should benefit from a university education, surely staff and others who can benefit by pursuing research should also be given the opportunity to do so? The government proposal is to focus research on intensive research institutions, those who obtained not just the highest rating in the last two RAEs but were the outstanding ones even among the very best. Funds, it is argued, must be targeted: '[It] is critical that we focus our resources on the strongest, who bring us best returns'. It affirms that research should be funded in 'larger more concentrated units'.[12] The most that is offered to the young researcher in a teaching and training institution is an opportunity to spend a few months in a research-intensive unit – though the anticipation is that only 100 people, across all subjects and throughout the country, will be given such an opportunity. Even for the chosen few, that is not a way to develop a substantial research programme or to equip the young researchers to fulfil their potential.

Again, in my opinion, the argument is based on the scientific model where research often depends on extremely expensive equipment. This is not the case in the arts and humanities. Libraries can be expensive, but in most fields there is not the need for daily access to them. The problem of access to books could be eased by more extensive agreements between institutions on access to each other's libraries. The White Paper refers to the importance of a critical mass in the social sciences. That is the received wisdom, but is it really necessary? The collaborative and inter-institutional work called for in the White Paper, as well as support for workshops and conferences, can overcome many problems of critical mass. In some arts and humanities subjects large units are not essential; indeed even in RAEs single-person submissions can receive a high rating where it is clear that there is collaborative and institutional support. Why should arts and humanities be subject to the same funding model, the same concentration of research, as is necessary in expensive sciences that require large well-equipped laboratories? Personally, I enjoy working as part of a team and do find stimulation from debates with colleagues, but in my field, work can be undertaken alone; indeed as a Parsi specialist I am – regrettably – alone in Britain. Why should the research of people like myself be constricted by the needs of particle physics? I learn a great deal from colleagues specialising in other branches of Indian or diaspora studies, but my major costing is of the order of an annual visit to India, periods in the British or Cambridge University Library and an occasional conference. Philosophers, and scholars in many branches of theology or English, are probably even less expensive than I am. Government policy on funding and research, as set forward in this White Paper, is being run according to the model of science, as was much of the design of the RAE.

The White Paper does include some references to the arts and humanities, promising, for example, the long-awaited creation of an Arts and Humanities Research Council funded by the Office of Science and Technology in the same way as the other research councils are funded.[13] The purposes for which it is to be created are, in my opinion, excellent, namely to encourage interdisciplinary research and 'more participation by the arts and humanities in national and international programmes'.[14] That step is itself a major development and makes the concentration of research in these fields even less necessary.

That major passage apart, there are relatively few references to the arts and humanities, and some of these are made just in passing.[15] Perhaps the strongest reference to the arts is at the end of a sentence on page 23: 'Research in the social sciences, and in the arts and humanities can also benefit the economy – for example, in tourism, social and economic trends, design, law and the performing arts – not to speak of enriching our culture more widely'.[16] It is good that the role of the arts and humanities in these areas is appreciated, but when this represents the sum total of the references to the arts and humanities, many, I am sure, will feel that this is but a partial indication of the value of our work. This restricted perspective is highly regrettable when it is the basis of our funding model, and will lead to the concentration of scholars in a few institutions while others have to forsake their research. It is perhaps unsurprising that a government policy should be based on such utilitarian considerations, but there is no mention of the importance of clear, logical, analytical thought, challenging assumptions, creative thought and writing. Reference to the performing and especially the visual arts is yet sparser. It is self-evident that governments have to give priority to such issues as economics, engineering and the like, but those of us working in other areas should not have funding limitations imposed on our fields because of the high costs of other subjects.

In the White Paper there are several references to the merits of the higher education practices and policies in the USA. They refer, for example, to the better record of Americans placing endowments in their old universities.[17] It is also said that in the USA, research-intensive departments are located in a relatively small number of large, well-endowed universities, while the smaller colleges concentrate on teaching. I cannot speak for the sciences, but TRS is certainly research-active in smaller colleges. (Some of the fine researchers I work with are in smaller colleges.) In the White Paper there is an implicit assumption that we should adopt the US model more closely. My American colleagues are horrified at such features of British universities as the RAE, TQA, benchmarking – even the external examiner system. It is rare for American colleagues to be asked to undertake any administrative duties. Perhaps there are other features of the American system we should call for in the UK!

Criticism of policies, on its own, is insufficient. The remaining part of this chapter, therefore, is devoted to how research might be given an important place in a relatively small college such as Liverpool Hope.

Each institution has its own conception of its mission. A crucial part of the Hope mission is outreach into the wider community, especially in the more deprived parts of the city, but also into the surrounding region, for example Blackburn or Wigan. In this it is clearly fulfilling one of the government's priorities. It is especially committed to enabling those who might not be in a position to study away from home, for financial or family reasons, to work for a degree. But not only should people be able to benefit from an undergraduate education; those who could benefit from postgraduate studies should also be enabled so to do. Surely, postgraduate research students can only be super-vised by a research-active teacher? If there were no research activity at Hope, how could the careers of those who wish to be research-active develop, as the White Paper says they should? One general criticism of the criteria for assessment in the last RAE (including, with the wisdom of hindsight, the panel on which I served) was that there was no requirement that institutions should show how they carry out their duty to nurture the careers of young academics. That ought to be addressed in the next RAE, otherwise universities seeking the highest grading will recruit only well-established scholars who already have a number of substantial publications. At Hope, each new member of staff who wishes to be research-active will have a mentor to work with their line manager in supporting their research as well as their other duties.

If institutions respond positively to the government's call to interact with the local community, then those which specialise in, say, making music or producing art for local exhibitions should not be penalised in the RAE for not engaging in 'international' activities. They should be assessed exclusively for their research or creative excellence on its own terms. Research in the social sciences should not be downgraded because it focuses on local issues, nor should it be considered academically weaker because it is applied research. Excellence, and excellence alone, should be the criterion for judgement.

One illustration of how Liverpool Hope plans to play to its strengths, serve the region and generate original research is the establishment of final-year and taught MA courses on religion, culture and migration. This could bring together colleagues from English (the study of Indian fiction in English), arts, social work, courses in applied healthcare (how should healthcare and bereavement practices take account of a multicultural society?), studies of Irish migration, and of refugees from countries of the former Yugoslavia. It will also involve the subject of education, as well as TRS. The aspiration is to generate original research relating to regional issues by using the course as a research-training course. Researchers in sociology are similarly forming a research cluster that will develop collaboration both within the college and with other institutions. In this way, small teams may become part of a larger unit, as the White Paper suggests, but funding will need to come into the college to achieve this.

Currently at Liverpool Hope, the funding gained from a single rating of 4 in the last RAE is being allocated approximately 50 per cent to the department which achieved the rating, and 50 per cent for 'pump-priming' promising research in other subjects or interdisciplinary projects. The smaller the sum of money available, the more important it is – in the words of the White Paper – 'to make use of the money by making sure that research funding is allocated, organised and managed effectively',[18] and the outcomes will be monitored strictly. There will be one round of bids per annum, which must conform to agreed criteria, and a sub-committee of the research committee will assess value for money and look to see that RAE-appropriate work is being undertaken which will achieve higher ratings for other departments in the future. In small institutions, especially ones with an outreach programme like that at Hope, which requires staff to travel to towns and cities across the North West, prob-ably the most common use of the money will be buying research time by employing teaching assistance, though obviously other uses will be considered. If there is no hope of pursuing research for those who wish to be research-active, staff morale will suffer. When academic salaries are so low, it is vital that there is job satisfaction and personal fulfilment. By removing the oppor-tunity to do research from those who wish to be research-active, the proposals of the White Paper will make recruitment and retention yet more difficult. The fact that the decisions are based on a funding model geared to expensive sciences, rather than on a model appropriate to most arts and humanities subjects, will cause yet greater dissatisfaction.

The White Paper calls for institutions to pursue their individual strengths. That has consequences for Hope. The University of Liverpool and John Moores University do not include religion in their teaching and research programmes. Liverpool does not have a substantial research programme in education. Growing as it does out of the amalgamation of church teacher-training colleges, it is natural that, at Hope, education and TRS should be priorities.[19] In the current academic year, three research-active professors have been appointed in the Education Deanery and two in TRS. But it does not follow that colleagues in other subjects should not be supported in their research interests. To ignore them would be to block colleagues' future prospects of gaining employment at research-active institutions.

Earlier I drew an analogy between a university and a football team. Here a parallel might be drawn between higher education and the football leagues. The big clubs in the premiership need the teams in the lower divisions because of the young players they bring on. Of course premiership clubs have their own youth academies – as the Russell Group universities bring on their own young researchers. But to exclude research from the smaller institutions would make as much sense as stopping all youth academies in clubs in the lower leagues. Research-active staff benefit from interaction with other researchers, even in different fields. Having only the odd research-active department in an institution weakens the research activity of the very good. Because of the importance of interaction between researchers, both staff and research students, a 'graduate centre' is being started at Hope, with an application to the Science Research Investment Fund. A weekly programme will link related research areas into a paired programme, with a social period in between, so that research students who live at a distance will be encouraged to come and meet others in the college, in order to avoid the loneliness of the long-distance researcher. Such an interactive day should aid the retention and monitoring of post-graduates. Presentations will not necessarily consist of polished papers, but will also invite discussion of research-grant applications, the early drafts of papers, chapters or books, in order to generate a mutually supportive research environment. It is in this setting, as well as in the departments, that we will give the essential high-quality research training.

A further weakness in the policy advocated by the White Paper is that it is only the departments overall that are rated publicly in the RAE, individual scholars' ratings never being divulged. But within a medium-graded department there may well be a scholar of real excellence who would, on these proposals, not have their research supported. The White Paper does not explain how the government will carry out their assurance of supporting quality research in isolated pockets.[20] Allowing more and smaller units to engage in research in the less expensive arts and humanities, rather than being held back by being tied inflexibly to the model of the expensive sciences, is surely a logical and easy amendment to make to the recommendations of the White Paper. For subjects in the less costly areas, it would be reasonable to allow departments with an RAE score of 3 (maybe including 3b) to have some funding to enable them to improve their rating. Further, the welcome Arts and Humanities Research Council should have as one of its concerns pump-priming research projects that show scholarly excellence by individuals or groups in smaller units.

The White Paper is the first serious attempt for some time to assess the funding and policies for higher education, and a number of its recommendations will rightly receive widespread support. But it does not address some serious concerns for research in the arts and humanities, and the work of smaller institutions. Big can be better, but there should always be a recognition of the place and potential of smaller units with clear social/educational/academic/creative missions to undertake substantial work with the hitherto disadvantaged, and with local communities; and, moreover, there is no reason why worthwhile activity of this sort should not extend so far as to include research work.

NOTES

1 *The Future of Higher Education*, January 2003, HMSO, 2003.
2 It is important to emphasise that this is a personal account. I am chair of the college's research committee and have discussed many of these ideas with the committee, but the document has not been through the committee and should be seen as representing a personal rather than an institutional position.
3 The Victoria University of Manchester – where I also served as Dean of Faculty – and London University, specifically the School of Oriental and African Studies, where I started a new department.
4 It is to be regretted that the target figure for the number of teaching fellowships is only 50 across all institutions and subjects.
5 I write as a disabled person who would have found it difficult to gain employment without a higher education.
6 *The Future of Higher Education*, pp. 18, 22, 87.
7 Ibid., p. 10.
8 Ibid., pp. 1–10, 16, 60.
9 Ibid., p. 29.
10 Ibid., pp. 33f.
11 Ibid., p. 34.
12 Ibid., p. 30 and p. 28 respectively.
13 The Office of Science and Technology does not seem an obvious funding body for the arts and humanities!
14 *The Future of Higher Education*, p. 32.
15 For example, on p. 29, after a list of points directed specifically at science, there is a single sentence: 'Some of these points are equally valid for the arts and humanities...'

Also, p. 37: 'We will continue to support higher education institutions in their role as community leaders celebrating the cultural and social contribution that they make.'

16 The same point is made on p. 21: 'At the same time it [higher education] needs to enable all suitably qualified individuals to develop their potential both intellectually and personally, and to provide the necessary storehouse of expertise in science and technology, and the arts and humanities which defines our civilisation and culture.'

17 The aim of changing the UK culture and encouraging people to make endowments to their former institutions is laudable. But institutions where research is not practised and which pursue foundation degrees and shorter practical courses are very unlikely to gain such endowments, however much the culture is changed.

18 *The Future of Higher Education*, p. 26.

19 For the position of TRS at Liverpool Hope see Chapter 10 of this book.

20 *The Future of Higher Education*, pp. 26, 29.

CHAPTER 12

Vocation and Profession
in Teacher Education

JOHN SULLIVAN

IN keeping with the different stances of their sponsoring churches, Anglican church colleges have always sought to equip their students to serve as teachers both in church schools and in mainstream schooling, while Catholic colleges were founded primarily to ensure a supply of teachers for Catholic schools. These Catholic schools were originally set up as a protective measure, in the face of what was then (in the nineteenth century) seen as a hostile society. A fortress church mentality led to an inward-looking and clearly distinctive approach to Catholic education. This required a fully Catholic staff, usually an overwhelmingly Catholic pupil population and an all-pervasive Catholic atmosphere. Anglican schools, starting from their links with an established and confident national church, have had a double focus: in particular, the nurture of Christian faith and, more generally, to provide an educational service to the nation. The balance between these two priorities has shifted from time to time and in different places. Despite this, it has been a constant feature of Anglican church colleges to address both priorities, with varying degrees of success. Therefore, many former students from such colleges have worked in church schools, while many have taught in other schools; some, of course, have worked in both sectors.

The gap between Catholic and Anglican education in this respect is rather less marked in practice than in theory. Even in theory, there appears to be not much of a gap over the guiding principles.[1] First, the vast majority of teachers currently working in Catholic schools have not been educated or received their professional preparation in Catholic colleges, but in secular universities. Furthermore, many teachers who have trained at Catholic colleges decide to work outside the Catholic system. This state of affairs is paralleled in the Anglican sector. Second, for all forms of teacher education, strictly enforced national ground-rules exist constraining the curriculum and competencies that must be covered. These national requirements ensure severe restrictions on the

152

degree to which any additional Christian perspectives, whether Anglican, Catholic or ecumenical, can receive much attention in state-funded teacher education and training, whether at initial, inservice or more advanced levels. Third, another practical constraint, one that is simultaneously a challenge and an opportunity for Anglican and Catholic schools and colleges, is that they usually find that their institutions could not function properly without the contribution of a significant proportion of men and women who come from outside the host faith community. This feature of church schools and colleges becomes more marked as the age level of students being served goes up. Thus they must accommodate, rely upon, collaborate with and engage constructively with a wide range of people who do not share their particular religious framework and all that flows from this. Fourth, a growing policy convergence between the approaches adopted in Anglican and Catholic education will receive further comment below. Both churches, at this juncture in their history, seek to address both distinctiveness and inclusiveness, to combine fidelity to their own tradition with an openness to the needs and perspectives of other people, to serve both the church and the common good.

With this dual focus in mind, one might justifiably claim that prospective teachers and leaders who undertake education and training programmes in church colleges such as Hope need to develop a bifocal vision and a bilingual capacity. That is, they need to be able to 'read' the educational and leadership tasks that face them both from the perspective of the church and also from the viewpoint of the nation. (It is a debatable point as to which of these perspectives one should attribute particularity and universality.) They also need to become confident in using language drawn both from a Christian and from a secular world-view, in order to mediate between these in their professional practice, both with their fellow professionals and also with other partners: pupils, parents, governors, dioceses, inspectors, the local education authorities and the wider public. In shorthand, they should be encouraged and invited to use the language of vocation as well as of profession.

In order to bring out Hope's significant contribution in this chapter, first, I review the dual role of church colleges in serving church and nation through teacher education. Second, I indicate how a constantly changing national educational policy context challenges church colleges to adapt how they prepare their graduates to exercise this dual role. Third, given their centrality to the work of church colleges in general and of Hope in particular, and as a contribution to the lively current debate about their role, I review the position of faith schools, show how they can serve both church and nation and bring out how their teachers and leaders can display both professionalism and a sense of vocation. Through offering this perspective from Hope, I seek to demonstrate what is meant by the claim that teacher education in the church colleges provides a distinctive contribution in developing bifocalism and bilingualism in teachers.

The church has for centuries – and throughout the world – been a leading agent in the provision of education. All kinds and levels of formal and informal learning have been sponsored by Christians as part of their response to the gospel and in service of God's Kingdom. Church colleges have a long history of making a major contribution to teacher education in the United Kingdom.[2] Although fewer in number at the start of the twenty-first century than they were in the middle years of the twentieth century, they continue to offer a very significant proportion of the total provision of teacher education in this country. Thus, one quarter of the nation's initial teacher education places at the beginning of the twenty-first century were located in Anglican colleges, which produce about 33 per cent of primary and about 17 per cent of secondary teachers in England.[3] Catholic colleges provided in 1998 for 6.5 per cent of primary and for 3.3 per cent of secondary students in initial teacher education.[4] Liverpool Hope University College came about as a result of bringing together in the 1980s what were originally three such colleges, one Anglican and one Catholic from the mid-nineteenth century and one Catholic college founded in the 1960s.[5] Hope has now diversified its curriculum in various directions and offers qualifications in many other areas than simply the field of educational studies. However, teacher education continues to represent a central priority within the institutional mission, as well as continuing to attract large numbers of students and to receive high praise for its quality.

The church colleges – and Hope among them – have always prepared teachers both for the church school sector and also for the main body of schools (formerly called county, now called community, schools) that maintain no formal links with churches. Thus they have sought to serve both church and nation. These twin priorities continue. If the church colleges were closed, the supply of teachers for mainstream schools would be seriously impaired and the government would incur a huge increase in costs in order to make up the shortfall. It remains crucial, for the health of the education system as a whole, that graduates from teacher education programmes in church colleges are equipped and motivated to contribute effectively to, and to comment wisely on, developments in mainstream schooling and the wider economic, social and political arrangements and framework for education. They should not perceive themselves as being concerned only about the church school sector, even if that is where some of them decide to focus their main efforts. At the same time, church schools and their sponsoring faith communities legitimately look to the church colleges to prepare teachers to work in and for the particular ethos they are trying to promote, one where Christian faith is celebrated, witnessed to, taught about, lived out, and where pupils can experience the opportunities and challenges of Christian community life.

In past times, it is probably true to say that links with the sponsoring churches were stronger, both at church school and at church college level, than they are now. The intake of students and the composition of staff was once more closely matched to the particular religious ethos of school or college. The prevailing ethos, rituals that marked the passage of the year, the centrality of chapel (formerly compulsory) and formal religious observance, the governing assumptions that underpinned professional practice and the salience of religion within the curriculum – all bore a more explicit Christian imprint than is currently the norm. One might claim that Christianity is less 'in your face' than might have been the case a few generations ago. It is possible to pass through a church college (and also a church school) and to receive an education (and professional preparation and training in the case of the college) with a minimal encounter with Christian faith and its diverse expressions. However, because Christian faith is neither imposed nor constantly intrusive, this does not mean that such faith is absent, invisible or insignificant. There are many opportunities in church colleges (as in church schools) to hear the gospel, to join in worship, to study theology, to explore the potential relevance of Christian faith for personal decisions and to experience community life. In particular, there are many opportunities to reflect upon the connections between faith and professional practice in teaching.

Not surprisingly, in church colleges both theology and religious education play an important part in the curriculum. In addition to the academic role they play in their own right as particular discourses or disciplines, theology and religious education also offer an architectonic role. That is, they articulate a framework of interpretation for the whole work of the institution, orienting attention to a source and goal beyond the remit of particular subject areas, offering coherence and interconnectedness. Such an architectonic role counters the fragmentation within the curriculum that specialisation tends towards. It also offers a way of linking a Christian world-view, first, to the perceptions and priorities yielded by, and the methods and approaches deployed by, all the other areas of the curriculum, as well as, second, to all features of institutional functioning and community life. A church college expects its theology and religious education teams to go beyond the pursuit of inward-looking academic interests – although these need to be of the same quality as in any other university theology and religious education department and operating at the cutting edge of developments in these disciplines. Theology in a church college is one of the places that the church does its thinking and where it brings this thinking to bear upon the wider curriculum and community life of that college, as well as prompting prophetic insight (and courage) and cultural discernment about developments locally, nationally and globally. I believe that the presence, confidence, liveliness and salience of theology in a church college is an especially important contextual factor influencing the distinctive contribution of teacher education. A parallel kind of role, mutatis mutandis, can be played in a church school by an effective team of religious educators.

Two quotations bring out some aspects of the central role played by theology. First, Scott Matthews argues that 'a religious tradition flourishes only to the extent that it is capable of making its central commitments available for public examination both within and beyond its boundaries. That is the condition for the public communication of those commitments, and also for their very survival.'[6] Without the presence of a high-calibre, confident, critical, imaginative and articulate theology team, the distinctive nature of a church college can easily be lost sight of and, as this happens, inappropriate forms of secularisation or of sacralisation can be accommodated or become prominent. Religious perspectives and commitments need to be communicated and exposed to scrutiny if they are to be engaged with and if they are to earn credibility. Without keeping in mind – and keeping critically alive – the nature of the special 'story' or world-view that underpins the institution, its mission can soon be swamped by other priorities and its conceptual capital become redundant through neglect. Second, David Cunningham claims that 'without occasional attempts to devote some sustained thought to the meaning and significance of a particular Christian belief, the practices that embody that belief can become hollow, insignificant, and ultimately unpersuasive'.[7] I take this to mean that mere repetition of religious terminology or reproduction of religious practice is no true form of fidelity. After all, the Christian conceptual or doctrinal 'toolkit' and the various spiritual, moral, liturgical and communal forms of response associated with this are articulated in constantly changing contexts. Changes in intellectual, economic, technological, social, political and cultural contexts force us to rethink what we mean by our Christian concepts and practices, how we perceive our priorities, the challenges that are posed by our circumstances, the misunderstandings we should refute, the tools we should deploy in communicating our message and the sources of renewal we should draw upon.

CHANGES IN NATIONAL POLICY CONTEXT

The state only slowly and with reluctance involved itself in education. Even after the introduction of compulsory schooling in 1870, with the Forster Act, this involvement had limited objectives and was on a relatively small scale in comparison with the major contribution being made to educational provision by the churches. Inexorably, though in fits and starts, the role of the state has gradually become more and more dominant. Now education is a major department within the government, disposes of billions of pounds each year, and relies upon a massive superstructure of monitoring and evaluation. So long as they met certain fairly limited expectations, church schools up until the last quarter of the twentieth century were mostly left free to develop their own ethos. Higher education institutions similarly had a wide degree of latitude as to how they constructed their own curriculum. This left room for church colleges to devote more time and energy to preparing student teachers for the special ethos of church schools.

In increasingly marked ways, the combination for church colleges of internal changes (in the composition and in the priorities of staff and students) and growing external scrutiny and pressure has led to secularisation, with an accompanying marginalisation of religion, together with the imposition of a heavily prescribed national curriculum for teacher education. This leaves very little time or opportunity to address the particular needs of church schools and the faith community. It takes a high degree of vision, commitment, energy and creativity to maintain a place for, let alone to enhance the role of, the Christian dimension within the life of a university college and in its teacher education work. Fortunately, Hope has been blessed with substantial amounts of these qualities in its staff and leadership, though complacency is never in order and must always be guarded against.

Changes in the wider educational context have to be taken into account. Not to do so leaves church colleges vulnerable to the complaint that they are preparing students for a world that has passed. They might also be accused of failing to meet the real needs and expectations of the schools which employ their graduates. What are some of the changing emphases in the wider educational context? Although it is always dangerous and at best slightly misleading to seek to outline major trends, it can be a risk worth taking, if one wants, by such a sketch, to indicate the adjustments that teacher education has had to make. Here I pick out a few themes.

First, education is associated with the passing on of skills, knowledge, sensitivities and commitments commended by society. Thus certain curriculum areas, social values and a cultural heritage were the focus of much schooling earlier in the twentieth century.

Then, second, during the 1960s, a strong wave of child-centredness emerged as a major emphasis in society and in many schools and this was reflected in teacher education. Relevance to the world of children and adolescents and starting with their experience became watchwords in educational practice.

Third, this was followed, as the movement towards a mostly comprehensive school system in the 1970s became all-pervasive, by some educators perceiving themselves as playing an important and necessary role in social reconstruction. Education was envisaged as a powerful tool in changing society, in liberating the disenfranchised, in overturning outdated institutions and in building a new and better world.

Fourth, by the early 1980s the government had introduced the technical and vocational initiative into secondary education. This sought to inject a heavily technological emphasis and entrepreneurial spirit into the curriculum, equipping pupils more effectively for the world of work by becoming adept in the use of new technology, and to reduce the gap between the worlds of school and of employment, thereby contributing to the economy.

Fifth, by the beginning of the 1990s a massively prescriptive national curriculum buttressed by an intrusive, complex and burdensome system of assessment was well established. This was soon followed, from 1993, by the introduction of a vastly more draconian system of inspection, with much more frequent scrutiny, on a larger scale, with rapid public reporting of results and judgements. League tables, showing schools' relative positions in relation to a range of criteria, were intended to aid parental choice of school, put pressure on those that were under-performing and reward those that seemed to be successful. Value for money as a slogan soon elided into value-added. An important question became: 'What difference are we making, bearing in mind where we started from?'

Sixth, paradoxically, just as some of these influences combined to make the notion of the educational 'market' a leading metaphor, along with associated notions of 'product', 'marketing', 'delivery', 'customer satisfaction' and the maximisation of choice as a social value, so there was a parallel emphasis on education as a prompt for spiritual, moral, social and cultural development. For the first time, all schools would be inspected with regard to these aspects of their work, in addition to their success in covering the national curriculum. This tended to counteract some of the worst excesses of the economic view of education just described.

However, it was not long before a seventh emphasis was promoted by government: this was the stress on basic skills, including literacy, numeracy and a facility in the use of information and communications technology. Time, energy, funds, attention and resources were pumped into these areas.

Even more recently, an eighth emphasis is the place of citizenship within the curriculum. Given the pace of change, it is likely that, in the time that elapses between the writing of this chapter (January 2003) and the publication of the book, further new priorities will have emerged. One might not unreasonably hope that, in the light of a careful reading of the signs of the times, there will be a renewed emphasis, as a curriculum priority, on the importance of religious understanding in a pluralist society and the development of the capacity to engage sympathetically, critically and constructively with believers from diverse religious traditions, as well as with those who do not adhere to any particular faith tradition.

These changes in national policy have had major implications for all schools and teacher educators, whether in mainstream or in religiously affiliated institutions. They have altered the climate, transformed people's expectations, led to a redeployment of resources and re-directed energies towards different goals. Not surprisingly, in focusing attention on so many new, different and rapidly changing areas, these variations of emphasis among educational priorities have had unfortunate side-effects. This is especially the case when the very survival of an institution is linked so closely with compliance rewarded with resources or non-compliance punished by withholding these resources. Thus, too often, the contemplative side of teaching has been neglected through excessive focus on the activist dimension. Institutional priorities have been privileged over personal ones. The arts and humanities have been downgraded as technological and functional skills have been promoted. Conformity has frequently triumphed over creativity. Intensification of workload has led in too many cases to the breakdown of health of many gifted and committed teachers who have been lost to the profession. The stress on standards tends to tempt some to rely on standardisation. The call for quality has led to damaging levels of prescription, when much of the best educational exchanges are unscripted, unpredictable, dramatic and spontaneous. The demand for more effective management has sometimes slipped into the heresy of managerialism, where detailed attention given to paperwork, to planning, measuring, monitoring, marketing, control and performance gets in the way of the person-centredness, the vision and the inspirational, motivating, facilitating, liberating and evaluating that should be features of educational leadership.[8]

Teacher educators in church colleges must always be willing to adapt to new professional requirements if they are to serve their students and their partner schools well. It must be admitted that some of the educational developments I have referred to have led to higher standards in schools (and in colleges), that more and more pupils and college students are achieving higher level results than previously, that the value added by institutions is more transparent, and that inadequate and lazy teachers are extremely and increasingly rare. At the same time church colleges should equip student teachers not only to meet the current professional requirements and to adjust to the contemporary policy framework, but also to critique these requirements and these policies in the light of a larger picture, a bigger story, broader principles, *sub specie aeternitatis*.

In other words, there has to be a double focus – on professionalism and on vocation.[9] Competence in their professionalism is essential for Hope's student teachers. In contrast, the sense of vocation, while desirable, cannot be compulsory: the spirit relies on the oxygen of freedom; vocation cannot be imposed. However, the possibility of connecting one's work to a sense of vocation can be articulated and advocated, modelled and witnessed to, fostered and encouraged. I am interpreting vocation here as something that combines several features. It entails an understanding of how God wants me to match my gifts with the world's needs. It helps me to clarify *what* my role is in co-operating with God's grace in building the Kingdom. It prompts me to discern *where* God wants me to work. It illuminates *how* I am to conduct this work. It reminds me of the priorities and principles that should govern and frame this work, no matter what the changing professional scene emphasises. Above all, it supplies an enduring sense of *who* God wants me to be. Furthermore I take the view that this sense of vocation draws upon, is boosted by and contributes to the ecclesial community, the Body of Christ.

FAITH SCHOOLS

Hope's aim in teacher education is not only to equip its students to take their place in mainstream schooling. A major priority is also to prepare prospective teachers to work in church schools – certainly as professionals and, if possible, as an expression of a sense of vocation. In order to bring out the bifocal and bilingual approach needed by teachers in church schools, I analyse some aspects of teaching and leadership that should be open to the language both of vocation and of profession, that is, open to a Christian and a secular interpretation. But before addressing this double focus on vocation and professionalism, required in a particular way in church schools, I expose for consideration some aspects of the wider debate about faith schools that is currently so lively.

Some members of various political parties, both in parliament and at the local level, secularists, some elements within teachers' professional associations, some people of religious faiths other than Christianity and, indeed, many Christians, have misgivings about or even object strongly to the existence, let alone the extension of, a system of separate, faith-based schools.[10] Such misgivings or objections might rest on concerns about the economic, social, political, ethnic, religious or educational effects of separate schools. One might ask various questions about them. Is it efficient or a good use of scarce resources to have a dual system? Is it corrosive of community for children in an area to go to different schools? Does a dual system end up by causing or exacerbating division or resentment of groups that appear privileged by separate provision? Is it a cause of or a reinforcer of racial disharmony? Does it adequately promote understanding of and respect for different religions? Is it an obstacle to tolerance and co-operation? Does it have damaging educational effects, perhaps by foreclosing too soon on religious options in a faith school, or by offering too superficial a treatment of religion in a mainstream school (because a deep examination is left to faith schools), or by failing to promote confident yet deeply probing questions and argument, out of a fear of causing offence?

From a Christian educator's perspective, one can pose three further questions. First, do denominational schools undermine ecumenism? Second, should Christians be putting all their 'eggs in one basket', that is, should they emphasise school less and other forms of and contexts for education in faith more? Third, does the concentration of Christians in some schools ultimately weaken witness elsewhere and overall supply a less effective testimony? In my view all these criticisms can be met by those church schools that manage to address both the vocational and professional imperatives already highlighted. The challenge for them is to combine distinctiveness with both inclusiveness and effectiveness. It is, however, incumbent on defenders of church schools to be sensitive to the nature of these potential criticisms and challenges and to be ready, not only to rebut them in advocacy, but, much more important, to work hard to ensure that, in practice, their schools are not vulnerable in this way because they demonstrably promote the common good as well as the needs of a particular faith community.

If teaching is conceived of as a vocation, if school leadership is envisaged as a form of ministry and if church schools are considered to be a central part of the church's mission and both drawing from and contributing to its living tradition, then church schools, to be authentic in their identity and purpose, require both a high degree of personal investment from each teacher and a substantially corporate approach from staff. There will be a strong brand and a strong culture. This poses difficulties for those who do not feel comfortable with this strong brand. Yet, 'if faith-based schools and agencies become conformed to government expectations and ways of doing things, they lose much that is valuable about their distinctive approach'.[11]

Thiessen admits that there are problems with particularity.[12] It can lead to isolationism, tribalism and over-determination of our lives. As he says, 'what is needed is an *equal* emphasis on our universal and our particular identities'.[13] In this respect, that is, in the attempt to stress the contribution that their schools should be making to the development of citizenship and to the promotion of the common good, I believe that Anglicans and Catholics have a creditable record. If generally Anglicans have stressed the service role of their schools, in contrast to their role in nurturing the faith of believers, more than and for longer than has the Catholic community, the gap between their two types of church school is rapidly diminishing. It seems to me that there is a real concern in many quarters to recapture the distinctive dimension of Anglican education, without loss of its traditionally inclusive style. And, in parallel fashion, there are real efforts to ensure that in Catholic schools the gospel imperative towards inclusiveness is properly engaged with, without loss of distinctiveness. In both sectors there is an acceptance that ecumenism should be an integral element of Christian life.

It is important that no impression is given that what is needed for church schools is an 'icing' on a 'cake' that is already baked. In that way, the additional elements are 'bolted on' after the main job of preparation is done. This could lead to a situation where the secular and the spiritual are kept in isolation from one another, to the detriment of both. Either there is an excessive accommodation to the secular agenda or an excessive spiritualisation of the way teaching and church school leadership is envisaged. For the individuals preparing for teaching and for leadership these need to be properly integrated, rather than kept in separate compartments. The range of professional duties – including classroom management, awareness of pupils' development and needs, subject knowledge, a facility in curriculum, pedagogy and assessment, team-building, development planning, strategic direction, performance management, communication skills and marketing of the school – need to be brought into dialogue with theological literacy, personal spirituality, communion with the church and a sacramental perspective, so that the apparently secular interacts with the apparently spiritual. A faith that takes seriously the belief that God entered fully into the fullness of the human condition in the person of Jesus Christ needs a proper appreciation of the material and the political, of technology and of the 'tools' of management, if it is to be fruitful, while effective educational leadership needs to be informed by a coherent, well-founded and inspirational vision, a core of values and a set of practices that connect a world-view to building a character and a community.

Just as the church's educational vision and priorities benefit from facing the challenge of real engagement with professional norms and the government's policy agenda, so too the alternative perspective offered by Christian views on human nature and needs, on education and development, on authority and leadership, on values and community, prevents too unquestioning an acceptance by teachers and school leaders of current agendas and assumptions. In the ongoing dialogue between church and state – and between other faiths and the state – on educational provision and on provision of leadership preparation opportunities, there is a gain for society in drawing upon, engaging with, though not in being dictated to by, the resources of the living traditions of the faith communities, for dwelling in these there is much practical wisdom for education, for leadership and for human flourishing.

If we start by analysing teaching as a human act, rather than as a technical form of communication, several features should emerge. These include the centrality of relationships, the importance of listening, the stimulation of curiosity, an awareness that we are all 'unfinished', opening ourselves and taking risks.[14] Without these features being part of teaching it is unlikely that much learning would take place. The whole process is based on a conviction that change is possible. None of these features depends upon, though all are compatible with, a Christian perspective. Our understanding of these features can be enriched by the theological, spiritual and ecclesial associations that are offered through Christian faith; but the features stand entirely as valid and worthwhile without such associations. One teacher might speak of sharing her humanity with students, in the interests of enhancing their humanity, while another might describe (to himself at least) doing much the same things as a form of evangelisation by witness. From a religious point of view the holiest thing that happens in a school, if it brings students into the light of truth and love, is simply teaching, per se, without further qualification. This does not require a religious label to be overtly attached. But neither should the religious interpretation be ruled out.

Christian educators will readily be able to share two major goals with their secular colleagues, learning about important aspects of life and the world and contributing to and improving the world, although their understanding of these is nuanced and coloured by a third goal that they do not share with these colleagues, that is, developing a critical appreciation and creative appropriation of the Christian world-view. Even if we start from the explicit goal of teaching discipleship, it can be seen that much of what this entails is open to secular interpretation and can be shared with colleagues who are not affiliated to any particular faith. Thus, in speaking of discipleship as being responsive to God, creation and humanity, one writer refers to the constituent features of such teaching for discipleship as being God-worshipping, idolatry-discerning, creation-enjoying, earth-keeping, beauty-creating, peace-making and justice-seeking.[15] Within this spectrum, there is much room for collaboration between colleagues who start their teaching from radically different premises about reality, human nature and morality.

Some of the purposes pursued in faith schools differ in important ways from those pursued in mainstream or common schools. I give just a few examples of different emphases. Thus, if all education imports, consciously or unconsciously, some idea of what it is to be human and some conception of human flourishing, then education based on a religious faith perspective, for example, Christian education, relates an understanding of humanity to its understanding of divinity. I should respect my pupils and colleagues, not only because of commitment to the principles of liberty, equality and fraternity, though this is a perfectly sound and adequate reason, but also because they, like me, are made in the image and likeness of God, are the recipients of God's love and the forgiveness and redemption offered in Christ, and are called by the Holy Spirit to grow ever more fully into the stature required for sharing in the divine life.

Christian education will aim for the holistic development of students, as do other types of education, but it will envisage this development as best happening in the context of discipleship. In promoting the all-round, or integral, development of persons, Christian educators will support and encourage, as other educators do, the intellectual, emotional, aesthetic, physical, moral, social and spiritual dimensions, but they will conceive of these as elements ordered in the light of their understanding of Christ as the Way, the Truth and the Life.

In aiming for a broad and balanced curriculum, Christian educators will wish to see interconnectedness and coherence, rather than isolation and fragmentation, brought out. For them, God is the ultimate environment, the reason for everything that exists, the source, sustainer and goal of its life, and therefore in the various subjects of the curriculum we are learning about God's world, God's purposes and God's people and creatures, whether we advert to this explicitly or not. Drawing from a sacramental perspective, education should alert and sensitise pupils to God's presence in all experiences. Furthermore, in the expansion of our powers and in the development of our capacities that education promotes, there is also necessary an ongoing conversion of the will, a turning away from sin, a disciplining of self.

From a religious perspective there are close connections between our metaphysics, our view of reality, our spirituality, that is, our response to and relationship with that reality, and our morality, that is, our behaviour, priorities and decision-making in the light of these first two. God, as known in Christ, makes all the difference; this difference is utterly hidden, misunderstood or distorted if the faith perspective is restricted to a slot on the timetable or relegated to the realm of the private option, on a par with a hobby.

Despite these differences of emphasis, faith schools also have many purposes in common with other schools. Therefore there will be at least some generic qualities and skills that prospective leaders for faith schools can usefully learn alongside other potential school leaders. Leaders of faith schools have, as has just been outlined, some purposes that differ in significant ways from those espoused in mainstream schools. The kinds of different purposes indicated briefly here imply additional specific leadership dimensions for faith schools, dimensions that cannot be addressed in the absence of joint affiliation to the faith community that sponsors such schools and from which they derive an important part of their identity.

Thus, all school leaders should ensure that the promotion of student learning is central to the deployment of resources and to all decision-making. In the UK such promotion of learning must address the requirements of the national curriculum and its associated assessment arrangements, even if these are considered inadequate as a basis for education, and therefore need supplementing. School leaders must comply with legislation, for instance, regarding health and safety, child protection, data protection and equal opportunities. They are accountable, in different ways, for the results achieved by pupils and for the effective use of resources, to various bodies, for instance, to government inspectors, to local education authorities, to parents and to school governors. Many aspects relating to the legal framework, to the local context, to support services, to curriculum, assessment, inspection, governance and management and personnel matters, should be learned in common by school leaders, regardless of the kind of school in which they intend to work.

I have written at considerable length elsewhere about some of the intellectual, political and spiritual qualities and skills required by leaders in church schools; therefore I seek exemption from repeating the case made there.[16] However, I hope it will be clear from the developing argument of this chapter that, if there are significant differences (from common schools) in the purposes being pursued in church schools, then there will also be important differences in the expectations of the leadership of such schools. Intellectually, effective church school leaders need a confident and articulate theological literacy. Politically, they must have the capacity to operate out of and to address the ecclesial community and its key stakeholders and gatekeepers. They should also be mature in their own spiritual development, sufficiently steeped in the faith community to be trusted as an elder and familiar with its liturgical 'repertoire' and style. The very terminology which best describes what is needed as preparation for church school leadership, formation for ministry, immediately shows that leadership for such schools requires opportunities for training, education and development that go well beyond what is offered and needed for common schools.

Formation implies an assimilation and an integration of four dimensions.[17] First, there is initiation into a way of thinking and understanding, the operationalising of a coherent conceptual 'toolkit' and 'story'. Second, there is a way of behaving, a set of practices into which we are inducted. Third, there is a way of belonging, affiliation to a particular community, with associated sharing, celebration, joint action and common life. Fourth, there is a way of worship to experience, to dwell within and from which to perceive the world.

This kind of formation cannot be provided by the National Professional Qualification for Headship, nor should it be expected. That framework, quite legitimately, has other purposes. It cannot deal adequately with the notion of spiritual leadership, beyond some rudimentary attention to the need for vision, for personal values and for self-knowledge. It cannot sponsor a sense of vocation, for it has no mandate to connect the educative task to the personal call of God to each person to match their gifts with the world's need. And, although it can stress the value of personal integrity, it lacks the rationale for grounding the coherent, integrated approach to the curriculum and learning required by a Christian world-view.[18]

Although mainstream leadership provision in many centres can be intelligent, principled, reflective, professional, practical, relevant, realistic and empowering – all of which is to be applauded, encouraged and supported – it still lacks dimensions I consider vital for effective leadership of Christian schools. These include attention to understanding informed by scripture, doctrinal and moral theology and spirituality, and insights illuminated by engagement with Christian witness, participation in the sacraments, liturgy and living tradition. Undergirding the existence of church schools, for instance, there is a particular, substantive, thickly developed and tightly integrated network of understandings which contribute to a shared view of life.[19] These understandings include a theology of creation, nature and grace, with an associated sacramental perspective, together with a Christology, and an associated anthropology and ecclesiology.

Mainstream provision of school leadership training programmes seems to me to attend quite well to the extra-personal and to the inter-personal dimensions of the work of leaders, but too little to the intra-personal, that is, to the inner dynamics that influence one's action, connecting this to meaning and motivation, to self-perception and self-acceptance, to over-arching purposes and a bigger 'story'. For leadership in faith-based schools, there is a need for more emphasis on personal formation, on orienting the curriculum for service, on modelling and fostering counter-cultural and prophetic witness, on community-building, and on coping with vulnerability, shortcomings, failure, forgiveness and healing – and on the role of prayer and worship in all of this.

Similarly, in teacher education more generally, it may be argued that some aspects of the key concept of responsibility are currently being addressed more successfully than others. Thus responsibility *for* learners' progress is often the focus of attention, with special emphasis given to inclusion and differentiation. We have to give an account of the difference we have made for others, the value we have added to their experience. It is not enough to say simply that we tried, that our intentions were noble; we have to be answerable for the outcomes of our work for others. At the same time, responsibility *with* is also emphasised. Teaching is a corporate activity, one that builds upon and contributes to the work of others. Teachers are encouraged not to operate as soloists, but to collaborate, to work in teams, large and small, to subordinate their idiosyncratic preferences and repertoires to a broader project which embraces the efforts of many other colleagues. Partnership with parents, pupils and other agencies is part of the role of a teacher, in order to bring out the best in pupils and to provide an effective education for all. Much less attention is given to the notion of responsibility *from*, the nature, character and personal *habitus* of the teacher. This forms the background and enduring environment to the teacher's ongoing series of interpretations, judgements, decisions and actions in the classroom. Who the teacher is, what she or he is like as a person, is bound to influence considerably their pedagogic effectiveness. Prospective teachers (and experienced ones during inservice and higher level courses) need assistance in 'reading' the personal dimension in teaching. This has two dimensions: first, the effect the personhood of the teacher has on the work, pupils and colleagues; second, the effect the work has on the personhood of the teacher. Both need to be taken into account in considering what I have called here responsibility *from*. Finally, from a religious perspective, responsibility *to* in teaching must include the sense of our being answerable before God for our use of talents and resources and for the exercise of whatever mandate we have been given in a particular teaching or leadership post.[20]

CONCLUSION

Liverpool Hope University College provides opportunities in teacher education at many levels. These include initial, inservice, master's and research degree work. Courses facilitate for students and teachers an integration of academic, professional and spiritual competence, intelligence and wisdom, paying attention to the inner self, to the group dynamics of daily school functioning and to agencies and factors beyond the school that influence its educational, religious and community responsibilities. The currently prevailing sense of 'vocational', that is, being relevant to, and equipping people for, the world of work, with careful attention to professional context and ground-rules, is brought into a serious engagement with an older sense of vocation, of living out one's life in response to God's particular call to us to match our gifts to the world's needs, giving witness to the gospel, offering a ministry of service and co-operating with God's grace in communion with the church.

Many features of Hope's provision in this area address issues similar to those dealt with in other, mainstream teacher education and school leadership courses, for example, strategic planning, curriculum leadership, staff development and the management of quality in learning and work. However, Hope also offers opportunities for students to immerse themselves in the church's developing understanding of the nature, purposes, scope and challenges of Christian education, by facilitating an in-depth engagement with the faith community's authoritative documents, at international and national levels, and relating these to the realities of current contexts for work, learning and living. Students can investigate the church's understanding of spirituality, of spiritual development and of spiritual leadership and explore ways to appreciate these critically and to appropriate them creatively. Theological perspectives are drawn upon in order to cast light on the educational endeavour, on moral dilemmas, on the school's relationship with the church, on styles of leadership and on relationships in classrooms and community.

Office for Standards in Education (Ofsted) reports (for example, that relating to religious education) regularly show that Hope is meeting the highest standards set for the teaching profession by equipping students with the necessary knowledge and skills.[21] Less obvious but equally important are the additional opportunities, taken up by many students, to relate their professional studies to other experiences at Hope: of worship, of engagement with one of the church colleges' certificates in Catholic and Anglican studies, of involvement in chaplaincy activities, of participation in Hope One World internationally, of participation in a range of community service activities, of widening horizons made possible through the weekly Foundation Hour which opens up different aspects of developing the whole person, mind, body and spirit. Students learn, through the formal curriculum as well as via college community life, that the living out of a vocation in discipleship, like professionalism, requires discernment and the capacity for initiative, responsibility, creativity and improvisation rather than mere conformity, repetition and obedience. In having the chance to examine the unfinished 'script' of the church's educational, spiritual and theological reflections, and using this to cast light on their teaching and school leadership, students not only come to see their work in new ways, but also to see differently elements within the tradition itself and to see new connections between the parts of its 'ecology' and the 'economy' of salvation. I believe that, in making connections and in raising questions, their insights make an important contribution to the cutting edge of (intra-ecclesial) applied theology, to the project of ecumenism as well as to the wider understanding of education.

NOTES

1 Cf. R. Dearing, *The Way Ahead*, London, Church House, 2001 with Catholic Bishops' Conference of England and Wales, *Education in Catholic Schools and Colleges*, Manchester, Gabriel Communications, 1996.

2 M. Eaton, J. Longmore and A. Naylor, eds, *Commitment to Diversity*, London, Cassell, 2000.

3 Dearing , *The Way Ahead*, pp. 65–66.

4 Naylor, in Eaton et al., eds, *Commitment to Diversity*, p. 14.

5 K. Lowden, 'Women religious and teacher education: a case study of the Sisters of Notre Dame in the nineteenth century', in Eaton et al., eds, *Commitment to Diversity*.

6 S. Matthews, *Reason, Community and Religious Tradition*, Aldershot, Ashgate, 2001, p. 213.

7 Quoted by A. Pauw in *Practising Theology*, ed. M. Volf and D. Bass, Grand Rapids, Eerdmans, 2002, p. 41.

8 For critiques, either of managerialism, or of the skills-based model of school leadership, see S. Pattison, *The Faith of the Managers*, London, Cassell, 1997; M. Loughlin,

Ethics, management and mythology, Abingdon, Radcliffe Medical Press, 2002; J. Sullivan, 'Wrestling with Managerialism', in Eaton et al., eds, *Commitment to Diversity*; J. Sullivan, 'The skills based model of school leadership', *Religion in Education*, Vol. 4, ed. W. Kay and L. Francis, Leominster, Gracewing, 2003.

9 J. Sullivan, 'Responsibility, Vocation & Critique', in *The Idea of a Christian University*, ed. J. Astley, L. Francis and J. Sullivan, Aldershot, Ashgate, 2003.

10 For a major survey and analysis about faith schools, see H. Judge, ed., *Oxford Review of Education*, 27 (4), December 2001 and also H. Judge, *Faith-based Schools and the State*, Oxford, Symposium Books, 2002.

11 C. Glenn, *The Ambiguous Embrace*, Princeton, Princeton University Press, 2000, p. 40.

12 E. Thiessen, *In Defence of Religious Schools and Colleges*, Montreal, McGill-Queen's University Press, 2001, pp. 209–19.

13 Ibid., p. 211.

14 S. Oxley, *Creative Ecumenical Education*, Geneva, World Council of Churches Publications, 2002, p. 95.

15 S. Vryhof, 'Traction on Reality: the Thinking behind Reformed Christian Schools', *Journal of Education & Christian Belief*, 6 (2), 2002, pp. 117–18.

16 J. Sullivan, *Catholic Schools in Contention*, Dublin, Veritas, 2000; 'Wrestling with Managerialism' in Eaton et al., eds, *Commitment to Diversity*; 'Living Logos: the Challenges facing Catholic school leaders', *Networking*, 3 (3), 2002; 'Leadership and Management' in *Contemporary Catholic Schools*, ed. M. Hayes and L. Gearon, Leominster, Gracewing, 2002; 'Leading Values and Casting Shadows in Church Schools', *Journal of Religious Education*, 51 (1), 2003.

17 J. Sullivan, 'From Formation to the Frontiers: the dialectic of Christian education', *Journal of Education & Christian Belief*, 7 (1), 2003.

18 J. Sullivan, *Catholic Education: Distinctive and Inclusive*, Dordrecht, Kluwer, 2001, pp. 86–92.

19 Ibid., pp. 105–17.

20 For a deeper analysis of these four types of responsibility in teaching, see Sullivan, 'Responsibility, Vocation & Critique'.

21 Office for Standards in Education, report on Religious Education at Liverpool Hope University College, 2002.

CHAPTER 13

... To Urban Renewal

R. JOHN ELFORD

B Y 1995, the inner-urban beginnings of Hope's predecessor colleges had become an exclusively suburban presence. This was no undesirable thing in itself, since it provided a campus which was soon to be enhanced and which, sited at one end of the M62 motorway, was well placed to serve the city and the wider region alike. The view was taken, however, that this exclusive suburbanism was not completely true to the founding colleges' original mission. For this reason, a development site was sought in an inner-city area, to which Hope might transfer some of its teaching and from where it could make its Access programmes more readily available. At the same time, Hope sought to play a wider role in creating, along with others, sustainable urban regeneration. The opportunity to do this was conveniently provided by Liverpool's Objective One status for European Regional Development Funding.

Numerous potential inner-city sites were considered. The one chosen, in 1997, was on Shaw Street in Liverpool 3. It contained, prominently, the stunning Victorian Gothic church, St Francis Xavier's, a Grade II* listed building dating from 1848, by the architect J. J. Scholes, and still in use. Equally impressive and overlooking the Islington relief road was the building of the former St Francis Xavier's School, like the church originally a Jesuit foundation, and commonly referred to as SFX. The school had moved to new premises in Woolton some forty years previously, and since then, although partial uses had been found for the empty building, it had not been restored or even maintained. As a result, the roof was gone and extensive weather damage to the interior had occurred. Like so many other such buildings, it symbolised the city's decay: the more so because of its prominent hillside location, highly visible from an arterial road. The rest of the site afforded space for two more buildings, as well as for a large open area in the middle. All this was surrounded by general dereliction, apart from there being some attractive modern houses along part of one side. Standing opposite was the former Liverpool Collegiate School building, also long in decay; as was a row of once fine Georgian houses further along Shaw Street. Apart from access to the church, the whole site was surrounded by high walls topped by barbed wire and posted with 'keep out' signs. The area generally was poorly lit and attracted a high incidence of drug abuse and soliciting for prostitution.

Clearly, the families that remained in the immediate vicinity had more than enough to put up with, and had also had the frustration of seeing successive plans for redevelopment of the site come to nothing. One of these had even included a proposal, supported by the Roman Catholic Archdiocese of Liverpool, partly to demolish the church, leaving only its spire. This had rightly caused local and national outrage at the time, and had duly been abandoned. No fresh proposal for the site was in prospect. The City Challenge initiative had failed to find a solution, until, that is, Hope came along. Minimal church maintenance and liability for the site were costing its owners, the Liverpool Archdiocese, considerable annual sums of money, and even more in embarrassment. It was, therefore, on the market for the proverbial sum of £1! Before the college made the purchase, it consulted extensively with local people about its interest in and proposals for the site. These were generally very well received. As this process of consultation developed, the college deepened its knowledge of the community. As a result, friendships were made and trust established – indeed, as staged phases of the project have been completed and buildings brought into use, including parts dedicated to community use, all this fostering of friendship and trust has continued. In due course the purchase was made and work started on site on a rainy but memorable day in September 1998. Amid all the dereliction, children from the local Friary Infant School, with beaming smiles, released balloons as the local MP Mrs Louise Ellman performed the opening ceremony. All this was a great act of faith in the future.

Initial funding came from the North Liverpool Partnership, English Partnerships and the college itself. This was soon followed by more college investment as well as grants from the European Regional Development Fund, the Higher Education Funding Council for England, and various charitable trusts, including those of Esmee Fairburn and Garfield Weston. Other grants were received from the English Heritage/Heritage Lottery Fund Joint Grants Scheme, from the Jesuit province and the Archdiocese of Liverpool, from the Historic Churches Preservation Trust and, again, from the North Liverpool Partnership. All this was over a period of about three years, and phases of the work had to be planned in advance, ready to be commenced as soon as elements of the funding became available. There was every reason, therefore, to believe that the 1998 'act of faith in the future' had not been a vain one. Reflecting on all of this, it seems to have been presupposed around the city and the region that communities in North Liverpool were somehow to blame for the absence of regeneration in their locality. The experience of Hope has been that the difficulty lies elsewhere. Local people and far-flung bodies have united in supporting the development of Hope at Everton. What was difficult was finding the keys to unlock the funding which ought to have been more readily available for one of the most disadvantaged communities in an Objective One region.

The first building to be completed was a student hall of residence comprising 188 en suite study-bedrooms. It is designed around the four sides of a quadrangle and the accommodation is organised as flats, each of six or eight rooms sharing a common kitchen and lounge. This hall is now named Hopkins Hall, after the poet and Jesuit priest Gerard Manley Hopkins who had been a curate at the SFX Church in the 1880s. Amazingly, this building was ready for occupation in September 1999. It was an immediate success with students, and remains so. This partly has to do with the fact that it is within walking distance of the city centre and main rail and coach stations. Regular free transport is provided to the main college campus at Hope Park.

Meanwhile, work had already begun on the restoration of the old SFX school. This is a Grade II listed, redbrick building dating from 1856 and designed by the architect Henry Clutton in what is described as French Hotel de Ville style. By any reckoning it is imposing, the more so because of its hillside position overlooking the city. The roof had to be totally replaced and the whole of the interior gutted. Minute attention was paid to the details of the re-design. Its focus was to be the central Great Hall, leading off from an atrium. From the entrance, this would create a dramatic vista of the whole scale of the building. The scheme was honed by the architects, Downs Variava, and the college design team, working closely together. This was facilitated by hours of lively discussion – perhaps really good buildings and refurbishments can only emerge from planning and design narratives in which architects and their clients participate equally. In this case, the clients centrally included academic members of staff, who made extensive contributions to the planning discussions and who now do so much to make the campus work as effectively as it does. One important design principle was the decision to reveal and preserve the integrity of the original building as far as possible. This has been achieved by exposing as much of the original brick and stonework as its condition would allow. The aesthetic result of this is much commented upon, and always favourably. None of this could have been achieved without the collaboration of all concerned.

This building is now called the Cornerstone, from the biblical text referring to the stone the builders rejected (Psalm 118:22). Here, it had also been rejected by almost everybody else. It now accommodates fine art and design, music, Hope in the Community and Urban Hope. Fine art and design is housed in new workshops and studios under the Great Hall, as well as in some of the rooms on the north side of the building. To the amazement of some, these facilities were largely ready in September 1999 when the first students arrived. These included those design students moving from their former location at Childwall as well as then freshers, who last year – 2002 – graduated as the first cohort to have completed the whole of their undergraduate studies for the Bachelor of Design degree at Hope at Everton. Reverting to 1999, the rooms on the west side of the building were occupied by the Deanery of Hope in the Community. This too had been re-located from Childwall and was soon busy with its Access courses and programmes. All this brought life and activity to the site and its environs for the first time in (all but older) living memory.

Very soon, the college had embarked upon collaboration with the city council and local residents to plan an improvement scheme for the adjacent Shaw Street. The pavement was widened to include a coach-parking facility and the provision of new street-lighting was of immediate benefit. Part of the open space next to Shaw Street was paved and further lighted, and the rest of the open space was turfed and laid out with tarmac paths. This space is now known as Josephine Butler Square. It is open to the community and provides a welcome pedestrian access through the local area and to the city beyond. Further land nearby has been acquired on the purchase and demolition of a derelict public house at what is likely to become the site of a major new pedestrian thoroughfare to the city centre. The project won a coveted Liverpool Architecture and Design Trust award for the best contribution to sustainability of the urban environment on Merseyside.

In January 2002, the remaining rooms on the north side of the building were completed and made ready for immediate occupation by staff and students in music. This, again, brought yet more life and vigour to the campus. It coincided with the reopening of SFX Church after re-roofing. On one memorable evening the national Church Colleges Choir Festival was held there, by candlelight. On the same weekend the Council of Church and Associated Colleges visited the campus during its annual conference. In all this, no time was ever lost between the completion of any phase of the facilities and their being occupied and brought into full use. This was achieved through excellent co-operation from the building contractors, Norwest Holst, and the project management team who were continuing the ongoing restorations. What could have been a logistical nightmare or disaster as the programme was rolled out presented nothing other than the occasional inconvenience to this group or that. Not surprisingly, but very necessary to say, the goodwill of students and staff alike did so much to make it all possible.

In the middle of all this, in February 2000, HRH the Prince of Wales was due to make a visit to the city and have lunch with young business people. Members of his staff came to the campus for a preliminary inspection and they asked about the closed-off central section of the Cornerstone. This was the Great Hall to be, from which the whole building was designed to radiate. They were told that it was not suitable for the Prince to visit because of its rough and ready, uncompleted state. To no avail! When they saw it they were sure that the Prince would want to look at it as it then was. So he did, during a prolonged visit in the course of which he spent time talking with students, staff and local residents. He also presented a short seminar to a small audience, during which he spoke passionately about his concerns for sustainable and architecturally acceptable regeneration. This was a memorable visit which was to do a great deal to give the project the publicity it needed as well as help to sustain the momentum so crucial to its success. The Prince had previously made a contribution to the project through the Prince's Trust, members of which were also present for the visit. In all, the impression was clearly created that the Prince approved of the project and wished it well for its completion and for the central role it was to play in the ongoing regeneration of the area.

The Great Hall was duly completed by Easter 2002. By common acclaim it is nothing less than stunning. The immediacy of its impact is achieved by the soaring view – right to the rafters eighteen metres up – from the floor of the main entrance. This entrance atrium contains a foyer and reception desk, seating, computer terminals and toilet facilities. The atrium is also designed as an exhibition and performance space, and has already proved successful in this function. A grand central staircase leads to the mezzanine and then up to a surrounding gallery. From the gallery there are dramatic views of SFX Church and away over the docks to the sea beyond. Surprisingly and most agreeably, the windows in the north face of the Cornerstone help to create ever-moving reflections, which vary during the changing natural light of the day and with the artificial lights of the night. There are then further reflections in the 12 square windows of the new screen separating the atrium from the Great Hall itself, which is accessed through two doors off the stairs at either side of the gallery. Here again the view is magnificent. The eye is carried to the far end, from where there are panoramic views of the city roofscape, including the two cathedrals. The Great Hall is floored in sprung beech-wood, and the symmetrical side arches have been retained, partly in their original brick. Doors lead off to other facilities on the north and south sides of the building. Like all good restorations and adaptations should, it even looks as though it were all designed for these new purposes in the first place! High-level heating and cooling ducts, blackout blinds, sophisticated lighting and comfortable seating for 400 in variable configuration complete the furnishing. Audio-visual and computer data points are located throughout. Happily, the acoustics have been found to be good, though it is thought that they might be further improved by the use of some curtaining, which is soon to be installed.

The Great Hall is one of the city's exciting new public spaces and is already attracting a varied programme of external users. These have included sections of the Royal Liverpool Philharmonic Orchestra and its choirs. The regional finals of the National Teaching Awards and of the National Mozart Song Competition have been staged here. Schools and other local groups use it almost daily. Two major art exhibitions have already been held: the first was the Methodist Church Collection of Modern Christian Art, in its entirety; the second was the travelling Cerda International Exhibition of Barcelona Architecture. Even all this has been topped by the exciting range of use by Hope students. One external examiner of musical performance commented that it 'makes some of them sound better than they are'. These performances have been enhanced by their taking place surrounded by displays of work by students of fine art and design. In late November and early December the inaugural Cornerstone Festival was held. This included some 16 separate musical, drama and fine art events. Plans are afoot to develop this into an even more major event in 2003. All this has been achieved largely as a spontaneous consequence of the enthusiasm of staff and students for their new venue. Its further potential is seemingly unlimited: it is clearly already inspiring new artistic achievements. Of course, this all takes sophisticated management, sometimes literally by the hour. Administrative staff, caterers and cleaners alike have responded enthusiastically. Seeing all this happen so quickly after some five years of planning is like seeing the proverbial dream come true.

St Francis Xavier's Church is phase three of the development, after Hopkins Hall and the Cornerstone. The church's future had hung in the balance for years: as noted earlier, it had survived Archdiocesan plans for its partial demolition. That it still stood at all was largely due to the loving commitment of groups of parishioners, many of whom seem to have devoted their lives to looking after it. The present leader of the parish is Fr Patrick Connors SJ, who has recently succeeded Fr Frederick Lane SJ. They have both been supported by the unflagging energy and vision for the parish provided by Brother Kenneth Vance SJ. He was born in the parish and served it as an altar-boy, returning in 1996. He breathes this parish, and in many ways is its modern lifeblood. It is impossible not to catch from him a great enthusiasm for the building and its central place in the life of the parish. His knowledge of its history is encyclopaedic.

When Hope was contemplating the purchase of the church, the school and the site, its first point of local contact was with this parish community. The college was made very welcome, if initially somewhat tentatively, and since those early beginnings great friendships have been made and trust has grown. At first, none of this was without difficulty, nor could it have been. Local people had, frankly, been let down in their expectations so many times that they could scarcely be other than doubtful about yet another proposal. As would be expected, there was no shortage of individual characters who could express all this in their own inimitable ways. One such was the much-loved and renowned Billy Thistlewood, now sadly deceased, who had been an altar-server in the church for over 72 years! While originally and understandably suspicious, he soon became a supporter of the idea of the college owning both the church and the rest of the site. For some months he was a daily visitor, along with other local people, to the refectory for his lunch. His health, however, was visibly failing and he knew that his life expectancy was shortening rapidly. When the scaffolding went up outside and within the church to facilitate its re-roofing, he remarked in passing to Brother Kenneth that he would not be able to die for a bit, because we would not be able to 'bring him home'. Die, however, he sadly did, within a very few weeks. The response of the college and the community alike was unanimous and immediate. He certainly would be coming home. And he did, his coffin lying in grand and traditional Roman Catholic state in the centre of the nave, attended by tall candles surrounded by all the scaffolding poles. It would have befitted a cardinal. Contractors kindly agreed to waive the quite properly draconian health and safety regulations to permit it. There was a moving eloquence in all this. Billy was home, amid the building works and developments that he had had the dignity to say what he thought about, the vision to support, and ultimately had worked so hard to help bring to fruition. At least one alleged sighting of his ghost in his beloved church has already occurred! Pray God there might be many more.

Billy Thistlewood was exemplary in the Hope at Everton venture, and he was not alone. Other parishioners brought their concerns and support to bear in similar ways. For example, at one meeting Philly Scott asked simply, 'Will we be able to light a candle?' This unselfconscious and in its way artless question articulated the thoughts and proper concerns of so many. The assurance was given, and there are now as many lighted candles as ever. These two personal narratives, which grew out of the collaboration between the college and the local community, are richly deserving of inclusion here in their own right. But they also illustrate an important wider point: no progress with the development could have been made without local support. Local people needed to be recruited to the domestic, catering and security staffs. All these helped to establish with the wider community that Hope was a good neighbour. For the most part this was accepted, though sadly some still felt potentially threatened by the scale of the new operations in relation to their own doings. Sensitivity towards that, on all sides, needs to be maintained. All this predominant good-will translated itself into visible benefits. Not the least of these was the absence of any vandalism to the exposed new construction work. This must have been linked to widespread local support for what was being undertaken. The recruitment of local people as excellent security personnel must, of course, have helped too.

All this and more is celebrated in a new stained-glass window in the church, entitled 'The Window of the Hidden Saints' – and not so hidden, one might add. This glass illustrates the story of the church from its beginnings through to the role it plays today in the life of the college. Some long-disused confessionals to the north of the nave have been tastefully converted into a suite of music practice rooms. Entry to them is from the old priests' passage at their rear, so the original doors facing the nave remain intact, though now sealed. Leaks in the bell-tower have been repaired, allowing the Liverpool Universities Guild of Change Ringers to recommence ringing, and further maintenance work and restoration of the peal is planned. The church roof has been totally retiled with Welsh slate, but will not be complete until high-level stonework repairs have also been carried out. As with most such buildings of its age, dry-rot control is ongoing. The church now caters for an increasing number of diverse uses, but is still visibly and primarily the place of worship that it has always been and, of course, will remain. Yet further restoration is still necessary before the building can be secured for the foreseeable future. Extensive exterior stonework repairs are urgently needed, and the electrical wiring needs total replacement, as does the heating system. Meanwhile, two adjacent Roman Catholic parishes, St Mary of the Angels (the Friary) and St Joseph's have closed their buildings and joined the SFX congregation. All this has brought welcome new life and energy to the parish. The church is also now clearly on lists of the city's heritage sites, and increasingly is even being visited by Liverpool people who were previously unaware of its beauty and importance. The college is privileged to own the church and has the expertise both to oversee its restoration and to manage it. However, the church will need all the support it can get from its many friends and well-wishers if its future is to be safeguarded.

The church organ was built in 1850 by Messrs Gray and Davison of Fitzroy Square, London, who at the time were considered to be the most fashionable and expensive organ builders in the country. The cost was £580. It was restored in 1907 and remains a fine example of its period. It is currently just about playable, but is not fit for regular use. Nothing short of full restoration costing an estimated £250,000 will achieve that. In the meantime, a substantial electronic organ has been installed in the nave. This is proving more than adequate for use at regular worship. Since its reopening on completion of the new roof, the church has again come alive at the heart of the community and many memorable events have taken place in it. One such was the Church Colleges Choir Festival mentioned earlier. Another was a concert given by the Chilingirian String Quartet during which a new piece, 'Aphrodite's Rock', by Professor Stephen Pratt of the college staff, was premiered.

The fourth phase of the project is the Rehearsal Rooms. This is to be a new building on the corner of Shaw Street and Langsdale Street. Construction is expected to begin any time now and will take eleven months. The building will principally be used for teaching drama and music. It will also accommodate numerous arts-related business start-up initiatives. A glass frontage facing onto the square will give access to a foyer and the central performance space, which will be surrounded by corridors on three floors leading to other teaching rooms. On the ground floor adjacent to the SFX Church a small bistro will open onto a patio. Part of the inspiration for this building came from a visit made by some of those involved to the City of Birmingham Symphony Orchestra's rehearsal rooms. While the new Hope structure is strictly a functional building designed to exacting specifications, every care has been taken to ensure that it sits well on the square and will be sympathetic to the imposing surrounding architecture. Once this is complete, the only remaining new building work will be to complete the flagging of the square and to introduce a water feature commensurate with the grandeur of the surroundings, and for which provision has already been made. Further environmental improvements to the area are planned by the city council, which is also aware of the increasing pressure on car-parking as the wider regeneration of the area takes progressive effect.

If all now goes according to plan, the completion of Hope at Everton will prove to have been a fine example of rapid urban regeneration. About 1,000 registered students will be using the campus. It will only take the expected modest proportion of them to remain in the area after their studies, as students so often do, for the college to be contributing effectively in yet one more way to sustainable local regeneration. Hope has already played its part in paving the way for wider regeneration of the area, as housing associations and private developers follow. It has also brought to the campus many activities that would normally have been associated only with the city centre. In this sense, it is properly often referred to as a 'gateway' development. Plans are in hand to celebrate all this, in collaboration with local people, through the erection of appropriate pieces of public sculpture – a fitting way to draw wider public attention to a renewed civic self-confidence. So many in the area who have toiled so long to achieve this can rightly be proud of their patience and vision. It is, perhaps, also fitting to remember that what has now been accomplished is in historical continuity with the educational activity that the nineteenth-century schools established and maintained for so long in the area. This is, in fact, often remarked upon by visitors to the campus, who recall the former times so vividly.

None of this is, of course, sufficient in itself; it is but a means to a greater end. This alone is good enough reason not to be too self-congratulatory about what has so far been achieved. Winning awards is not the point of it all. That point is to work, year-in, year-out, with all people of goodwill to ensure that Hope at Everton, as well as delivering courses to students coming from wherever, makes a visible and lasting difference to the educational aspirations and achievements of significant numbers of local people of all ages. Putting these two objectives together has already begun, but doing it as well as possible over the years will be no easy task. Succeed, however, it must, if the college is to make the most of the opportunity and responsibility now vested in it. Forming partnerships with other agencies for regeneration, however tenuously at times they might seem to be related to higher education, is crucial to reciprocal success. In an area like this, every effort for the good needs the help of every other if any of them are to succeed. While, of course, this is true of urban regeneration in general, it is excitingly the more so in such a well-defined geographical area as this. Numerous forums for achieving this have long existed in the locality. Just two such are the West Everton Community Council and the Everton Luncheon Club. The latter meets monthly at Shrewsbury House, the home of St Peter's Parish Church. The college has been welcomed into these communities from the beginning and has benefited tremendously from them.

As outlined already, the campus is designed principally for teaching the performing and visual arts: fine art and design, music, and drama. Together these form an administrative school, but there is far more to their conjunction than that. By existing alongside one another and wherever possible interacting, they create further dimensions of artistic frisson which tangibly add up to more than the proverbial sum of their parts. The design of the campus has had this in mind from the outset. The Cornerstone atrium with its mezzanine and gallery, and the Great Hall with its own gallery are all designed as performance and exhibition spaces which can function simultaneously. This generates a serendipity that is marvellous to experience. It is an inspiration to all those performing, contributing or looking and listening. Some drama performances have already produced much integration, and this will be further developed when the Rehearsal Rooms are complete and all the college's drama teaching and researching takes place on the Everton campus. If the modularisation of learning programmes and their increased use of electronic methods of delivery tend to fragment the learning experience, work at the Cornerstone is a complementary reminder of what can happen when individual learning programmes are juxtaposed. This is something that all students and staff should have the opportunity to engage with at some point during their learning processes. There is nothing new in this emphasis, of course. Distance learning programmes such as those of the Open University have always stressed the importance of summer schools and other such shared learning opportunities. What is perhaps new here is the excitement of its being so focused, and designed from the outset to be so. In an age when, sadly some will think, campus-based higher education is on the decline, all this is a counter-example which turns back to older notions of collegiality and to what Hope's mission statement calls the 'education of the whole person'. Writing about all this is the easy part; realising it is rather more difficult. Hope at Everton has already amply demonstrated its ability to make it real during these few recent months when the combined educational activities have been up and running.

A further dimension of the performing and visual arts that is essential to this vision is that they are interlinked as fully and as often as possible with cognate activities across the city. Collaborations with the Royal Liverpool Philharmonic Orchestra, its subsidiary ensembles and choirs are now regular. This is equally true of the way that drama works with Liverpool theatres, and of how the fine art and design team collaborates with the city's galleries. For example, the annual college-sponsored Tate Gallery Lecture is now attracting larger audiences and wider attention. All this is mutually enhancing and provides students and professional artists alike with a sustained range of activities for professional improvement. For the college, this means that its students tap into and are an active part of the city's wider arts community. With Liverpool a short-listed finalist in the current competition to become European Capital of Culture in 2008, this clearly has great potential that should be developed and celebrated constantly. Again, other HEIs will be emulating some of this, but few will have a dedicated new inner-city campus to facilitate it with quite the same intensity. In turn, these links can lend enrichment to the many local schools belonging to the network that the college maintains as a major local and national provider of initial teacher education and training. The growing collaboration with the Philharmonic Orchestra in its educational programmes and activities is just one example of this. When professional musicians visit schools in the company of teacher educators and trainee teachers, who knows how much more all of these partners can achieve with their pupils than when they visit separately?

There are other vital aspects of Hope's vision for this venture. One is its situation at the heart of a community that has virtually open access to the campus. This is the very opposite of the way many HEIs have come to locate themselves. For all their original pioneering civic spirit and innovation in the nineteenth century, the so-called 'redbrick' universities mostly now exist on campuses that are seemingly impenetrable to the casual passer-by. They are massive and can be impersonal, and often have few real working relationships with those on their doorsteps. There are, of course, exceptions to this, but the general picture will be familiar to anyone living in their physical shadow. The Hope at Everton campus is a deliberate attempt to redress this tendency.

Another key feature of the work of Hope at Everton is its involvement with primary and secondary schools. The campus is designed to allow pupils ready access throughout the day. It is never more alive than when this happens. It creates an obvious and exciting educational chemistry that breaks down so many of the traditional barriers between the several educational stages. As is well known, the British government is currently committed to narrowing the FE/HE divide. It sees this as the principal means whereby it will achieve its stated intention of getting 50 per cent of 18–30-year-olds into higher education by the year 2010. While the ultimate desirability of this is open to debate, it remains the policy. The erosion of this particular barrier, however, is only a minor part of the problem in an area like West Everton. The reason for this is quite simply that hardly any young people from this locality go into further education in the first place. The anti-educational culture here really is that strong, in spite of persistent heroic efforts by the schools to change it. It is, perhaps, almost impossible for those who have never encountered this to comprehend it. Educators simply have to accept this, if they are even to begin to understand it.

The complex attitudes buttressing this mind-set are deeply ingrained. The first thing we have to do is to understand why this is the case. It is, perhaps, an understandable defence mechanism for communities that have been denied opportunities for so long. The stronger the sense of community, the more entrenched the attitude can be. Strong communities hang on to their own, including their young. While this produces admirable family life, even if in many modern alternative forms, it can also have a stifling effect. Around here can often be heard the remark, 'We don't go over there'. For historical reasons, some of which have to do with thankfully long-gone sectarian divisions, such communities have a natural respect for territorial boundaries. Individuals are imbued with ingrained attitudes which remain in local folk memory long after the original reasons for them have ceased to exist. Such territorial isolation is the more insidious because so many people are unconscious of it. They will willingly go away for reasons such as work and holidays, but at home the territorial boundaries remain. Anti-educational attitudes are an integral part of all this and, no doubt, of so much more were we able to analyse it fully. People therefore find other ways to succeed in life. Unfortunately, many of these alternative avenues now lead into the drug and prostitution underworld. It is sad that civilised society persists in its failure to decriminalise such activities, thereby colluding in making them so lucrative for criminal exploitation.[1] Perhaps one way to make some inroads into all this is to create a higher education facility in the heart of such a community. This, after all, is why community colleges are so successful at what they do. The difference here is that higher education is also part of the wider local, national and international networks which are ever the more essential as an individual's education advances. With all this in mind, it might just be possible to create and sustain learning experiences which become such a natural part of everyday life that people can take them almost, as it were, for granted, to their immense benefit.

One might not even be aware at the time that these are learning experiences at all, or of the lasting effect for the good that they might be having.

This last point is central to the educational philosophy of Hope at Everton, and this book has touched upon it throughout. The essence of education is never more powerful than when it is elusive. Its providers busy themselves with preparing and delivering courses, with maintaining all the complex arrangements that this demands, and with building into this all the devices required by endless inspections, audits and the like. This all consumes so much effort and professional dedication that it is little wonder that we are seduced into thinking that all this is the stuff of education itself. It is assuredly not. It is but a part of the necessary prolegomenon to education, if we reserve the word 'education', as we should, to refer to a personal and socially transforming power. Education is nothing unless it is a life-transforming experience. Of course, we do not have to be conscious of this on a Tuesday morning or when-ever, and if we were, life would be so unbearable as to frustrate the educational enterprise anyway. That transforming experience has to be something we acquire in an accumulation of different ways. Some of these, as we have men-tioned, will be obvious. We *do* courses, we *get* qualifications, and so on. We also get things that we are less aware of, and these are precious. These are things like a kindness, a personal word of understanding in a difficulty, a surprise moment of insight, enjoyment or appreciation. It is not possible to programme the delivery of these things as such. Attempts to do so invariably kill them. All that educators can do is to create an ambience which allows them to happen. They are the stuff of the sublime serendipity mentioned earlier. The sound of a clarinet as we walk along a corridor, or the glimpse of a picture or performance as we have coffee, can give us just the lift in spirit which is as close as we might ever get to understanding what it means to become educated. The much laboured word 'ethos' is often used to encompass something of all this in educational philosophy, and it is difficult not to resort to it here. Perhaps the word 'awareness' is better. An awareness, that is, which is shared sensitively by all who engage in educational activity. Practically, this means that all we have to do on the proverbial Tuesday morning, when the campus is alive with all manner of educational undertakings, is to be aware that just one of the primary-age pupils coming into the building might be changed for the lifelong better by some passing and barely noticed experience.

Those of us who work in church colleges and schools should be particularly sensitive to all these things. They are what is required of us if we believe that all human beings are created in the image of God and are, therefore, capable of revealing the love and grace of God in their lives. These things are of the tangible ephemera that make up an educational experience. They are not, as we began the book by noting, the exclusive possession of Christians or anyone else. They are what all human beings become aware of when they seek to educate one another. Christians do this as part of their life of worship and prayer. This is how, for them, it is sustained and never forgotten, as it can so easily be in the face of life's other pressures. It is nothing less than golden. If about £20m of investment in inner-urban educational regeneration can go on actualising that, year-in, year-out, in even modest measure at the heart of a community, then not a penny of it will have ever been wasted.

NOTES

1 See my *The Ethics of Uncertainty*, Oxford, Oneworld, 2000, Chapter 6.

CHAPTER 14

Impressions of Hope

SIMON LEE

EACH picture of a cathedral painted by Monet, or by anyone else, tells us something about the cathedral, something about the artist, something about the particular vantage point and something about the light at that time. Monet's studies of the cathedral at Rouen capture the view at different times of the day. He explained that he was trying not to paint the cathedral so much as to capture the atmosphere, the *enveloppe*, through which we see the cathedral. In my inaugural lecture as Professor of Jurisprudence at Queen's University Belfast, I developed this imagery to say that we understand the cathedral (whether of law or of Northern Ireland) all the more if we have many studies from different perspectives, not just from the one angle and the one person of Monet's Rouen series. This applies also to our understanding of other phenomena, including higher education. Painting from the outside, however, can never capture the point of a cathedral or of a community such as Liverpool Hope University College. It helps to go inside, to explore the cathedral of Hope also from a variety of internal perspectives. Even then, the cathedral will remain a mystery, despite the most meticulous examination, if its purposes are not understood. A full appreciation benefits from a mixed exhibition containing the impressions of both outsiders and insiders.

In my time at Hope, we have been under such constant and intense scrutiny from the serried ranks of quangos that much is known about our performance, as judged from the viewpoints of externals. In my first year, 1995–96, our overall quality was being audited by the Higher Education Quality Council, and the Research Assessment Exercise was upon us. In the 1996–97 academic year, the University of Liverpool ran its re-accreditation exercise. The late 1990s saw subject reviews across the arts and sciences matched by Ofsted inspections of our teacher training partnerships. Then it became possible to apply for taught degree-awarding powers in the 1999–2000 academic year, following which we were assessed in 2000–01, while further subject reviews, Ofsted inspections and another Research Assessment Exercise were conducted, before receiving the powers in 2002; whereupon the cycle begins again with a

University of Liverpool re-re-accreditation process in my penultimate month, June 2003. Along the way, the HEFCE audit service twice reviewed us, we received Investors in People recognition after a thorough investigation and HEFCE checked further before giving us major estate grants. Less formal scrutiny has included the attentions of the local and national media, sister or rival institutions who turn up at open days to see what we are doing, league tables, stories about comparative percentage increases in applications or the pay of the chief executive, objections to applications for planning permission, defences at industrial tribunals and attacks in court cases. More formal scrutiny has come from governors, trustees, churches, external examiners, bankers and auditors. Irate scrutiny comes from the occasional student who fails or the occasional neighbour who rails against the students. The mother of all scrutineers is often the mother of a prospective student who has an impressive grasp of all the above information but still wants to know what it is really like.

If this sounds like a litany of over-inspection, then the truth is that it is easier to lead and manage an institution when it is under such constant, rigorous scrutiny. External inspection and assessment build team spirit beyond compare. Students and governors, as well as staff, rise to the occasion on such visits. Now, of course, inspectors are sharp enough to realise this is happening and will doubtless discount for it, but the development of team spirit through inspection is still a powerful factor. If Monet were encamped outside your cathedral, you would probably spruce it up a little and, though he was painting rather than video-recording, you would probably make sure that the atmosphere included your best cathedral music.

As the editor has explained, this collection of essays from a few of those *inside* the cathedral of Hope can only be another series of views, necessarily incomplete. Other series will no doubt emerge in years to come. If a pewful of middle-aged male theological researchers has only a partial understanding of what Hope is like, that will be complemented in due course by a procession of younger, female researchers, stretching round the cathedral as at graduations. If senior managers predominate in one series, then another will eventually explain what it is like to be one of a team of more than 200 teachers at Hope, or more than 500 staff committed in student support services.

Any future volumes are likely to follow the example of the editor and the Chair of the Governing Council in prioritising student voices. My generation's impressions of higher education may be influenced a little by campus comedies, such as the TV series *A Very Peculiar Practice*, in which a gloomy university estate was depicted without students. The only movement seemed to come from litter being blown in the wind (whereas we are keen, at Hope, to control litter and to present our students with beautiful learning environments) and from nuns in full habits scuttling across the campus. A familiar sight in Hope is a Sister of Notre Dame, Sr Eileen Kelleher SND, Chair of the Governing Council. She carries the charism of her order's foundress, St Julie Billiart, not in a habit of cloth but in a lifetime's habit of commitment to inclusive and rounded education. In her contribution to this collection, she gives some inkling of what a more balanced series of portraits would tell us about Hope, as she quotes the students and staff, female and male, old and young, whom she meets through her daily involvement in life at Hope.

In the same spirit, I would like to frame my impressions around the perspective of one student who wrote to me after her graduation in the summer of 2002:

> This is just a little note to say thank you for my time at Hope. I got a D and an E for my A levels and graduated with a First. I just wanted to let you know that I have thoroughly enjoyed my three years at Hope. I have made wonderful friends and have loved learning about new subjects... Thank you for always smiling and saying hello when walking around campus. Finally, thank you for an amazing Graduation. I think it was probably the most enjoyable day of my life. The best bit was leaving the cathedral and being applauded by all the Hope staff. I felt so proud. Thank you.

This letter is so delightfully modest and grateful that I am protecting the author's identity. Of course, the head of an institution receives occasional letters complaining about this or that, such as from neighbours wishing students would not park (lawfully) outside their house. The praise as well as the criticism must be taken on behalf of the institution and one of the joys of being a principal is to pass on such thanks to the colleagues or students who are primarily responsible for good practice. Indeed, a significant part of any senior role in higher education is to give proper, meaningful thanks and encouragement to fellow staff and students (just as I have been grateful for the encouragement given by governors, especially successive chairs). It is only meaningful if genuine, and if all know that constructive criticism will be honestly given instead where that is merited. Reports from across the country suggest that students are increasingly likely to complain in an era of tuition fees, but it is our experience at Hope that they are also quick to praise. In a few sentences, this letter-writer captures so much about Hope at its best that her generosity might be the only answer needed to any questions which remain in the minds of neutral or sceptical readers of earlier chapters of this book. The editor believes, however, that my successor and I might wish to have the last words ourselves. In my case, my brief is not even to attempt an overview. Much as I have enjoyed the development of Hope at Everton, for instance, there is no point in duplicating the excellent account in the preceding chapter. Instead, my task is to offer some glimpses of the cathedral which might not have been so easily seen from the perspectives of earlier writers. The vantage point which I would choose above all others is this privileged one of being the recipient of last resort of student thanks.

It is worth dwelling at the outset on the second sentence of the student's letter: 'I got a D and an E for my A levels and graduated with a First.' One of the reasons why Hope has been hitherto content with our students pursuing University of Liverpool degrees is that their worldwide reputation has acted as a guarantee of the quality of the achievement of this student and of all who have added value during their studies at Hope. Cynics are ready to doubt the standards of some newer degrees whereas the traditional university degree's proven quality enables this student with modest grades on entry to leave not only with a first class degree but with one of unimpeachable standing. The time may now be right for Hope to have the courage of our own reputation, initially in such fields as education or theology, and in the widening participation initiative of foundation degrees, to develop a mixed economy in which some students take Hope degrees. We would never, however, forget the importance of the partnership with the University of Liverpool as illustrated by the rein-forcement it gives to this student's story. It is possible to do badly at A level and improve all the way through a degree course. Such a profile is a tribute to the determination of the student, her potential and the encouragement which she has enjoyed at Hope. Indeed, the accomplishments of this particular student were recognised by the decision of another top-class higher education institution to offer her a postgraduate place. Almost all Hope's 7,000 students go on to such postgraduate study or straight into employment, putting us among the top few universities and colleges in the country for employability, even though our mission commits us to accepting students, including the letter-writer, who have not necessarily shone at A level.

We do not do this because the government now offers financial incentives to widen participation. We have done it for more than a century and a half, whatever obstacles have been put in our way by governments. They have now changed their approach, partly because Hope and others have shown the way. There are hundreds of thousands of students who can achieve better university degrees than their school records would indicate. Sometimes, it takes decades and patient work by further education colleges or Access courses before the student is ready to embark on higher education. In other cases, it only needs a short bridging opportunity to take a student who lacks confidence, or at least lacks grades, into constructive use of a place on a university degree course.

Hope students graduate not only with that quality 'kitemark' of a university degree certificate but with their whole experience of the Hope ethos. It is a privilege to play a part in creating the atmosphere, the *enveloppe*, the ethos, in which our students thrive. My role of wandering around our campuses, 'smil-ing and saying hello', has been simple enough, as is developing Graduation

Days which celebrate student achievement. Ensuring that all staff are there, and that almost all staff want to be there, helps students offer thanks, along the lines quoted, to the people who have made a difference. It is not only one of the most enjoyable days of many students' lives; Graduation Day can also be the most rewarding occasion for staff, for students' families and all others who come together to applaud graduands.

Our rhythm is to hold three Graduation Days in the second week of July, with about 400 graduands attending on each day, together with three guests each. Graduands wear their gowns all day. Over 100 staff process each day and a further 100 are working in the cathedral. Hundreds more are working at our campuses. The catering team prepares breakfast, lunch and dinner for those staying at Hope Park (since we have had 'widening participation' summer schools in residence during graduations) while simultaneously putting on a special graduation lunch for 500, originally in a marquee on the lawns but more recently in the new sports centre, suitably adapted for the week, and then a champagne and strawberry tea in the Great Hall of the Cornerstone, Hope at Everton. Apart from the informal opportunities to meet fellow graduands and one another's guests, everyone has the chance to attend an ecumenical mid-morning chapel service followed by the presentation of prizes and then a group photograph and opportunity to meet staff. Within the graduation ceremony, which alternates in a two-year cycle between the Anglican and Roman Catholic cathedrals in Liverpool, the Vice-Chancellor of the University of Liverpool and I address the graduands. When staff process out of the cathedral, they form a guard of honour and applaud the graduates as they emerge. It is not only the letter-writer who finds this to be a moving finale to a student experience.

It only works, however, because it is true to the spirit of Hope through the years of a student's time with us. It is well organised and carried off on the days themselves with goodwill as well as minute attention to detail. For example, for weeks beforehand and on the mornings of each Graduation Day, provosts and other senior colleagues will work with the estates and domestic services teams to ensure personally that the campuses are in perfect condition. The marketing team have worked through the night to make certain that the arrangements in the cathedrals, including the preparations for the video-coverage, are perfect. We hold debriefing sessions every day and try to improve each day each year. Great sporting teams concentrate to the very end of the game which is why they can so often win in extra time. In higher education, similarly, we should be committed right through to the last minutes of students' experiences, including the moments when they graduate and when they return their gowns. Hope has this approach because we understand the significance of the day as a whole and especially of those few seconds for each graduand when their name is read out and they walk across to shake hands and collect their certificate.

Students and their families repeatedly volunteer the opinion of the letter-writer, that these are among the happiest and proudest moments of their lives. The words of another graduand last year, 'I will remember this day always', are an encouragement to all who work to make graduation a fitting celebration of a well-rounded education.

On high days and feast days, then, and especially at graduations, anyone who is inside the cathedral will be able to understand what is special about this ecumenical university college called Hope. The grace of the letter-writer's repeated thanks reflects so well on her that it will enlighten any picture of a rounded student experience. Yet interested observers who have not shared Graduation Days with us, especially those working elsewhere in higher education or the churches, or our home city or wider region, and particularly assessors scrutinising us, repeatedly ask the same questions, which could be grouped into the following lines of inquiry.

- Why the name Hope?
- Is it all marketing, or is Hope really distinctive? (the brand of Hope)
- What is the point of physical changes of estates? (the place of Hope)
- How has it been achieved? (the people of Hope)
- What would happen if you were run over by a bus? (the sustainability of Hope)

The answer I have always given to the last of those questions is that after the colleague driving the bus had reversed and those on the bus had cheered, life would go on for the rest of the Hope community much as before. This was indeed the first question on the last day of our scrutiny for degree-awarding powers. A more precise answer can now be given, in that Professor Gerald Pillay will take over the privilege of leading Hope. The other questions are more serious. In what follows, I will offer my impressions in answer to them, trying to complement the insights offered by my colleagues in the preceding chapters in order to present my successor with a wider range of sketches of this work in progress.

WHY HOPE?

When I was interviewed in 1994 for this post, staff, students and governors established two priorities – that a new name needed to be agreed for the federation of S. Katharine's College and Christ's and Notre Dame College, and that the profile of the institution needed to be raised. The latter would be difficult, of course, without the former. On my first day, in a talk to all colleagues, I proposed Hope as expressing the mission and values of this ecumenical university college based in Liverpool and we put up rough and unready signs which called the estate Hope Park, partly to establish that the whole campus was to be integrated and partly to put the word Hope in the public arena. The Governing Council agreed to the name at its first meeting in my period of office, on 31 October 1995. The academic board and the students' union had already supported the choice of Hope, no doubt with some private misgivings in some quarters. So, why was Hope chosen and why had the question of the name not been resolved sooner?

The two cathedrals in Liverpool, representing the Church of England and the Roman Catholic church, are joined by Hope Street. The Sisters of Notre Dame began one of our founding colleges in 1856 at Mount Pleasant, on the corner of that same Hope Street. Hope, properly understood, is the essence of widening access to higher education and of working towards ecumenism. Liverpool FC supporters, and increasingly the wider city of Liverpool, have appropriated the song from *Carousel* that encourages us to 'Walk on, with hope in your heart', and the then chairs of the Governing Council, the late Archbishop Derek Worlock and Bishop David (now Lord) Sheppard, had adapted it in the title of their latest book at the time of my appointment. I knew that Hope College in Michigan was a church foundation for whom the name had worked. In family discussions, our son Jamie observed that Hope has the rare advantage among university or college names of being both a noun and a verb.

Some colleagues were sceptical, expecting local humour to fasten on to 'no hope', 'hopeless' or simply the weak sense of hope, as when people say 'I hope (meaning I wish) I win the lottery'. My argument was that we had to project the stronger, deeper meaning of hope, whereby we believe in a better world and then do something to make it happen. Moreover, it would be a challenge to live up to such a title in all that we do. We stopped using 'hope' in weak senses (for example minutes do not say 'X hoped that Y would ...') leaving space for the strong form. I personally do not use abbreviations or acronyms for such aspects of Hope life as our electronic newspaper, *Hope Virtually Daily*. This helps to keep building up awareness of our name and the mission it represents. I reject the notion that principals should not be bothered with the minutiae of college life. On the contrary, it is in such details as minutes and litter-collection that the overall vision of the institution is expressed.

Perhaps the little detail of the name had eluded the federation for twenty years because those inside the cathedral were preoccupied with rearranging the church furniture; perhaps at some level those who came from one or other of the founding colleges would have liked 'their' name to prevail or at least did not want one of the others to be perpetuated in preference to theirs. I prefer to put it more positively, that the timing was not right for my predecessor or previous chairs of the Governing Council to take that decision. By 1995, however, the need was pressing for a clear identity to be built around a new name.

Learning from the peace process in Northern Ireland, which had also convinced me that there was always hope, it seemed important to have a deadline, the first meeting of the Governing Council, and a proposal. I emphasised to colleagues that it was not a referendum or a beauty parade in which they could make an irrational or personal choice. The names S. Katharine's, Notre Dame or Christ's were ruled out of contention. The arguments for Hope were put and better arguments for a better alternative would be needed if the choice were to be anything but Hope. Simply not liking the name would not be enough: negative moaning about the world or the options within it is never helpful to the development of a community. 'Hope' set the tone and style, in the spirit of our mission.

In fact, the mission statement had been agreed not long before I came and the Chair of the Governing Council at the time, Bishop David Sheppard, was understandably insistent that it could not be reopened. Asked if we could instead offer a summary of it, the Chair agreed. I suggested summaries in not more than five words, ten words, and so on: educating the whole person; educating the whole person in mind, body and spirit, and so forth. A later chair agreed that we could expand the summary to form the current full version of the statement, a necessary two-step to achieve an appropriate contemporary expression of the traditional values and purposes of Hope's founding colleges.

The mission statement alone is not the whole story. Later in the 1990s, we explored what this mission meant in terms of the values of Hope. In my last year at Hope it has been a particular delight to enjoy a series of six inaugural lectures by new professors. At the end of one of these, the lecture by Professor Anne Campbell, one of her referees, Professor Anne Edwards, a distinguished professor from the University of Birmingham, gave a most gracious vote of thanks in which she chose to talk about how she had read these values on our website and had now experienced them personally, values such as being 'welcoming, … intellectually stretching, … full of Hope'.

The values include the declaration of intent that we will be 'challenging'. On Graduation Days, we video students talking to camera about their experiences of Hope. No one has ever said it had been easy. Very many graduands offer variations on the view that 'the work has been hard but worth it'. The staff and governors interpret this commitment to being challenging as applying not only in our work with students but also in standing up for disadvantaged communities in Liverpool and beyond. If necessary, we are also prepared to stand up for Hope and other church colleges by challenging quangos or the government. Part of higher education's role in a democracy is to challenge governments, often through the academic freedom of individual lecturers but sometimes through institutions. David Blunkett, Secretary of State for Education in the 1997–2001 Labour government, appointed me to two roles, as a member of the Standards Tasks Force nationally and as the chair of the

Independent Monitoring Board for the Liverpool Education Authority locally. These were privileges that I greatly valued, but I did not hesitate to tell him and others that there was a glaring inconsistency at the centre of the government's educational policies. They were busy at secondary level encouraging diversity, with incentives for schools to become specialist colleges, yet their actions at the tertiary level were favouring a dull conformity. Not only were they sponsoring mission drift through financial inducements for old universities to become interested in widening access and for newer universities to chase research funding, but their reversal of the historic understanding of university colleges was a threat to church colleges and the diversity of the sector.

The government's approach was also unfair. Whereas historically a university college was one that awarded degrees from another institution, they were now going to make the test the exact opposite, that you had to have taught degree-awarding powers in order to retain or acquire a university college title, and this about-turn was being effected while there was no opportunity to apply for these powers. A slow review of the criteria and process, to make both much more stringent, was the excuse. Hope made the point that we would pass any test, we just wanted to have the opportunity to prove our worth. Since we had been happy with our partnership with the University of Liverpool for a hundred years, we had had no reason to do this hitherto by seeking our own powers. Our governors and Tony Grayson, Secretary and Clerk to the Governors (and now also Registrar), showed great courage and determination in standing up alone to government as Hope argued this through the courts. This gave us two years of grace and, along the way, forced the government's hand in unfreezing the process. After the Court of Appeal had refused leave to the House of Lords, at the point when we would have had to take our case to the European Court of Human Rights, we were almost at the end of the scrutiny process for the powers. Hope was the first institution in the country to secure the powers under this new, severe test of quality, just ahead of Imperial College London, which also had a good reason for not having sought the powers previously, as it had been comfortable within the federation of the University of London. Our challenge to government was all of a piece with our challenges to quangos and our interventions on behalf of communities around Liverpool whose projects were running into difficulties. For example, Hope acted as the accountable body for community endeavours in Granby and Toxteth. The spirit of improving opportunities for students and communities is the essence of Hope. Sometimes that requires challenging the authorities. If others challenge similarly, circumstances can be changed. For instance, the Labour government's second term, beginning in 2001, has seen an acceptance of the need to reverse their first-term policy and now foster diversity in higher education. Hope played a part in that welcome U-turn.

As students, staff and the wider community began to see a university college called Hope live out its values through such challenges and, by direct action in urban regeneration, challenge the conditions of Everton, so they began to absorb the deeper, stronger meaning of hope and of Hope. Impressions of the cathedral of Hope became more rounded. Visitors saw what Hope meant by increasingly open-access campuses as the walls came down from Childwall to Everton. The views of insiders and outsiders changed. By that, I mean that what they could see changed, and therefore what they understood by the concept of Hope also changed. That in turn led more and more people in our home city to talk about Hope. In a small way, such changes can affect the mood of a community. Watching Hope turn dreams into reality, transforming an area of under-privilege at Everton into a thriving campus, influences the community's understanding of hope, of how we do not need to accept second best environments or restricted opportunities but can make a difference.

THE BRAND OF HOPE

On our last day of scrutiny for degree-awarding powers, the Quality Assurance Agency panel asked whether our 'Hope Springs' bottled water illustrated that our marketing was just too slick. There was vigorous support for the brand-building qualities of our water. More generally, cynics suspect that many successes in higher education are an illusion, generated by marketing, and that all higher education is much the same, a tepid water. These two impressions from sceptical vantage points do not, in my judgement, offer clear views of the cathedral.

Our Queen's Anniversary Prize for the work of the Hope One World charity gives a different, I would say more revealing, glimpse of the foundation of Hope. Students and staff each summer go to places such as Ladakh in northern India where they help Tibetan refugee communities by teaching and presenting inservice courses for teachers. Until invited to apply for a Queen's Anniversary Prize, we did not once seek to make any capital out of this or 'market' it in any way, even though it was highly successful. Of course, when we won publicity followed. The venture was as successful the year before the publicity came and it was a success thanks to the goodness of those involved, not courtesy of marketing. Similarly, there are many domestic, student-led activities which are distinctive to an ecumenical church university college and are not simply what anyone would expect from any higher education institution. On the evening of St Patrick's Day, to take just one recent example, students from Catholic and Protestant backgrounds celebrated the feast together, distinctively, across the Irish Sea in ways, including religious services, which would be inconceivable in most other universities.

Every detail of the learning environment and every human interaction matters because what influences us the most at university is often what we are least aware of at the time it happens, a point I make repeatedly from open and interview days through to graduations and beyond. It may be a chance encounter with another student which leads to a lifelong friendship or a working relationship, a trip round the world or a marriage. It may be an insight in a book, lecture or seminar which encourages a lifelong interest in a topic. It may be that a sporting, theatrical or musical experience leads to a career or a leisure interest. It may be that the aesthetics of a campus influence the design of an institution students help to develop in their subsequent careers.

One of my formative influences as a student in Oxford was a series of well-attended evening lectures by a visitor, the great ecumenist Cardinal Suenens. This may be why I appreciate so much the way in which the Archbishop of Canterbury, the Archbishop of Liverpool, the Bishops of Liverpool, Rochester and Oxford and many other visitors have taken time to speak here at Hope in this academic year. For I had the privilege of hearing Cardinal Suenens say in the magnificent setting of the Sheldonian a version of the phrase which we have displayed on scaffolding above Liverpool during the building of Hope at Everton – 'to hope is not to dream but to turn dreams into reality'. This is the strong, theological meaning of the word 'hope'. Of all the phrases which we have used to explain hope and Hope, this is the one which most appeals to the widest range of friends of Hope. Attending a packed lecture with a guest star is what our statement of values would call a collegial, stimulating, intellectually stretching experience. A quarter of a century later, I have just listened to another passionate speaker, this time at Hope, the Revd Professor Duncan Forrester, again in the company of students. It is easy not to turn up for any lecture in the evenings and, sadly, too often nowadays it is impossible for students who have other commitments, but I would have missed a moving experience in either case. I only became aware of the impact of the Suenens lecture on me in the 1990s, first in Northern Ireland and then on coming to Liverpool. So the work of the Oxford chaplains in organising the lectures continues to have a knock-on effect, most recently through the brand and example of Hope. For example, the head teacher of a secular school in another regeneration area explained at the launch of a Sure Start partnership that the spirit of that quotation, allied to the witness of urban renewal at Everton, had inspired her to begin transforming the start in life for her pupils' younger siblings.

To give another personal example, when I was a postgraduate student at Yale Law School, I read a book by the theologian Henri Nouwen, *Clowning in Rome*. Twenty years later, I have adapted this to 'clowning in Liverpool' and used it in one of my graduation addresses in July 2002 when Hope had a record number of PhD students graduating, one of whom, Michael Ford (another contributor to this volume) had been researching Nouwen's life. Why did I read the book? Nouwen had been a professor at the Yale Divinity School. Other students were talking about him. When we decorate our new World of Difference lecture theatre complex at Hope Park with the covers of books written by our lecturers and former students, part of the message of Hope is about the scholarship of our community and part is an encouragement to read your institution's teachers. Nouwen had a different, hope-ful perspective on life:

> This large, busy, entertaining and distracting city keeps tempting us to join the lion tamers and trapeze artists who get most of the attention. But whenever the clowns appear we are reminded that what really counts is something other than the spectacular and the sensational. It is what happens between the scenes... Clowns are not the centre of events. They appear between the great acts, fumble and fall and make us smile again after the tensions created by the heroes we came to admire. The clowns don't have it together, they do not succeed in what they try, but they are on our side...

This is a more inspirational way of making the point that every little smile around campus makes a difference. For Hope, marketing is not primarily about selling the institution to the outside world but is a way of deepening students' participation in their own rounded development. Several people who have worked in our small marketing team during my eight years have been former students, for Hope regards marketing as 'celebrating the student experience'. If we draw the attention of students and staff to all the clownish activity going on around our campuses and in our community work, using the intranet version of *Hope Virtually Daily* and the internet on-line magazine, *Hope Direct*, students will find that 'what really counts is something other than the spectacular and the sensational'. Modern media can play a part in developing a new form of collegiality. With 7,000 students, many of whom are in part-time employment and 1,000 of whom study in Blackburn and Bury, not everyone can come to every distinctive event. Our experience is, however, that they appreciate knowing about it in real time.

On that final day of QAA scrutiny for taught degree-awarding powers, there were two other unsolicited testimonies to the spirit of Hope which are relevant to this context. We had had unstinting support from the then Vice-Chancellor of the University of Liverpool, Professor Philip Love, successive Pro-Vice-Chancellors and their Dean of College Studies, Dr Jimmy Chubb. I am told that, in a session at which I was not present, Professor Love spoke of the respect in which Hope's distinctive mission but university quality was held throughout Liverpool. It is part of the civic glory of the 'redbrick' universities that they discharge their role of nurturing, partnering and then liberating other institutions with such grace. Clare Dove, Principal of Blackburne House, which does such wonderful work in opening up access to lifelong learning for women, also gave a moving tribute to the reputation of Hope in disadvantaged communities across our home city. It is not the public image projected by marketing, but rather views such as these, usually privately held, that shape a full understanding of the cathedral of Hope. One of the benefits of such processes as seeking degree-awarding powers or Investors in People recognition is that they give opportunities for governors, friends and a wide range of insiders and outsiders to offer their impressions more openly. In almost all cases, what emerge are stories about individual students, which is why our internal and external marketing has such a fund of stories to relate. This is how higher education should be – focused on celebrating student experiences.

John Henry Newman made the point just after Hope's first founding college had begun in the mid-nineteenth century when he said, in his lectures on *The Idea of a University*, that a 'university is an Alma Mater, knowing her children one by one – not a foundry, or a mint, or a treadmill'. A university college, on our approach, has university standards of academic excellence but also everyday interactions on the scale of a small Northern Irish town or village with a main street where you will know who everyone is, a village in a city, for our campuses are only a few minutes away from the centre of one of the most famous cities in the world. It is not a parochial community for, helped by easyJet, 500 students come from across the Irish Sea and, helped by all manner of airlines, another 500 come from further round the world. They all interact with one another and with local-born students. Some of those students, for instance from Sri Lanka, joined the recent Catholic and Protestant celebrations of St Patrick's Day. It must be an education to live and study and be known in such a community. This is the brand of Hope. It is not a marketing invention. Rather, its substance is increasingly well captured by marketing. Its essence comes from constant good communication and interaction. I talk to my senior colleagues, including the editor of this book, every day including at the beginning and end of every day. I walk around campuses every day. I begin every day at our collective ecumenical Morning Prayer. I observe in the middle of every week our Foundation Hour. I eat every lunch-time in the refectory with guests, colleagues and students. So I absorb the light from the mission of the college on a daily basis and try to reflect it in my smiles and greetings to students and staff. The Chair of the Governing Council is a model of the same approach. That is easy to market. It is pure Newman, whose idea of a university was so heavily influenced by his idea of a college community. It is also pure Hope, one of whose founding colleges, S. Katharine's, chose as its motto the psalmist's refrain, 'In thy light'.

Yet still outsiders will question whether that is any different from any other higher education institution. Is the ecumenical Christian mission distinctive?

There is much confusion behind such a question. Some of the misunderstandings are due to not grasping what Christianity is about, some are to do with mistaking what a mission is and some rest on a misapplication of distinctiveness. For example, not only church colleges but also specialist institutions, such as those focusing on the creative and performing arts, have the advantage of a clear mission and distinctive niches in British higher education.

With this comes the perennial challenge of deciding whether to embrace other activity which more generalist universities undertake. A senior Marks & Spencer executive, a fellow participant in a management training session, convinced me in 1995 that sometimes institutions have to move beyond their distinctive positions in order to survive and compete. His example was the struggle to convince the Marks & Spencer board to stock tinned tomatoes to deter customers from going to Sainsbury's. Both stores had all the other ingredients for cooking pasta and sauce. If Marks & Spencer had insisted on no tinned foods, given their expensive niche-marketing of themselves as providing fresh and high-quality food, they would have lost customers to their rivals. As a church college which originally trained teachers only, some of the modern subjects might seem far removed from the core mission of Hope, but business studies, for instance, was introduced only in the late 1990s yet received the highest possible grading in our last subject review by the Quality Assurance Agency in 2001. Mission distinctiveness must never be an excuse for anything less than the highest quality that we can offer our students. University college life is more rounded than simply being about securing a degree certificate, however, and so the narrative of developing our mission in the spirit of our founders to open up access to a well-rounded education of the whole person in mind, body and spirit does have meaning. It is distinctive, which is not at all to say that there are not others acting in good faith to provide higher education in the spirit of their missions. It is articulated daily in the life of Hope. The complex interactions of broadening horizons are not all about what overseas students bring to Hope, valued though they are, and are not all about publicity. To give but one example from the week in which I am writing this essay, our influences from across the Irish Sea do not affect only Irish students in Liverpool but also a local student from the North West, a British Muslim woman, who has been participating in a Hope module playing Gaelic football in Germany. This opportunity would never have happened but for the crisscrossing of influences in the cause of Hope's commitment to diversity, widening participation and opening up opportunities. Hope works as a brand not because of some clever marketing but because Hope works as an ecumenical university college in its own right. Hope, branding and mission all have their place in contemporary higher education.

WHAT IS THE PLACE OF HOPE?

Where exactly is that place? Are we confined to Liverpool? Does it matter how the place looks? Should a church university college glory in poverty or is it Christian to invest in beautiful campuses? The Anglican founding college of Hope began in 1844 in Warrington, chosen partly because it was in the middle of the North West. After a fire, much of the 1920s was spent in exile in London before the current location in Childwall was ready. Soon, the college was evacuated to the Lake District while the Liverpool buildings were used as a military hospital. Then there were campuses around the North West during the postwar boom in teacher training. So we delight in our Liverpool home, and we are exceptionally honoured by the Freedom of the City of Liverpool bestowed on us, together with the University of Liverpool and Liverpool John Moores University in the 1996–97 academic year, but we are at ease in the wider region and the future of Hope under Professor Pillay's leadership will almost certainly see further developments with our partner colleges in Blackburn, Bury and Wigan.

It is not just a question of where Hope is to be found but also a question of how we can express the mission of Hope in our various settings. A feature of the last decade at Hope has been the transformation of our learning environments. The main campus, Hope Park, has a good claim to be one of the most improved in the country. As the previous chapter chronicles, we have also created an award-winning campus which is pioneering urban regeneration, Hope at Everton, thanks particularly to huge support from HEFCE's Poor Estates funding. We have state-of-the-art accommodation at a third location in Liverpool, our Aigburth halls of residence. Our Welsh activity centre, Plas Caerdeon near Barmouth, has been reinvented in dramatic fashion. There is now a Hope Zone at St Mary's, Blackburn and the next is expected at Holy Cross, Bury. There is much which could be said about any of these. The pathway through Hope Park, in particular, is a simple, practical way of developing that vital *enveloppe* of a community, a village in the city. This is where I 'walk around the campus'. Yet if I have to choose one estate development to illustrate my impressions of Hope it would be one which has come and gone yet which lives on in the memories of all who enjoyed it.

The tag about Sir Christopher Wren (looking around to see an architect's monument) is not the whole story in the context of higher education. For sometimes in university life and probably also in architecture, it is the case that important memories are not reflected in what is still around to be seen. It may be a location but it could be a course which is no longer running but which was vital and vibrant in its time, or the example of a lecturer who has moved on to promotion elsewhere, or one of the many guest lectures which touches a particular individual but of which there is no other lasting record. The conversation between lecturer and student can be life-changing even if there is no plaque to record it. Hope on the Waterfront was a concept whose time came and went but which has had a lasting influence. Before we could create Hope at Everton, it was important to establish a temporary presence in the centre of the city of Liverpool. We therefore took over the 'Richard and Judy' studio from Granada TV to secure the prime location in the Albert Dock. The dock dates from the middle of the nineteenth century, as do Hope's founding colleges, yet was flourishing in the 1990s after a contemporary renewal (a project inspired by Michael Heseltine in the wake of the Toxteth riots of the early 1980s). As far as I am aware, Hope was the first to use the now commonplace expression in Liverpool of 'waterfront' to describe the Mersey river frontage which is now being considered as a world heritage site. In the spring of 1997, we created an attractive and vibrant internet café, ahead of its time, with a huge video-wall and aesthetic grace at every turn, from the wooden and original cobbled floors to the beautiful views of the water and the Liver Building from the full-length glass front. For four years, from 1997 to 2001, this was the setting for many moments of grace, especially as graduates each year rounded off their day of celebrations by re-viewing their passage across stage on the giant screen. From the beginning, Hope on the Waterfront was a partnership with the Churches' Anchorage and with Liverpool's experiment in educational collaboration, City of Learning.

Internally, it was also a partnership of various Hope teams, from catering to IT services, from marketing to estates, to finance and resources. Many members of staff from across the college community volunteered to help serve the public at weekends. Cleaners from Aigburth, for example, received training and then worked alongside senior managers from Hope Park. There was a proper pride in the institution being on display in a form which was accessible to the general public of Merseyside and to visitors from around the world. If you work as a cleaner in a hall of residence, it is difficult to show visitors your workplace, but Hope on the Waterfront gave a flavour of the institution to all-comers day after day, round the year.

Moreover, team-building and awareness of the institution's primary role were fostered by all manner of staff waiting at tables. They had to deal with questions from the public about our status as a university-in-waiting. The vagaries of government policy on university title needed to be known by everyone who was volunteering to be an ambassador of Hope. The line that we were worthy of university college and indeed university titles which we would demonstrate at the first opportunity has been borne out in practice. It takes some confidence to make the point, however, while serving customers who have a garbled (or even accurate) version of government changes from the media. The most common question was whether Hope offered a particular course which might interest the customer or a member of their family or circle of friends. So the domestic services team and others began to become more and more aware of the curriculum, some would say of its limited or dated nature. Again, this influenced in turn our belated efforts to revolutionise our portfolio of courses.

Our theologians were quick to embrace the opportunities which the Waterfront provided for bringing together interested parties from around the city and beyond. The Hope Theology Society lectures and seminars were regularly located there. The institutional churches followed suit, most notably introducing the accomplished media figure of the Rt Revd James Jones as the Bishop of Liverpool in the setting of Hope on the Waterfront.

At first, we constantly played two video-clips on the giant video-wall to illustrate the two elements of the title. The word 'Hope' was illustrated by the US Democrat Convention where Bill Clinton (born in Hope, Arkansas, and speaking before his disgrace) won the nomination for the Presidency, concluding his speech with the line that he still believed 'in a place called Hope'. Extracts from the film *On the Waterfront* explained something of our mission as a teacher training institution founded by the churches. One exchange had the leading woman explaining to the leading man that she was going to become a teacher at a college run by nuns. Even the tough young man accepts that this is a noble endeavour. The second exchange is the one where those involved in corruption on the dockside tell the priest to go back to his church but he says that he must be where they are and where Christ is – right there, on the waterfront. Having the courage to show what Hope on the Waterfront means in these graphic ways was itself a statement about our distinctive mission as a church university college and our relevance to Liverpool which had just granted us the honour of the Freedom of the City.

The most regular volunteer was one of my most senior and busiest colleagues, Sean Gallagher, Director of Finance and Resources. Despite living the farthest away from Liverpool's waterfront, in his home town of Bolton, Sean Gallagher regularly gave up his weekends to clean tables and serve customers in Hope on the Waterfront. Few universities or colleges have such senior members of staff who would show this commitment to teamwork, but it is part of the success of Hope that senior colleagues are so involved in the front line of customer care. It was not surprising, therefore, that Sean should be on duty when a Sri Lankan businessman was looking for something to do one Sunday in a windswept and largely closed Liverpool. He came into Hope on the Waterfront and struck up a conversation with Sean. He was so impressed that he sent his daughter across the world to study with us. She took an undergraduate degree, then a master's and is now pursuing her doctorate while working as a resident tutor. Meanwhile, her positive experiences of Hope have led to more than 20 other Sri Lankan students joining the Hope community.

In these and other ways, Hope's involvement in the Albert Dock through Hope on the Waterfront was true to the roots of both Hope and the dock, each of which began in the middle of the nineteenth century at the height of Liverpool's international reputation among seafarers for welcoming those borne here on waves of hope. I still believe in a place called Hope and I still believe in Hope on the Waterfront.

HOW HAVE CHANGES WITHIN HOPE BEEN ACHIEVED?

Hope is privileged to have the backing of many external people, among them local civic leaders who support the college in numerous ways. The leader of the city council, Mike Storey CBE, is an alumnus and former governor. His colleague Councillor Lady Doreen Jones has taken a proper interest on behalf of neighbours in the planning issues surrounding Hope Park. Our newest governor is Councillor John Coyne who promises to do much the same for Aigburth. The MP for the constituency which includes Hope Park, Jane Kennedy, is often to be seen at events, despite the burdens of ministerial office. The MP for the constituency which encompasses Hope at Everton, Louise Ellman, has been an invaluable champion of that project from the beginning.

Internally, we have not relied on too many newcomers to change the culture, but instead have spent millions of pounds investing in our estates. We have spent to the absolute limit of what we can afford, we have benefited from HEFCE and other grants and we have borrowed. It is not right that we should hoard surpluses and only spend money provided by one generation on the learning environment of the next. Instead, we try to balance the funding of developments, partly from the current income, partly from that saved in the past, partly by mortgaging within limits the income we expect in the future. This seems equitable. It is also necessary given a highly competitive market and a welcome emphasis on facilities.

Of course, traditional accounting can seem to work against this. In my eight years we have doubled our turnover yet tripled the depreciation charge for the very reason that we have invested so much in our estates. As the estates become more valuable, the accounts can look worse because provision has to be made for maintaining (and preferably enhancing) those higher standards. This is part of the answer to the perennial question of why there is not more money to spend on more lecturers when we can afford to invest in the campuses. Another part of the answer is that higher education probably employed too many staff in too inflexible a way whereas the institutions which will flourish are those that can adapt to a world in which IT for instance has altered the balance and distribution of employment and capital investment which students need. Moreover, we live in an age in which the increasing focus on customers by successful commercial enterprises has led consumers to expect 24-hour opening coupled with first-class facilities and first-class service. This has implications for our library, for example, in which my predecessor invested. In my time, we opened the new building, opened the contents up through the gifts of generous donors and have finally come to opening up the hours through the night.

There has not been the money available, given the need to transform our campuses, to buy in new players whenever a gap in our skills has been discerned. Sometimes a new subject or a renewed commitment to research means that we rightly look outside Hope for people such as some of the authors represented in this volume, for example (in order of their arrival) Professors Markham, Sullivan, Sagovsky and Hinnells. In not doing the same for areas other than theology, we have until recently accepted that our research in other areas is more modest. We are now at the point of developing a second strand of research, in education, which is to be pitched at the level of national and international excellence. The recent appointments of Professors Campbell and Fairbairn begin this process. Nonetheless, we have not neglected existing members of staff who have the capacity to develop such research reputations, and not all first-class researchers are professors. Thus, Kenneth Newport has emerged through the ranks at Hope as a world-renowned Professor of Christian Thought, and some of our lecturers, such as Drs Mark Elliott and J'annine Jobling, have established formidable research reputations early in their careers.

Indeed, a significant part of the enjoyment of leading the scholarly community of Hope comes from liberating the talents of long-serving colleagues on the same principle as giving students a chance. In other words, there are twin principles underpinning our investment in people: we take risks to give staff and students the opportunity to flourish and we insist on the highest standards of professionalism which we can muster, accepting always that more could be done. My job has involved not only dreams but turning them into reality through taking risks and encouraging professionalism. In particular, it is important that the principal of a church college knows the staff team one by one and knows what is happening. If these two tasks can be achieved, the twin principles will be embedded in the daily life of the community.

The risks taken by both employers and employees are not accidental but should be related to the foundation, mission, values, tradition and future of Hope, in all of which potential can trump past experience. It is vital that we focus on potential and opening up opportunities in staffing as well as in student recruitment. In the same spirit, I have tried to encourage staff, students and prospective students to aim high in their own careers, whatever their age or gender or ethnic background, using their talents to the full. Sometimes the risk is to appoint someone who is perceived by others to be too young or junior, but sometimes it is that they are considered to be too old or too set in their ways. A high moment for me came on the morning after my successor was appointed, the last Friday before Christmas 2002, when chairing a panel for the post of Deputy Registrar. For all the five internal candidates being interviewed were an enormous credit to themselves and to the ethos of Hope. Throughout my time at Hope, however, the same spirit has been palpable, of a willingness of women on the staff, for example, to take on further responsibilities once given the opportunity. The four senior officers were all male as were 14 of the 15 heads of department when I arrived. Since then, senior women at Hope have included Registrars in Mary Ford and Joy Mills, all the Assistant Registrars, Deans in Pro Torkington, Sue Zlosnik and Kathy Hodgkinson as well as three of the four current Heads of School. Two of the authors contributing to this volume, Sharon Bassett and Helen O'Sullivan, have undertaken a variety of ever more senior roles with distinction while pursuing their own lifelong learning and other interests. We have benefited from some outstanding women governors and resident tutors through to female presidents of the students' union and a female Pro-Rector.

Risk is present not only in the appointment of externals to the staff and in the promotions of internals but also in the deployment of colleagues. Again, potential needs to be discerned and flexibility needs to be developed. Those staff who are most afraid of change which affects them are often unnerved by the observation that their conservatism sits uneasily with the self-image of those who profess to be radical in their politics. Yet all staff deserve the support of employers in adjusting to, and preferably in anticipating, change. Compulsory redundancies are a last resort where change has not been foreshadowed in these ways. Sometimes staff will be so uncomfortable with change, or will listen to siren voices claiming that higher education can be frozen, that there is no alternative. The truth is that tomorrow's students will not pay for the preferences of yesterday's appointments to preserve their status quo. Hope in my time has not until recently adjusted our curriculum as swiftly as we should have done. Even when I did grasp the importance of this, my first instinct was to encourage additions to the portfolio without removing yesterday's subjects as quickly as others have managed it. By my last year at Hope, we had begun to make progress on both additions and subtractions in such a way as to leave my successor more of an expectation and more of a process to suit the pace of change in the wider sector. The onus is now firmly on subjects to argue for their place in the portfolio of subjects offered in the prospectus each year. For too long, the burden of proof seemed to be on senior managers to stop a subject which had had its day. This change of emphasis will make a difference in our responsiveness to students.

Beyond the curriculum, the paradox of those professing radical politics hiding in conservative corners applies in reverse. That is to say, there are heartening examples of those colleagues who see themselves as respecting tradition actively embracing change. For example, the editor of this volume, Dr John Elford, had rightly been given responsibility within the Rectorate team for Information Technology by my predecessor. This was a far-sighted move which might at first have seemed strange to those used to Dr Elford's normal routine. Prompted by the merest hint from me, however, he willingly transformed his working practices from longhand and dictaphone to become the most avid user of laptop and desktop computers, mobile phones and digital cameras. There was great personal risk involved in someone leading from the front in this way after a long and distinguished career which had flourished without personally having to use such technology.

At every turn in Hope, and no doubt in other thriving universities and colleges, there have been similar examples of people having a go at the un-known. Several members of our domestic services team have become reception-ists. Colleagues originally employed as technicians and secretaries are now lecturers and administrators. Gardeners have become security patrollers. At the most senior levels, Sean Gallagher has accumulated responsibilities for a range of functions from catering to estates to the library to personnel, while Tony Grayson is integrating our Registry and our Secretary's Office. Professor Bill Chambers has led two deaneries in succession, Arts and Sciences followed by Hope in the Community. Dr Sue Thomas has directed two subject areas, management and business followed by psychology. She was succeeded as head of the management and business team by Dr John Brinkman, a mathematician. The self-assessment document was submitted under the leadership of the former and the assessment visit came under the leadership of the latter. That the outcome, as mentioned earlier, was highly successful and earned a glowing report demonstrates that colleagues have potential to give and to achieve in areas other than that of their original subject.

Nowadays, every HEI needs a policy on risk management. Hope's policy is on risk-taking and risk-management. It begins with a preface by the Presidents of Hope, the Bishop and Archbishop of Liverpool, who explain a theology of creative risk-taking. This distinctive approach represents the church colleges at their most adventurous. Hope at Everton or the Network of Hope would not have happened if we had not been willing to take risks, to trust that funds would come to support the idea of higher education leading urban regeneration or to trust that partner FE colleges with a shared mission could create HE opportunities in their localities. Both risks have proved to be well worth taking. Our founders would have expected nothing less for they had the courage to create opportunities for women to continue their education in order to serve the next generation of schoolchildren at a time when those few universities which existed banned women. The church colleges in general and the founding colleges of Hope in particular are the outcome of outrageous risk-taking. I know that my successor will similarly find ways to take risks which lead Hope in unimagined directions which nonetheless turn out to be good in themselves and in keeping with the spirit of our founders' risk-taking creativity.

For often the risk lies in returning to that strange country, the past, whether at an institutional or personal level and reinterpreting its lessons for the contemporary era. At the personal level, Dr John Elford did not just adopt the unknown in technology, he also had the courage to return to the academic lathe and craft a new series of research publications in the manner of his earlier career but very much adjusted to the challenges of the current age. This interplay of past and present explains at the institutional level my interest in regenerating Liverpool and Hope through re-using splendid buildings of the vintage of our founding colleges, the middle of the nineteenth century, in what I would like to think of as imaginative ways befitting the turn of the millennium. First, Hope on the Waterfront and then Hope at Everton send out the subliminal message that Hope, like the Albert Dock and St Francis Xavier's Church, has been around for 150 years serving the people of the city, the region and beyond. Second, they are self-evidently part of the contemporary urban renaissance. Third, their modern manifestations are accessible, inclusive, well-rounded, again in line with Hope's mission. Fourth, the risks involved in such pioneering work would not be contemplated by universities around the world which do not have such strong missions and especially community links. Fifth, at the same time, the risk is intimately connected to the twin spires of university excellence, teaching and learning on the one hand and research and scholarship on the other. For research into the history of these developments, especially the longer-term one of Hope at Everton, has played a significant part in their use (see, for instance, the invaluable doctorate by Maurice (now Professor) Whitehead, Head of Education at Swansea and now once again a regular visitor to inaugural lectures at Hope), while their re-emergence as visible, accessible learning centres has a teaching role to play.

This takes us on to a more general point about the ethos of Hope, including the wandering around campuses saying hello and smiling. Everything we do as members of a university college community can have an impact on our students. We must therefore try to foster professionalism in every way. This requires daily energy, stamina and commitment to improvement. Too many workers in higher education are allowed to become too complacent as if it is self-evident that their teaching must be good on the flimsy basis that their research is not, or vice versa. Instead, as a sector, we could learn from professional sportswomen and sportsmen who know that if they stop working at their fitness or their

skills, they will lose their reputations. Alison Kervin wrote of Jonny Wilkinson, the England rugby player, in *The Times* (15 February 2003) that he

> has surrounded himself with experts and he listens to their advice while
> remaining clear about his objectives. 'People talk about the number of balls I
> kick but it's not a matter of how many… I have to kick until I'm satisfied.
> You can't put a time limit on when you are going to be satisfied.… I do the
> same thing every day. It's not interesting or exciting …'

Wilkinson might eventually emulate Rob Andrew, one of his predecessors as
England fly-half, who is now his director of rugby at Newcastle, by going into
management. He is already a leader. In higher education, as in sport, the
unexciting truth is that constant vigilance is necessary behind the scenes for
every public performance. It helps in professional sport, of course, that the pay
and conditions are usually good and that managers and coaches know their
team one by one as well as collectively. It has been important at Hope, I would
like to think, that I know the staff team, not just their faces and names but also
where possible their aspirations and their potential. It is also important that I
know what is going on and that colleagues know that I know. Wandering
around campuses helps with this as does a comprehensive e-newspaper so that
everyone knows where to wander at what time.

To give just one illustration of what I mean by professionalism, my emphasis on punctuality in beginning (and usually in ending) meetings is recognised
by the Hope community but has perplexed some. Nonetheless, as we strive for
perfection in all areas, punctuality is indeed one indicator on which I have
focused. Why? Punctuality is a constant challenge, many times a day, every
day. Being on time is part of respecting the time of others, which is part of
respecting those people as ends in themselves. Punctuality is a discipline against
verbosity and an aid to sharp thinking. It is objectively measurable by all in the
community. By and large, those who are consistently late for meetings are
consistently sloppy in other respects. Often, they are subconsciously or deliber-
ately drawing attention to themselves, the message supposedly being that they
are more hard-pressed than others. This should not work in higher education
any more than it would be accepted in the part-time jobs which so many
students do to pay their way through higher education, where turning up on
time is expected in the interests of professional customer service. Punctuality is
such a good indicator of professionalism because it depends on preparation,
thinking ahead, not simply responding in situ when a question arises, as some
in university life can do brilliantly. It is possible, on the other hand, to be both
punctual (sporting stars have to be there on time for kick-off) and able to
improvise (as illustrated by Jonny Wilkinson again).

There is a wider symbolism in punctuality, for it is a close relation of a more nebulous concept, 'timing'. Church colleges and other HEIs have sometimes given the impression of complacency, of moving slowly if at all, even as the pace of change in higher education and wider society accelerates. To borrow the title of a novel by C. P. Snow, *The Sleep of Reason* is an accurate description of too many sleepy colleges and universities. My predecessor took the colleges as fast as they could bear to go; faster, in merging two or three departments into one for each subject. Meanwhile, however, former polytechnics multiplied their student numbers and changed their approaches at a formidable pace. Punctuality was part of a broader response which included insisting, in a speech to all staff on my first day, Friday 1 September 1995, that all those paid a full-time salary had to work a full day for a full week for a full year.

For the leisurely summers or short days punctuated by long coffee breaks and even longer teas, attributed fondly by some staff to the founding colleges, were over during the leadership of my predecessor. The last rites now had to be administered. There is much to be said for the relaxed world of intellectual senior common room discussions but now that students are paying for the privilege of higher education they do not want to subsidise leisurely staff gossip behind closed doors. It is refreshing for students and staff to enjoy conversations in Fresh Hope, where all can see who achieves a balance between the extremes of not participating in collegial life and of not seeming to have any work to do. We deceive ourselves in higher education if we think that Microsoft or a broadsheet newspaper do not have a culture of intellectual excellence among their staff. The former will have a more laid-back style than the latter but each of these private sector environments is as stimulating as the most research-intensive university's self-image. There is a time for relaxation in a well-organised scholar's day but there must also be a full day's work in the interests of our students. Malcolm Bradbury's comic novel, *Cuts*, published in 1987, talks of the 'summer-empty university car-park'. That description of a campus should not be recognisable fifteen years later.

At an even broader level, the emphasis on timing takes us back to the lessons of risk-taking and Hope on the Waterfront. It is no longer enough to keep up with the pack. We must be ahead of the game. Timing was crucial to Hope on the Waterfront. It needed to happen before others understood the need for higher education to position itself in unusual locations. The experiment needed to be brought to a conclusion before a more permanent presence in the city could add extra value by linking the centre to a disadvantaged community. This was the task achieved by Hope at Everton, a sequel to Hope on the Waterfront on a grander scale, the story of which has been told elsewhere in this volume. Hope at Everton would not have been possible without the confidence engendered by the successful risk-taking of Hope on the Waterfront. Cumulatively, these ventures made possible the even bolder step of the Network of Hope. Yet even what many regard as the greatest of risks, establishing Hope through the partnerships of the Network in the wider North West, especially at Blackburn, Bury and Wigan, is in keeping with the original spirit of the founding colleges. For our Anglican forebears began their training college in Warrington, then and now at the centre of the North West.

Returning to the scene where it all began is a common phenomenon in literature. In that C. P. Snow novel, *The Sleep of Reason*, to which I referred, the fictional character Lewis Eliot returns to the Cambridge scene of his donnish days for a meeting of the University Court. This is tedious until it reaches the sixth item on the agenda, 'Extension to Biology Building'. Suddenly, the mood is transformed:

> The voices round me didn't sound as though they could have enough of it. The UGC! Architects! Appeals! Claims of other subjects! Master building plan! Emotions were heated, the voices might have been talking about love or the preservation of peace. Of all the academic meetings I had attended, at least half the talking time, and much more than half the expense of spirit, had been consumed in discussions of buildings. Whatever would they do when all the buildings were put up? The answer, I thought, though not that afternoon, was simple: they would pull some down and start again.

C. P. Snow and Lewis Eliot have been accused by one of my predecessors in an earlier role, William Twining, when he was Professor of Jurisprudence at Queen's University Belfast, of giving academic life a bad name. Twining's critique came in an address to the legal scholars' annual conference and was based on the perception that Eliot never seemed to teach, research, write or go into a library. My first defence of Snow and Eliot came when I had the opportunity to address the same conference half-way through my time at Hope. The meeting was in Leeds and my lecture was given in Leeds Metropolitan University, where I am now going as Vice-Chancellor. I used the passage quoted above to show that Snow and Eliot understood academe only too well.

The story of Hope in recent years could similarly be recorded as a property trail of pulling buildings down and putting others up, with passion and commitment. Important though the learning environment is, however, a higher education institution flourishes primarily through its people and ideas. Snow and Eliot understood this also. Eliot moved seamlessly between what could be described as the little world of petty academic politics and (in Snow's memorable phrase) the 'corridors of power' at another time when the discussion in those corridors was about weapons of mass destruction. Snow had a rounded career as a novelist, a scientist and a leading public servant. If the relationships between institutions, their buildings, people and ideas can be crafted into a rounded, coherent narrative, so much the better for any university or college community seeking to understand itself.

My predecessor, Dr James Burke, the Chairs of Governing Council, the late Archbishop Derek Worlock and Bishop David (now Lord) Sheppard, together with successive Pro-Rectors and Heads of Colleges and the wider college community had all laboured to great effect in federating and then integrating three colleges into a single constitution by 1995. Prudent financial management had buttressed all this good work. At one level, all that was needed in the last five years of the last millennium was to pull down some structures and build up the new identity in keeping with the spirit of our founders' distinctive mission and values.

Yet the transformation from hope-less to hope-ful does not need buildings being pulled down or erected or reinvented. It can happen in the grace of a tutor's encouragement, of a burden shared by a chaplain, of brass cleaned every morning, of brass neck in risk-taking, of prayers said every day, of students supporting one another, of an image of student life accessed on-line through *Hope Virtually Daily*. We hear increasingly of these moments of hope as families share their stories of transformation at graduations. This essay began with one graduate of 2002 and would not be complete without the heroic tale of a graduate of 2001. Suzanne Kelly's determination to graduate on time despite serious injuries in the Omagh bombing was inspiring, the story of a young woman teacher from across the Irish Sea triumphing over all adversity in the spirit of our founders opening up opportunities 150 years ago. The cornerstone of Hope is the conviction that individuals and communities who have experienced rejection or worse can walk the corridors of culture, of reason, of faith and it is they, the excluded, who thus bring to us all a sense of hope. With that spirit, there is no question that Hope is sustainable, that Hope can flourish under the leadership of the inordinately gifted Professor Gerald Pillay. We sustain ourselves not just with visionary dreams for the development of campuses (although we have those for Hope Zones at Blackburn and Bury) but with clowning in Liverpool and all through our activities, trying to get the little graces right, trying to see the cathedral of university college life in a different light, encouraging students in their first steps and throughout their journeys of lifelong learning.

The journey imagery takes us back to the other question, the one about the bus. It is a way of asking whether Hope is sustainable without a particular principal. We have had some fun with this question over the years. Some people take the view that the test of a flourishing institution is whether it can survive without noticing the demise of a principal or two. Others consider that if nobody notices the end of a principal's contribution, then the incumbent was probably not offering value for money. My own view, hitherto unarticulated, is that there has never been the slightest chance of a bus running me over – as years of cowardly rugby have shown, one of my limited abilities on the rugby field was to dodge out of trouble or, to put it another way, to cause more trouble than I was caused. Nor has there ever been any doubt in my mind that Hope would escape any lumbering threat from a merger-bus. If all else failed, we would hop on the bus, hijack it and take it on a journey of Hope.

That is the essence of opening up access to higher education. Some conferences give the impression that widening participation is a device to serve the interests of institutions. It should be instead, as our founders appreciated more than a century and a half ago, a way of encouraging those who are in the way of life's juggernauts to find a way of escaping what seems to be their fate, of taking control of their destiny, of using that energy and momentum to drive in a direction of their own choosing.

To vary the metaphor, when others praise governors for taking the risk of appointing me, they routinely say that this was more courageous than opting for a 'safe pair of hands'. If, perish the thought, I were the kind of principal who was easily irritated by daft comments, this would have grated. For a common element in my rugby, cricket and still in my soccer goalkeeping (in the weekly game between international students and Hope staff) has been that my hands are perfectly safe, thank you very much. There is an assumption in this misuse of metaphor that it is the plodder in a sporting team or higher education leadership who has safe hands whereas the risk-takers have unsafe hands. Tell that to great sporting heroes, from Jonny Wilkinson backwards. Ian Botham, for example, was an outstanding risk-taker who had exceptionally safe hands. He is still remembered for outrageously successful risk-taking in 1981 at Headingley, the location of my next job. My belief and, I would like to think, my experience is that the more you work at your game, the safer your hands become. It must, however, be '*your* game'. There are too many individuals and institutions in higher education who are tempted by facile comparisons with others to play on the wrong, unlevelled field, rather than to play their own game to their own strengths. Likewise, there are too many people who belittle the efforts of others who are playing their own game. We should not be chasing government funding, fashion or favour. We should play our own game and encourage our students similarly to value their own talents and endeavours.

Our game is most obvious at Graduation Days. I have enjoyed explaining Hope's game on those occasions by reference sometimes to people such as St Julie Billiart, the foundress of the Sisters of Notre Dame and St Benedict whose birthday and feast-day respectively fall in the second week of July, the time each year when we hold our Graduation Days. In other years, I have focused instead on the place(s) of Hope, on the locations of our ceremonies, one or other of Liverpool's magnificent twin cathedrals, linked by that street called Hope. At others, I have used the insights of a person in the news to illustrate the mission of Hope. In the summer of 2001, for instance, the British Lions' rugby tour was in full swing and Keith Wood, the Irish hooker, had excelled in the first test. Incidentally, he is another character who takes extraordinary risks but who has safe hands. I quoted to students his philosophy, honed in his early years of club rugby when old stagers would put him down by reference to his father, who also played in the front row of the forwards for Ireland and the Lions, saying that Keith Wood may have thought he was good but he would never be as good as his father. 'That's fine,' he used to respond, 'I don't want to be as good as my father, I just want to be the best that I can be.' That is the spirit of Hope. Each student and the whole institution should strive to be the best that each can be, not worry over much about how others judge us. The external scrutiny can shed some light, so can comparisons with other cathedrals. We can see ourselves or others in The Window of the Hidden Saints (and sinners and scholars) at St Francis Xavier's Church, Hope at Everton. Yet what really counts is whether we have the courage, fostered by en-courage-ment, to make the best use of our talents, to be the best that we can be. It is good occasionally, in the silence of the inner sanctum of a cathedral or a church or a chapel or a soul, that we reflect on this. Sometimes, we take the time to do that immediately before we burst into the light of a celebration, for instance at graduation.

In a way, this book has been an opportunity to go through such a process just before the inevitable public rituals of handing over responsibilities from one principal to another, and I am extremely grateful to all involved, especially the editor Dr John Elford, for the opportunity to reflect together. To borrow from another source of Newman's wisdom, we do all this in the spirit of being led by a kindly light. The candle will be kept burning. My impression in 1995 was that the torch or flame was being passed to me not only by my predecessor but also by governors, trustees and the student body. In 2003, we would include not only the Student President but also the Presidents of Hope, who have so kindly written the preface to this volume, as we collectively hand over a living tradition of Hope to my successor. It is not for me, from this vantage point of departure, to map out my impressions of the next phases of the journey. Rather, I am simply grateful for the company I have been able to keep on each step thus far, and I have every confidence that Hope will be led by the light in directions as yet unknown which will enable the individuals within Hope, and the whole community of Hope, to be the best that they can be. I have faith in Hope and its sustainability, indeed its flourishing, under the leadership of Professor Gerald Pillay. With Newman, then, I can say, 'I do not ask to see the distant scene; one step enough for me.' Finally, I would like my own last step for Hope to be the adoption of the words of the Hope graduate quoted at the beginning. Mine is just one more view of the cathedral of Hope but I will always watch the distant scene with interest, affection and gratitude. Meanwhile, this essay is 'a little note to say thank you for my time at Hope'.

Hope in the Future

GERALD J. PILLAY

THIS rich collection of memories and reflections celebrates the pilgrimage of a remarkable British institution. It is a story of courage, sacrifice, commitment, service and compassion that eludes public reviews and assessments, corporate plans and even the very best attempts to capture it in this fine and fitting tribute. However, two key words – 'hope' and 'community' – recur throughout these pages in the testimonies of academic and administrative staff, students and graduates. It appears that the experience of this university college has become inscribed in the lives of the people associated with it.

Hope is not a Christian virtue or a quality like goodness, gentleness or mercy. It cannot be cultivated like self-discipline or patience. It has nothing to do with either nature or nurture. Hope is the Christian's philosophy of history. It can only be measured by time. To 'have hope' or, more correctly, to live in hope is to live in the confidence of the end result. In theological terms it means living eschatologically; in the full assurance that the end (*telos*) is assured and fulfilled in God. Wolfhart Pannenberg, the German theologian, would say that in Christ we have 'proleptically' encountered the end. To live and work anticipating that all may turn out well or that our efforts may not be futile is wishfulness, not hope. To live in hope is to let the fulfilment of the end guide and illuminate our way. Hope is the basis of this institution's confidence and commitment to 'educate in the round' – to entrench its foundational vision in the whole scholarly process in all its depth and breadth.

During these past few months I have become gradually educated into the culture and ethos of Liverpool Hope University College and three things have become very obvious to me. First, Liverpool Hope has one of the most lucid and succinct mission statements I have encountered anywhere. The notions of 'vision' and 'mission', which have now passed into common university parlance, were originally theological ideas. There is a clear and unambiguous synergy between this university college's mission of hope and its academic vision. During the 1990s it became fashionable to establish a mission statement to appear at the foot of letterheads. This statement was designed for marketing purposes, to make an institution stand out from the rest. Like business executives, some vice-chancellors also appeared in advertisements. It helped, according to the publicity consultants, to put a face to the institution. But seldom do these corporate intentions become the habits of the heart or evolve into conventions that guide and nurture the aspirations of the staff to be better teachers and more impassioned enquirers willing to publish the fruit of their reflections. The pages of this volume tell a different story. The writers freely quote the mission statement and constantly refer to it. Liverpool Hope's vision and mission infuse all aspects of its practice and planning, whether of expensive capital investments or of tending the gardens.

Any self-respecting university has to be creditable in the three areas of standard university competence: teaching and learning, research and community service. The last is sometimes referred to as the social or public responsibility of the university or its 'ethical vision'. It is currently fashionable at some universities to require in the 'graduate profile' of its degrees an explicit statement on an academic course's ethical and social contribution. Universities are places absorbed in teaching and researching, trusting that in this process they fulfil their service to the community and meet their social obligations. In practice, though, research and teaching are often competing interests dependent on what attracts more students or more money. Community service too is often 'commodified' and exploited for research and commercial dollars. At Liverpool Hope, community service is not an appendix to its profile or a by-product of its corporate plan but is the a priori of its mission. It adopts what might be described as a circular or 'dialectical' model to explain its purpose. The commitment to serve focuses its teaching and research which in turn extends its mission to serve. It is 'mission driven' and its scholarly ambitions are nurtured by its vision for service to Merseyside, to the North West, to the UK and beyond.

The Secretary of State for Education has stated that there may be too many postgraduate providers in Britain compared to the USA. Even if that is a valid comparison between these two countries, institutions such as Liverpool Hope have few parallels in the largely secularised higher education sector in the UK. In fact, the founding colleges that united to form Liverpool Hope, together with a handful of other colleges that took root in the nineteenth century, pre-dated the 'redbrick' universities and persisted in providing an alternative to them. At their best, this distinctiveness of vision has been their raison d'être ever since and it must, rightly, remain at the heart of Liverpool Hope's future.

Second, Liverpool Hope has a unique ecumenical foundation. Against a background of denominational suspicion and years of sectarian conflict, the educational partnership between the Catholic and Anglican churches in Liverpool is a unique and invaluable Christian witness for generations to come of what is possible. Liverpool Hope's ecumenical foundation is both a valuable inheritance and a task requiring constant effort. Its location in Liverpool is not incidental. It was here under particular circumstances that notable visionaries made it possible for hitherto self-contained colleges to open up to each other and to pool their resources to achieve a greater good. This coming together is graphically illustrated in the living parable of Hope Street linking the two magnificent cathedrals in the city. It is of historical and national importance to uphold this ecumenical witness to the world.

Third is Liverpool Hope's new status as a *university* college – a status earned after undergoing stringent testing. It places Liverpool Hope in a new league with new challenges and opportunities. As we anticipate the future, we may well ask whether this new status means that we have here the makings of just another British university.

We ought to bear in mind that the university world, in spite of actively creating knowledge, publishing, and patenting innovations, has in fact ceased to be a happy world. A third of the academic staff, we are told in a recent survey, would leave if they could.[1] They feel unappreciated – their ideals seem to have lost their lustre and their work its meaning. Much time is dissipated managing the numerous forms of scrutiny through ever-refined assessment measures introduced in the name of accountability and increasing productivity – all well-intentioned and some quite necessary – but hardly encouraging of the inner motivation that fosters creativity. Through a decade or more of imita-ting 'cutting edge' business measures, popularised through MBA programmes, roving higher education experts, professional facilitators and consultants (the money paid to these last has been profligate), administrators have now become quite proficient 'managers'. We have arguably become more efficient but not necessarily more effective.

The 'changing of the guard' at Liverpool Hope is taking place at a time when the government has promised widespread changes to the higher education system. What new opportunities are there for Liverpool Hope? Besides the all-important funding formula that government will settle on and which naturally preoccupies heads of higher education institutions in the UK, there are some new opportunities. One should go behind the White Paper to Estelle Morris's mandating speech at London Guildhall on 22 October 2001, Sir Howard Newby's keynote address to vice-chancellors and principals at the HEFCE annual meeting in April 2002 and the discussion papers that the Secretary of State, Charles Clarke, made public in December 2002. The storm over top-up fees has drowned out what all three actually agree on and have been advocating over the last two years. They agree that teaching and learning should be properly and better funded with appropriate incentives in place to encourage excellence in teaching as a good in itself, in the way that research is funded and acknowledged as a good. They also agree that diversity within the higher education sector is crucial in order to 'fit it for purpose' to provide tertiary education to a larger section of the UK population; 50 per cent of 18–30-year-olds by 2010 with appropriate skills for the social and economic health and survival of the country, that is, almost 400,000 extra British enrolments by 2010. Liverpool Hope features in the *THES* list of those higher education institutions with a rate above the average on the access tables. Its outreach and development programmes beyond Hope Park, its excellent new inner-city presence in a context of urban renewal and its presence further north and east all prepare it to be the university for the wider North West. This access achievement will be an abiding asset given global student trends. In recent US research it was found that 75 per cent of undergraduate students were 'non-traditional' students in terms of age, financial status and when they enrol. They were usually older and studying part-time. Only 27 per cent were traditional students, that is, straight out of high school, studying full-time and dependent on their parents for support. In Britain, New Zealand and Australia many students who enrol as full-time students work for ten or more hours a week and a significant number for up to 20 hours a week. Yet the system treats them as traditional students and the whole teaching and learning process functions on that premise.

Yet further, Morris, Newby and Clarke all agree that universities and colleges should be encouraged to have a bifocal vision: to collaborate and achieve international standing while making a real and tangible contribution to the community and the region; to be both global and local. There is a need for higher education institutions to make strategic decisions about what they want to be. Newby's 'core-plus' approach is the driver here. Not all institutions can be excellent in everything; neither, we should add, can all units within the same institution be equally good at everything. Choices have to be made about the 'core' where excellence can be achieved. The 'plus' must be judiciously chosen, and built on the solidity of the core.

Liverpool Hope, thanks to the sterling efforts of Professor Simon Lee, is well placed to gain from all the 'funding pots' described in the White Paper. In the years ahead, Hope will have to continue making its case for these different funding options and on achieving the national objectives laid out in the White Paper.

The separation of research and teaching in the White Paper remains, nevertheless, a vexing issue and is compounded by a seemingly narrow definition of 'research' to refer to research that, in the main, might produce national economic benefits. 'Technology transfer' seems to be the goal. Unfortunately, the word 'research' in many places in the White Paper could be substituted by 'science and technology development' without substantially altering the meaning intended. In New Zealand, for example, the current 'higher education strategy' tries to distinguish teaching from research institutions in order to alienate funds from polytechnics and colleges in favour of universities where research will be concentrated. The rationale behind profiling higher education institutions as research institutions or not remains a problem for the government, which aspires at the same time to foster a 'knowledge economy' based on appropriate skills development. However, the antithesis between research and teaching is both false and unnecessary, and for any serious degree-awarding institution the distinction is disastrous. The university is where *research-informed teaching* takes place. Sir Howard's more sober stance 'not to profile institutions or make them prisoners of one or other stream or type of education' makes very good sense. The quid pro quo, of course, is that institutions cut their suit to fit the cloth, consciously decide their modus vivendi and make explicit their contribution to a diverse and effective higher education system in Britain. Liverpool Hope's vision and mission is its hermeneutical guide for determining its distinctiveness and how best to fulfil the roles of research, and teaching and learning. HEFCE has affirmed that it will not impose missions or assign higher education institutions to categories but will provide a range of incentives to encourage particular outcomes.

Under Professor Simon Lee, Liverpool Hope University College has, quietly and purposefully, made several key decisions addressing the Dearing Compact and has gone a long way in implementing these plans. The Compact includes:

- lifelong learning
- creation of a learning culture
- regional economic regeneration
- pure research and scholarship across disciplines
- technological innovation
- social cohesion
- public accountability

While still Vice-Chancellor of the University of Southampton, Sir Howard Newby, in an influential address, maintained that 'coming to terms with diversity is one of the major challenges for UK higher education in the twenty-first century'. This book is a record of how Liverpool Hope has dealt with diversity. Its vision and, in turn, role are indispensable to a diverse higher education sector mindful of the educational tasks Britain has set itself.

The question 'How can the uniqueness of Hope's vision infiltrate its academic planning and intellectual pursuits?' has to be constantly asked. A university with a Christian foundation, as any good university, must remain deeply committed to the scholarly task in all its facets and to the rigour of enquiry. But in this case, as George Marsden reminds us, 'we are not talking about bringing a secret Christian knowledge into our scholarship but rather about cultivating sensibilities'.² *Scientia* (knowledge) is important but *sapientia* (wisdom) is indispensable.

The so-called 'secular' university is a late and relatively modern contrivance. Within the secular university the knowledge discourse has become more truncated rather than broader. The methods of the natural sciences dominate the way academic legitimacy is conceived. 'Method' in general still determines what constitutes truth and knowledge. A new ideological Procrustean bed has come to replace what Immanuel Kant perceived to be 'the conflict of the faculties' in the eighteenth century. In place of 'conflict' is a new conformity narrowing rather than broadening or deepening the discourse about knowledge today. Issues of utility have been elevated above those of meaning and purpose. In this connection, Sir Walter Moberley's pronouncement of 'a crisis in the university' in the 1940s is as relevant now as it was then. He wrote:

> Our predicament... is this. Most students go through our universities without ever having been forced to exercise their minds on the issues which are really momentous. Under the guise of academic neutrality they are subtly conditioned to unthinking acquiescence in the social and political status quo and in a secularism on which they have never seriously reflected. Owing to the prevailing fragmentation of studies, they are not challenged to decide responsibly on a life-purpose or equipped to make such a decision wisely. They are not incited to disentangle and examine critically the assumptions and emotional attitudes underlying the particular studies they pursue, the profession for which they are preparing, the ethical judgements they are accustomed to make, and the political or religious convictions they hold. Fundamentally they are uneducated.³

Moberley's comments do not seek to affirm mindlessly old ways of doing things. Rather, he suggests that the modern university with its present challenges discourages rather than protects the 'community' of learning – the other word that recurs in these pages. The preservation of community is one of the main safeguards against the functionalism and pragmatism that govern the modern university. Professor Lee rightly reminds us of Newman's moving description of the university as an Alma Mater 'knowing her children one by one – not a foundry, or a mint, or a treadmill'. True to its Christian roots, authentic community is where individualism and selfishness are transcended and where human creativity is fostered. Authentic community nurtures human freedom and is the necessary and sufficient condition for personality. Liverpool Hope's emphases on its foundational vision, forming a 'village' in the city, going the second mile in caring for students and its goal to 'educate in the round' are a celebration of community. Here Jerusalem has much to do with Athens! Liverpool Hope's emerging university status will make it part of an illustrious alliance of universities in the world with a similar Christian vision. These institutions exist in all three areas of the world that Hope has targeted in its internationalisation plan and in the UK and North America. Such alliances can offer mutual benefits such as cross-credit, collaborative research, student exchanges, sharing of best practice, joint supervision of research students and joint ventures with the private sector.

These are some of the outcomes that the head of HEFCE has been advocating. His reference to the Wisconsin model to illustrate these benefits is relevant when Hope has to decide about co-operation with institutions locally (Cheshire, Merseyside, and the North West) and internationally while treasuring its 100-year-old relationship with the University of Liverpool, an extremely important alliance. In a diverse higher education sector there is no longer the need to put all one's institutional eggs into one basket, even though one may have a primary partner or alliance. The recent ministers, Blunkett, Morris and Clarke, have all echoed Newby's views in different ways and at various times, namely, that a well-articulated higher education system must allow for collaboration, shared practice and effective use of limited resources rather than perpetuate the competitive models of the 1990s driven by 'the market'. In the Wisconsin model, institutions in the city have a non-hierarchical relationship to each other. There is open cross-transfer and pathways across campuses, which is far better than the unacceptable binary relation between research and teaching institutions 'trapping institutions in their roles' and creating an institutional caste system.

Every grand scheme, no matter how well intentioned, creates its own perversities. One must, therefore, maintain a critical solidarity with governments. Educational institutions and cultural symbols generally outlast them. Yet the recommendations of the White Paper on Higher Education, when they do take final legislative shape, will set the limits on what it is possible to have funded from the pubic purse. There are a few political battles yet to be fought before those lines are drawn. For Liverpool Hope its mission will guide it in making its own strategic choices. Where there are synergies between its mission and public policy it will no doubt be the exemplar of support and solidarity.

The much-vaunted benefits of mergers for reasons of economies of scale and removing duplications are over-rated. After some initial savings the larger institution often swallows up the smaller one. Realignments and restructuring invariably lead to 'asset stripping' and the death of those unique traditions important for the diversity the government seeks. In their place there can only emerge a featureless sameness. One has still to discover the logic behind the bureaucratic belief that putting all needy relatives together in the same room will somehow make them richer. Liverpool Hope is already the result of the *purposeful* mergers of older colleges whose foundational vision remains a shared and life-giving vision, uniting and empowering those who identify with it. As an institution which has come of age, Liverpool Hope is free to partner enterprises with other institutions here and abroad and even form alliances, but it does so confident about its own standing and vision.

Søren Kierkegaard, the Danish philosopher, once recorded in his Journal that

> It is perfectly true, as philosophers say, that life must be understood backwards. But they forget the other proposition, that it must be lived forwards. And if one thinks over that proposition, it becomes more and more evident that life can never be really understood in time simply because at no particular moment can one find the necessary resting place from which to understand it – backwards.[4]

No particular moment can be a resting place! Liverpool Hope's future in the envisaged new higher education sector in Britain, despite the new challenges ahead, is optimistic. The government states that it seeks to 'foster proud and autonomous institutions, confident in their differing missions and meeting the need of students'. The White Paper is envisaged as 'taking another step along the road of moving universities and colleges from their old missions of being elite and giving opportunities for the few, to being in the heart of our communities, the key to individual life chances, and that serve the heart of the country as well'. This is precisely what Liverpool Hope has been busy doing for 150 years.

The vision of Liverpool Hope is best expressed in the lives of the people represented in these pages. Among these are Bishop David (now Lord) Sheppard and Archbishop Derek Worlock whose bona fides graced this ecumenical foundation; their successors, now Presidents of Liverpool Hope, who preserve this ecumenical heritage; the staff, both academic and administrative, among whom extraordinary commitment exists; the governors whose support is typified in the tireless efforts of Sr Eileen Kelleher SND, the present Chair of the Governing Council; and the remarkable departing Rector, Professor Simon Lee, who has left indelible memories on the minds of staff, students and all who have had anything to do with Liverpool Hope. In Bishop Sheppard's words, Simon Lee has 'brought flair, imagination and a higher profile to Liverpool Hope'.[5] In his concluding chapter, Lee compared the writing of this book with trying to describe a cathedral. Those of us who continue his work should do so in the spirit of anyone entering a cathedral – prayerful, expectant, and hopeful.

NOTES

1 *The Guardian*, 10 March 2003 (reported in *THES* news under the heading 'One-third of academics want to quit'): 'Nearly half the academics said morale had worsened in the past two years, while an overwhelming majority complained that they suffered from work-related stress.'

2 G. M. Marsden, *The Outrageous Idea of Christian Scholarship*, New York, Oxford University Press, 1997, p. 94.

3 W. Moberley, *The Crisis in the University*, London, SCM Press, 1949, p. 70.

4 S. Kierkegaard, *The Journals of Søren Kierkegaard* (a selection, ed. A. Dru), London, Collins, 1958, p. 89.

5 D. Sheppard, *Steps along Hope Street: My Life in Cricket, the Church and the Inner City*, London, Hodder & Stoughton, 2002, p. 267.

Notes on Contributors

The writers who have contributed to the book are listed below in chapter sequence.

Dr R. John Elford is Pro-Rector Emeritus of Liverpool Hope. He was also the inaugural Foundation Dean and Provost of Hope at Everton.

Sr Eileen Kelleher SND is Chair of the Governing Council of Liverpool Hope.

Ms Sharon Bassett and Dr Helen O'Sullivan are former Directors of Student Services. Ms Bassett's substantive post is that of Director of Marketing and Dr O'Sullivan is now Deputy Registrar.

Dr Bernard Longden is Director of Funding and Planning.

Dr Michael Ford is an author, news journalist and broadcaster for the BBC.

Bishop Ian C. Stuart is the Co-ordinating Chaplain, Provost of Hope Park and Director of Student Services.

Dr Ian Sharp is Foundation Dean, Liverpool Hope.

Professor Ian S. Markham was the inaugural Liverpool Professor of Theology and Public Life, and was the second Foundation Dean. He is now Dean of Hartford Seminary, Connecticut, and Professor of Theology and Ethics there. He remains a Visiting Professor at Hope.

Professor Nicholas Sagovsky is the present Liverpool Professor of Theology and Public Life.

Professor Kenneth G. C. Newport is Professor of Christian Thought.

Professor John R. Hinnells is Professor of Comparative Religion.

Professor John Sullivan is Professor of Christian Education and Foundation Dean designate.

Professor Simon Lee is Rector and Chief Executive of Liverpool Hope University College. He is soon to become Vice-Chancellor of Leeds Metropolitan University.

Professor Gerald J. Pillay is currently Executive Head of the School of Liberal Arts at the University of Otago. He is Rector and Chief Executive designate of Liverpool Hope.

Index of Names

Subject Index